Walter Scott
and the
historical imagination

Walter Scott
and the
historical imagination

David Brown

Routledge & Kegan Paul
London, Boston and Henley

First published in 1979
by Routledge & Kegan Paul Ltd
39 Store Street, London WC1E 7DD,
Broadway House, Newtown Road,
Henley-on-Thames, Oxon RG9 1EN and
9 Park Street, Boston, Mass. 02108, USA
Photoset in 11 on 12 Garamond by
Kelly Typesetting, Bradford-on-Avon, Wiltshire
and printed in Great Britain by
Redwood Burn Ltd,
Trowbridge and Esher
© David Brown 1979

British Library Cataloguing in Publication Data

Brown, David
Walter Scott and the historical imagination.
1. Scott, Sir Walter, bart. Waverley novels
I. Title
823'.7   PR5341   79–40661

ISBN 0 7100 0301 3

Contents

Acknowledgments

I would like particularly to thank Myrddin Jones, of the Department of English in the University of Exeter, for the help he gave me during the time spent working on the thesis which was the original of this book. His encouragement, constructive criticism, and useful suggestions were deeply appreciated.

I must also thank Peter Garside, of University College, Cardiff, and Claire Lamont, of the University of Newcastle, for their help on a number of points of detail.

Author's note

1 All references to the Waverley Novels in the notes are in the form

Rob Roy, XXXV, p. 353

where chapter and page numbering is that of the Dryburgh Edition of the Waverley Novels, published in London by Adam & Charles Black, 1892-4, in 25 volumes.

The chapter numbering (in roman numerals) will be standard for most editions; although in a few cases where other editors have changed Scott's 'introductory' first chapters into Introductions in their own right, the chapter numbering will be found to be one chapter out.

2 In the notes and bibliography an author's name in parentheses, e.g.

(J. G. Lockhart), *Peter's Letters to his Kinsfolk*, Edinburgh, 1819, ii, p. 143.

indicates that the original publication was anonymous.

Chronology of the Waverley Novels

Waverley, 1814
Guy Mannering, 1815
The Antiquary, 1816
The Black Dwarf, 1816
Old Mortality, 1816
Rob Roy, 1818
The Heart of Midlothian, 1818
The Bride of Lammermoor, 1819
A Legend of Montrose, 1819
Ivanhoe, 1820
The Monastery, 1820
The Abbot, 1820
Kenilworth, 1821
The Pirate, 1822
The Fortunes of Nigel, 1822

Peveril of the Peak, 1822
Quentin Durward, 1823
St Ronan's Well, 1824
Redgauntlet, 1824
The Betrothed, 1825
The Talisman, 1825
Woodstock, 1826
Chronicles of the Canongate:
    The Two Drovers, The
    Highland Widow, The
    Surgeon's Daughter, 1828
The Fair Maid of Perth, 1828
Anne of Geierstein, 1829
Count Robert of Paris, 1832
Castle Dangerous, 1832

Introduction

In 1819 J. G. Lockhart, the future biographer of Scott, wrote in *Peter's Letters to his Kinsfolk* of the unhappy effect that the Edinburgh establishment's blindness to the greatest poet of the age had had on Scottish opinion: 'The reading public [in Edinburgh] do not criticise Mr. Wordsworth; they think him below their criticism; they know nothing about what he has done. . . .'[1] Lockhart would have found it ironic and incredible had he known that exactly the same fate was to overtake the greatest established novelist of the day – his friend and mentor, Sir Walter Scott. Yet, by the beginning of this century, Scott was not only largely unread, but simply dismissed by the British reading public in the same way that educated Scots had dismissed Wordsworth a century earlier. Only Scott's inferior, medieval, novels remained in school classrooms, supposedly to entertain the young, but more often encouraging them to avoid the Waverley Novels in later life.

Over the last twenty-five years, however, Scott's accepted stature as a novelist has been steadily increasing. It would still be wrong to suggest that he is 'widely read' today in the way that Jane Austen, George Eliot, and the Brontës (among nineteenth-century classic authors) continue to be read. On the other hand, a number of paperback editions of the great Scottish Waverley Novels have appeared in recent years, and the casual reader of Scott is now more likely to have come across one of these than he is to have been bored by a school edition of

Ivanhoe. This represents a real improvement in Scott's chances of being read with interest by a wider audience in future: for too many years he has hardly had a fair hearing.

Behind this resurgence of interest in Scott lies a large-scale revaluation of his work by the critics. Scott had influential admirers throughout the nineteenth and early twentieth centuries, of course (notably among the major novelists), but even his champions among the critics did not then seek to challenge the conventional image of Scott inherited from the Victorians. Carlyle's damning criticism of the Waverley Novels, his allegation that they lacked intellectual weight or moral seriousness – that in short, they were fit only for 'harmlessly amusing indolent, languid men'[2] – was not refuted. Virginia Woolf, for example, seems to have admired Scott principally for his 'sentiment', if Mr Ramsay's feelings on reading *The Antiquary* in *To the Lighthouse* can be taken as her own:[3]

> This man's strength and sanity, his feeling for straight-forward simple things, these fishermen, the poor old crazed creature in Mucklebackit's cottage, made him feel so vigorous, so relieved of something that he felt roused and triumphant and could not choke back his tears.

Here Scott is seen solely as a novelist of the heart: no claim to intellectual interest for him is made, or felt to be appropriate. Among modern critics, at least Frank Jordan has followed Virginia Woolf's reaction to Scott,[4] and it would be wrong to discount sentimental interest altogether in a novelist whose first novel was dedicated to Henry Mackenzie. On the other hand, most modern critics would agree that such a reading distorts and underestimates Scott's true appeal.

The revival of serious interest in the Waverley Novels is due principally to the work of two critics, George Lukács and David Daiches, who first successfully challenged the received wisdom about Scott and rehabilitated him on new grounds as a novelist of importance. Moreover, although Lukács's section on Scott in *The Historical Novel* (written in 1937, but not available in English until 1962) and Daiches's essay, 'Scott's Achievement as a Novelist' (written in 1951) in many ways represent very different views on Scott's work, both men are united in their attempt to approach the Waverley Novels in a new way, concentrating on Scott's achievement as an *historical* novelist. According to Lukács:[5]

> Scott's greatness lies in his capacity to give living human embodiment to historical-social types. The typically human terms in which great historical trends become tangible had never before been so superbly, straightforwardly, and pregnantly portrayed. And above all, never before had this kind of portrayal been consciously set at the centre of the representation of reality.

This is Scott's great, 'poetic' achievement. On the basic issue, Daiches is in complete agreement:[6]

> His imagination, his abundant sense of life, his ear for vivid dialogue, his feeling for the striking incident, and that central, healthy sense of the humour of character, added, of course, essential qualities to his fiction. But it was his tendency to look at history through character and at character through the history that had worked on it that provided the foundation of his art.

Both essays attack the conventional notion of Scott's history as essentially romantic and fanciful – the *histoire Walter Scottée* of his French detractors of the late nineteenth century. Taken together with Duncan Forbes's article on 'The Rationalism of Sir Walter Scott' (1953), which first pointed out Scott's close connections with the eighteenth-century Scottish 'philosophical' historians,[7] these essays (whose similarity of direction is remarkable, considering that they were composed quite independently) constituted a revolution against the accepted idea of a 'romantic' Scott.

Much of the critical interest in Scott in recent years has been due to a new awareness, largely derived from these articles, of his original genius as an artist of the historical process – hence, for example, the number of articles published in the last ten years on the general theme of 'Sir Walter Scott and history'. Yet at the same time, the full-length studies of Scott's work which are a result of this new interest have all more or less drawn back from the implications of, particularly, Lukács's book. The prevalent attitude to Lukács's theories is of polite, but patronising, scepticism. The large theories put forward by

Lukács, it is suggested, although very interesting, do not stand up to detailed scrutiny when the novels are examined in depth. My own feeling, however, on reading some of the 'detailed' criticism which has recently been produced, is that while such critics have often, quite rightly, brought out the complexities of Scott's work, they fail to do justice to the 'coherence' of the Waverley Novels – the subject treated by both Lukács and Daiches.

I do not believe that this is an inevitable result of 'detailed' examination of the Waverley Novels. In fact, on the contrary, it seems to me that many of the situations and events in the novels, and nuances of Scott's presentation, only become clear and make sense as part of a larger pattern. This book is an attempt at a study in depth of the Waverley Novels specifically in terms of Scott's historical imagination – looking at the novels as the imaginative working-out of Scott's understanding of history and of the historical process.

In particular, I have tried to develop three connected ideas. First, I have tried to show, through a detailed critique of eight novels of the Scottish series, some of the ways in which Scott skilfully dramatises the social relations of the historical period with which he is dealing, through his characters and their interaction in the novels. Second, I have tried to show that Scott's art does develop both in outlook and expression through the novels, broadly in the direction of greater 'historical realism.' Last, in the two concluding chapters, I have tried to define theoretical criteria for Scott's varying successes and failures in the Waverley Novels, considered as a whole, and to suggest some reasons for the limits that seem to apply to him as an historical novelist. This last point inevitably brings in the influence on him of the Scottish 'philosophical' historians.

The eight Scottish novels that form the subject of the detailed analysis in this thesis are those in which I feel Scott's essential qualities as an historical novelist are most fully displayed. It is perhaps a fairly conventional choice; most recent critics have concentrated on the Scottish novels more or less intuitively, although some would have included *A Legend of Montrose*, *St Ronan's Well* or *The Fair Maid of Perth* in their choice, and others, perhaps, have omitted *Guy Mannering*, *The Antiquary*, or even *The Bride of Lammermoor*. Although I have tried to set

Introduction

down grounds for distinguishing critically between the novels, it will be seen from the nature of my argument that I do not believe that hard and fast lines can be drawn. To this extent, the choice of the eight novels considered remains, in the end, a personal one.

1

Waverley

The full title of Scott's first novel, *Waverley, or 'Tis Sixty Years Since*, warns us that we are about to read a double history: the story not just of one man, but of an historical epoch. The novel is easily divisible into two plots on different scales. On the personal scale, it covers the events of Edward Waverley's life, and the development of his character from early youth to manhood. On the public scale, *Waverley* depicts the failure of the Forty-Five Jacobite rebellion to reinstate in Britain an older political order – the Stuart absolutist monarchy, overthrown with James II in 1688. In this chapter I will suggest that the novel's seemingly disparate plot elements in fact share a common movement, and that by inter-relating them Scott is able to make certain assertions about the fundamental processes of human history.

The history of Edward Waverley is a story of character formed by experience. An early critic makes this point about him:[1]

> we can only say that his wanderings are not gratuitous, nor is he wavering and indecisive only because the author chooses to make him so. Every feature in character is formed by education, and it is to this first source that we are constantly referred for a just and sufficient cause of all the wandering passions as they arise in his mind.

The first six chapters of *Waverley* deal with the unusual conditions of Edward's education. Edward is the unwitting casualty of the Waverleys' disruption as a family after his father abandons their High Tory principles in order to pursue wealth and preferment in the Whig parliament of George II. Brought up in the splendid isolation of his uncle's home at Waverley-Honour, Edward is completely protected from the realities of the outside world. His uncle, Sir Everard, is a picture of aristocratic impotence in more senses than one: just as he shuns the idea of matrimony after an early disappointment, finding that 'the labour of courtship did not quite suit the dignified indolence of his habits',[2] so he also resigns his seat in parliament after the accession of George I, effectively withdrawing in disgust from political life. In both cases Sir Everard has opted out of battles in the real world, preferring to preserve his chivalric ideals and political faith in the isolation of a leisured existence. It is in this honourable, but ethereal, atmosphere that Waverley's 'education' takes place. Aunt Rachel's nostalgia for the family's Royalist heroes mingles naturally with Sir Everard's strict notions of honour, and with Waverley's own Quixotic absorption in romances, to exert their influences on the character of the hero.

Waverley's enlistment in the army, which ultimately ends his state of innocence, is actually intended to preserve it. When he is forced to leave the vicinity of Waverley-Honour as a result of his infatuation with the socially inferior Cecilia Stubbs, his father specifically rejects the idea of a Grand Tour, viewing the Continent as a place 'where all manner of snares were spread by the Pretender and his sons' and which is thus unsuitable for the son of a Whig partisan.[3] Ironically, the 'safe' option turns out to be the dangerous one, a result that is due at least as much to Waverley's character as to the circumstances in which he finds himself. His adventures in Scotland, on leave from his hated military duties, allow him progressively to indulge his romantic fantasies at the expense of reality.

With an attraction for the primitive and the picturesque which would have been all too easily appreciated by Scott's readership, Waverley's head is carried away successively by the physical grandeur of the country, the Gothic 'monastic solitude' of Tully-Veolan, the wild heroism of the Highland clansmen, and finally by the seeming epitome of romantic Scotland, Flora MacIvor. Waverley's meeting with Flora at a Highland waterfall results in a disastrous infatuation: the encounter takes place, however, in an obviously ironic context:[4]

> It was up the course of this last stream that Waverley, like a knight of romance, was conducted by the fair Highland damsel, his silent guide. . . . Around the castle, all was cold, bare, and desolate, yet tame even in desolation; but this narrow glen, at so short a distance, seemed to open into the land of romance. The rocks assumed a thousand peculiar and varied forms. In one place a crag of huge size presented its gigantic bulk, as if to forbid the passenger's further progress; . . . In another spot, the projecting rocks from the opposite sides of the chasm had approached so near to each other, that two pine trees laid across, and covered with turf, formed a rustic bridge at the height of at least one hundred and fifty feet. . . .
>
> While gazing at this pass of peril, which crossed, like a single black line, the small portion of blue sky not intercepted by the projecting rocks on either side, it was with a sensation of horror that Waverley beheld Flora and her attendant appear, like inhabitants of another region, propped, as it were, in mid air, upon this trembling structure.

If Waverley is like a 'knight of romance' at all here, it is only in his imagination. It is through his eyes, of course, that Scott depicts the whole scene. The Highland scenery is transformed into a Spenserian Faerie world, a 'land of romance'; the Gaelic maidservant (so allusively named Una!) is transmuted into a 'fair Highland damsel'; rocks turn into giants threatening to block the way, while Flora finally appears as a fairy spirit. Narrative objectivity is maintained here wholly through the ironic presentation: Scott wishes us to share Waverley's romanticised view of the world only to an extent that we may understand and sympathise with his predicament. The episode is certainly a 'pass of peril' for him, reinforcing his illusory idea of his own actions in a way that robs his brain of any vestige of cool consideration.

Waverley's passion for Flora and his associated obsession with knight errantry are both unmercifully exploited by Fergus MacIvor in his attempts to recruit him to the Jacobite cause. An exactly parallel 'seduction' to that practised on Waverley by Flora in the foregoing passage is the scene in which the Pretender overwhelms him with a chivalric appeal for his fealty:[5]

> 'But,' continued Charles Edward, after another short pause, 'if Mr. Waverley should, like his ancestor, Sir Nigel, determine to embrace a cause which has little to recommend it but its justice, and follow a prince who throws himself upon the affections of his people, to recover the throne of his ancestors or perish in the attempt, I can only say. . . .'

This appeal to his ancestor Sir Nigel, the esteemed hero of Aunt Rachel's most poignant tale, is the one most likely to strike Waverley to the heart. Scott comments drily that the Prince's 'words and his kindness penetrated the heart of our hero, and easily outweighed all prudential motives.'[6] Flattered by the condescension shown to him, unused to Charles's courtly manner, mindful of his uncle's loyalty to the Stuart cause and most of all, of his own position, an outcast from his regiment and interdicted by the established government, Waverley devotes himself to following the Prince in a flood of emotional loyalty. It takes the remainder of the novel for Waverley to disengage himself from this double commitment – to Flora and the Prince – commitments that are parallel examples of Waverley's impulsive, romantic character.

Waverley's fate, however, cannot be considered in isolation from the broader historical situation of 1745, against which Scott places his hero. This is the other 'half' of the novel, which has not often been examined in any depth, even though attempts to see the narrative of Edward Waverley as the sole unifying design of the novel are bound to fail. Thus Stewart Gordon, who has taken the 'individual fate' plot-line as far as it can go, is finally forced to admit that the most striking episodes which conclude the novel, the trial and execution of Fergus and Evan Dhu, are strictly 'inappropriate according to this reading of the work'.[7]

The fact is, of course, that against the ironic narrative of Waverley's 'progressive enchantment and disenchantment', Scott sets a strikingly realistic picture of Scottish society and the political events of 1745. Often this picture contrasts strongly with the view of things we are given through Waverley's eyes. The scene in which Waverley passes through the village of Tully-Veolan, on the way to the Baron of Bradwardine's house, is a good example. Scott begins with a finely objective description of the depressed hamlet:[8]

> As Waverley moved on, here and there an old man, bent as much by toil as years, his eyes bleared with age and smoke, tottered to the door of his hut, to gaze on the dress of the stranger, and the form and motion of the horses, and then assembled with his neighbours, in a little group at the smithy, to discuss the probabilities of whence the stranger came, and where he might be going.

This naturalistic depiction of peasant life would not be out of place in Maupassant. Yet the scene is gradually transformed as we come to see it through Waverley's eyes:

> Three of four village girls, returning from the well or brook with pitchers and pails upon their heads, formed more pleasing objects; and, with their thin short-gowns and single petticoats, bare arms, legs and feet, uncovered heads, and braided hair, somewhat resembled Italian forms of landscape. Nor could a lover of the picturesque have challenged either the elegance of their costume, or the symmetry of their shape; although, to say the truth, a mere Englishman, in search of the *comfortable*, a word peculiar to his native tongue, might have wished the clothes less scanty: the feet and legs somewhat protected from the weather, the head and complexion shrouded from the sun, or perhaps might even have thought the whole person and dress considerably improved by a plentiful application of spring water, with a *quantum sufficit* of soap.

The ambiguity of this description is obvious. On the one hand is the romantic English response to the 'picturesque' – obviously Waverley's response; on the other, the rational, Augustan observation of the poverty and dirt of the village. When Scott continues, he temporarily abandons Waverley in order to describe the villagers with an unusual power of observation and analysis:

The whole scene was depressing – for it argued, at the first glance, at least a stagnation of industry, and perhaps of intellect. . . . Yet the physiognomy of the people, when more closely examined, was far from exhibiting the indifference of stupidity: their features were rough, but remarkably intelligent; grave, but the very reverse of stupid; . . . The children, also, whose skins were burnt black, and whose hair was bleached white, by the influence of the sun, had a look and manner of life and interest. It seemed, upon the whole, as if poverty, and indolence, its too frequent companion, were combining to depress the natural genius and acquired information of a hardy, intelligent, and reflecting peasantry.

In this passage, Scott is suggesting that the state of the peasantry in Tully-Veolan is far from 'natural': that it is, in fact, a social result of the village's economic depression. Waverley, of course, sees none of this. As the village recedes, so his irrepressible dreams return. Typically, as he enters upon the decayed grandeur of the baron's feudal estate, his usual associations envelop him again, and erase the unpleasant impressions of the village. For Waverley, the grounds of the baron's mansions are a retreat from the drabness of the village, with which he imagines they have nothing to do:[9]

The solitude and repose of the whole scene seemed almost romantic; and Waverley . . . walked slowly down the avenue, enjoying the grateful and cooling shade, and so much pleased with the placid ideas of rest and seclusion excited by this confined and quiet scene, that he forgot the misery and dirt of the hamlet he had left behind him.

The ironic sting in the tail of the sentence, however, ensures that the reader does not also forget the village.

Instead, we become progressively aware of the gulf between the appearance of things to Waverley and the reality of the situation. In the aftermath of the *creagh*, for example, having joined Evan Dhu to track down Donald Bane Lane, Waverley is left for a while by himself on the banks of a loch. Sitting in darkness, he immediately begins to exercise his fancy, imagining himself another Marco Polo on a perilous journey to the den of a romantic bandit, 'a second Robin Hood, perhaps' Scott comments:[10]

> What a variety of incidents for the exercise of a romantic imagination, and all enhanced by the solemn feeling of uncertainty, if not of danger! The only circumstances which assorted ill with the rest, was the cause of his journey – the Baron's milk-cows. This degrading incident he kept in the background.

Robin Mayhead has pointed out that Scott satirically punctures Waverley's illusions here, but he does not quite do full justice to the irony of the passage.[11] For, just as Waverley fails to see that the ramshackle state of the baron's home is intrinsically connected with the depressed state of the village of Tully-Veolan through a decaying social system, so he here fails to perceive that, far from being just a romantic 'incident', the *creagh* is an integral part of the economic system which supports the Highland clans. It is highly significant that the first contact we see between the Baron of Bradwardine and Clan Ivor is antagonistic, for the only way Fergus can provide for the huge number of clansmen in his 'tail', while keeping up the open hospitality displayed at the feast Waverley attends, is if the clan survives at the expense of the feudal estates like Tully-Veolan, either by raiding them or by blackmailing their owners. Milk-cows, in other words, instead of being 'incidental', are the main means of subsistence, and the prime cause not only of Waverley's journey but of much of the Highland way of life.

The baron's hostility towards Fergus over 'blackmail' at the time of Waverley's arrival at Tully-Veolan, coupled with the Baron's references to his family's former open warfare with Clan Ivor (one result of which is a lasting enmity between him and one old clansman), further suggest to the reader that the *creagh* is in fact only the tail-end of an ancient dispute between the clans and the feudal estates that has continued, on and off, for centuries. The long-standing antipathy of the clansmen to the baron's own retainers, and vice versa, is never entirely eradicated, even when both groups attempt to bury their differences in order to take concerted action in the Prince's cause. Their mutual hostility surfaces very quickly during the march into England, as a result of Waverley's quarrel with

Fergus over Flora. Only Charles's exemplary diplomacy on this occasion averts a potentially disastrous clash between the two main factions of his supporters, and the incident serves as an excellent reminder of the essential fragility of the Jacobite alliance.

It is on account of this history of conflict between clan and feudal estate, and not just because Clan Ivor is known to be behind the *creagh*, that Scott has Evan Dhu appear at Tully-Veolan as 'An Unexpected Ally' in the title of Chapter XVI. His meeting with Bradwardine serves to explain to the reader (though not to Waverley, of course) that these previously opposed social orders are prepared to combine to face a common enemy. In their opening parley, the Baron and Evan Dhu appeal to the common feature of both their cultures: the aristocratic hierarchy based on birth, which they both respect absolutely, and which is threatened for both of them by the power of the emergent middle classes in the Hanoverian parliamentary system. Thus, to Evan's richly metaphorical offer of conciliation, the Baron replies, with suitable dignity[12]

> that he knew the chief of the clan Ivor to be a well-wisher to the *King*, and he was sorry there should have been a cloud between him and any gentleman of such sound principles, 'for when folks are banding together, feeble is he who hath no brother.'

This alliance between 'gentlemen' finds its natural political expression in their support of the supreme representative of the old hierarchy of birth, the exiled 'King' James III, the Old Pretender. For both the Baron and Fergus, their present situation is untenable. Both are increasingly impoverished and powerless in the new Scotland – a prospect particularly galling to Fergus, whose education in the French court has made him impatient to exercise his political genius beyond the limited sphere of Clan Ivor's influence, but who is forced out of necessity to put his energies into ensuring the clan's subsistence from day to day.

In fact, the differences between the clans and the Prince's supporters from the Lowland estates come to appear relatively unimportant once the rebellion begins. What Scott impresses strongly on the reader is the obsolescence of the whole Jacobite party when it confronts the society of the Scottish Lowland towns. It is an obsolescence both of methods and ideas, a reflection of the antiquated organisation of society which is all that Charles's supporters understand. Ominously, Waverley's first meeting with the Prince's occupying forces takes place in the ruined castle of Doune, where a gentleman introduces himself to Waverley, without any hint of irony, as the 'governor of the garrison.'[13] The occupation of this dilapidated monument clearly displays the doomed strategy of the commanders of the Jacobite forces, for to occupy the ancient centres of feudal power in the countryside is quite useless when economic changes have transferred real power to the towns. Holding the castle of Doune is an illusory success, because the Prince's opponents are not even disputing the ground. In contrast, the British government's strategy in Edinburgh is adroit: the gold from the city's banks is simply moved into Edinburgh castle before the Jacobites occupy the rest of the city. There is a strong contrast between the fortress, a symbol of the Hanoverian government's financial impregnability, presiding over the city, cannons firing at any Highlanders who show themselves, and the Prince's own base in the old palace of Holyrood, outside Edinburgh. The character of the palace with its 'long, low and ill-proportioned gallery, hung with pictures, affirmed to be the portraits of kings who, if they ever flourished at all, lived several hundred years before the invention of painting in oil colours'[14] gives not only an obsolete but an inescapably fake cast to the proceedings of Charles's 'court': an impression which the extravagance of his Restoration-style ball, covering as it does his desperate impecuniosity, does little to dispel.

Notably, support for the Prince in the Lowland towns is practically non-existent. In Cairnvreckan, that centre of Presbyterian industry, the only sympathetic voice heard is that of Mrs Mucklewrath, whose drunken carousing is really a personal rebellion against the sexual mores and the hypocritical propriety of the town's petit-bourgeois kirk-elders. Only too obviously, her mind is running on the potentialities of the 'lads in kilts' rather than on the political consequences of 'Charlie's' restoration. Similarly in Edinburgh, while Mrs Flockhart, Fergus's landlady, does display a real affection for the chief, she nevertheless considers him only as a courteous and handsome lodger – hardly the attitude towards feudal 'authority' upon which the Jacobite rebellion depends for any lasting success.

Even the troops the Prince eventually raises from the Lowland counties (in which officers ominously outnumber men) are less than whole-hearted in their enthusiasm. Waverley questions one man, Lieutenant Jinker, thus:[15]

'You perhaps act as quarter-master, sir?'

'Ay, quarter-master, riding-master, and lieutenant,' answered this officer of all work. 'And, to be sure, wha's fitter to look after the breaking and the keeping of the poor beasts than mysel', that bought and sold every ane of them?'

'And pray, sir, if it be not too great a freedom, may I beg to know where we are going just now?'

'A fule's errand, I fear,' answered this communicative personage.

'In that case,' said Waverley, determined not to spare civility, 'I should have thought a person of your appearance would not have been found on the road.'

'Vera true, vera true, sir,' replied the officer, 'but every why has its wherefore. Ye maun ken, the laird there bought a' thir beasts frae me to munt his troop, and agreed to pay for them according to the necessities and prices of the time. But then he hadna the ready penny, and I hae been advised his bond will not be worth a boddle against the estate, and then I had a' my dealers to settle wi' at Martinmas; and so he very kindly offered me this commission, and as the auld Fifteen wad never help me to my siller for sending out naigs against the government, why, conscience! sir, I thought my best chance for payment was e'en to *gae out* mysel'; and ye may judge, sir, as I hae dealt a' my life in halters, I think na mickle o' putting my craig in peril of a St. Johnstone's tippet.'

'You are not, then, by profession a soldier?' said Waverley.

'Na, na; thank God,' answered this doughty partisan.

This brilliant and humorous piece of dialogue (Waverley's dawning of understanding with his last question is particularly amusing) speaks volumes about the state of the Scottish

Lowlands in 1745, and about the motivation of the men who make up Charles's army. The Laird of Balmawhapple's evident impoverishment (even his estate is no security for a debt), Jinker's shrewd calculation before coming 'out' for the rebellion as a financial necessity and his contempt as a tradesman for both military activity and the Jacobite cause ('a fule's errand'): all this manifests a decay in the old feudal system and its authority which is not to be reversed. Later, Jinker has 'a vehement dispute upon the price of hay with a farmer, who had reluctantly followed his laird to the field, rather than give up his farm, whereof the lease had just expired.' The gentry have had to exert every scrap of power over their tenants to turn out even these dubious supporters.

Moreover, the march into England, despite its speed, is disastrous in terms of support:[16]

> Waverley could not but observe that in those towns in which they proclaimed James the Third, 'no man cried God bless him.' The mob stared and listened, heartless, stupified and dull, but gave few signs even of that boisterous spirit which induces them to shout upon all occasions. . . .

The quotation here, from *Richard II*, is from Shakespeare's description of the mob's treatment of Richard when he is brought into London a prisoner by the victorious Bolingbroke. It is a deftly ironic parallel with the English townspeople's silent rejection of Charles Stuart and the *ancien régime* in favour of the established Hanoverian 'usurpers'. Indeed, only the few local Tory gentlemen actually feel compelled to make the decision not to support the rebellion. For the majority, so remote is the culture of the Highland clans and the Scottish feudalists from their own way of life, that the appearance of the rebels strikes them only as an alien intrusion. The 'astonishment, mixed with horror and aversion' with which they greet the sight of the Highlanders spells the death of the rebellion; for their first reaction is not even antipathy, but sheer incredulity.

The depth of Scott's portrayal of the failure of the Forty-Five in *Waverley* is achieved by his paralleling the decay of the clan system and of feudalism with the changes in the psychology of the Jacobites themselves. The dilemma of the leading Jacobites is that of men placed inevitably on the 'wrong' side of historical development, their traditional social positions negated by the material changes which have taken place in society. In many ways, Fergus MacIvor embodies the contradictions of the Jacobite cause. Brought up in exile in the French court, Fergus displays an alienation from the very clan culture of which, as chief, he is supposedly the *raison d'être*. The satirical tone he adopts with Waverley over his bard's prophetic powers (which hold the rest of the clan in a mystical rapture) is a symptom of his cultural rootlessness;[17] as are his continual, opportunistic attempts to extend his influence beyond the traditional patriarchal sphere into national politics. Hoping to make the rebellion a realistic proposition for himself, Fergus joins the army of hangers-on which surrounds Charles in Edinburgh, seeking titles, positions, and rewards for their services from his solitary money-ship. The reader is not allowed to forget the pre-eminence of the profit motive and its sometimes absurd consequences: amazingly, Fergus actually regards the few men who do join the rebellion in the Lowlands with suspicion, as additional claimants on the Prince's bounty.[18] With the women also, Fergus's attitude is distastefully mercenary; he is quite ready to use Flora's beauty to gain influence, and regards his own intended marriage to Rose Bradwardine as a sound business proposition.[19]

Scott's irony here is that this self-seeking mentality in Charles's supporters is implicitly in direct contradiction to the ideology of the Jacobite cause. As Charles says, his cause 'has little to recommend it but its justice' – his only claim to the throne is his lineage, and the celebrated philosophy of Stuart absolutism which maintains that his family has the God-given right to rule. By manipulating the Prince, and especially by using him as a means to their own monetary advantage, his supporters show they no longer really believe in the ideology of their own cause, and that the values of the bourgeois Lowlands and England have in practice become their values. Fergus's frustrated exclamation to Waverley, when baulked in his attempt to have his earldom confirmed, amply illustrates the confusion of feudal and commercial ideas in his mind: 'I'll tell you what I *could* have done at that moment – sold myself to the

Devil or the Elector, whichever offered the dearest revenge.'[20]

The influence of commercial society on Fergus here is not, however, merely a result of the peculiarity of his personality or individual position. Inexorably, the same pressures are being exerted even on the clansmen themselves, as an inevitable result of contact with the more advanced state of society in the rest of Britain. When Waverley first enters the banqueting hall at Glennaquoich, we are told that he was made the traditional offer of having his feet washed ceremonially:[21]

> but by a smoke-dried skinny old Highland woman, who did not seem to think herself much honoured by the duty imposed upon her, but muttered between her teeth, 'Our fathers' herds did not feed so near together that I should do you this service.' A small donation, however, amply reconciled this ancient handmaiden to the supposed degradation; and as Waverley proceeded to the hall, she gave him her blessing in the Gaelic proverb, 'May the open hand be filled fullest.'

Robin Mayhead, referring to this passage, argues that the old woman views Waverley's gift here, 'not as a bribe, but as a symbolic substitute for orthodox ties (in her society's scale of values) which would make her perform the service without question'.[22] Yet though Mayhead is perhaps right in this particular instance, the passage also suggests that the accumulated effect on the Highlanders of incidents like this one will inevitably be far-reaching. If money is repeatedly accepted as a 'symbolic substitute for orthodox ties', a reassessment of the strength of those ties in comparison with monetary advantages will be the eventual result.

Try as they may, the characters in *Waverley* cannot isolate themselves from the effects of the modern world. Only the Baron of Bradwardine makes a real attempt to ignore the changes which have taken place, and Scott's tragi-comic treatment of him reflects the ambiguous nature of his success. The baron's feudal ideas, 'greatly strengthened by habits of solitary and secluded authority', make him the only true feudalist of the Jacobite party. Unwaveringly true to the feudal forms – so far as it is within his power to be so – it is the baron's fidelity to the feudal organisation of society that finally underlines its lack of credibility. His refusal to compromise over what he sees as his traditional duties makes him notorious: he even quite disinterestedly applies his notions of Salic Law to Rose, preparing to disinherit her in favour of a distant male nephew of suspiciously Whiggish sympathies. On the other hand, it is the same ideal of honour that leads the baron to take Waverley's place in the duel with Balmawhapple, over an issue on which he in fact agrees with his opponent. On his own feudal holding, he is incorrigible:[23]

> For, as he used to observe, 'the lands of Bradwardine, Tully-Veolan, and others, had been erected into a free barony by a charter from David the First, *cum liberali potest, habendi curias et justicias, cum fossa et furca* (lie – pit and gallows) *et saka et soka, et thol et theam, et infangthief et outfangthief, sive hand-habend, sive bak-barend.*' The peculiar meaning of all these cabalistical words few or none could explain; but they implied, upon the whole, that the Baron of Bradwardine might, in case of delinquency, imprison, try, and execute his vassals at his pleasure. Like James the First, however, the present possessor of this authority was more pleased in talking about prerogative than in exercising it; and, excepting that he imprisoned two poachers in the dungeon of the old tower of Tully-Veolan where they were sorely frightened by ghosts, and almost eaten by rats, and that he set an old woman in the *jougs* (or Scottish pillory) for saying 'there were mair fules in the laird's ha' house than Davie Gellatley,' I do not learn that he was accused of abusing his high powers. Still, however, the conscious pride of possessing them gave additional importance to his language and deportment.

But he equally takes the obligations of his position seriously, even if (as over the *caligae*) he is the only one to do so. Our reaction to the baron is curiously ambivalent. An antique figure in the 'modern' world, he is ridiculously anachronistic, because he takes seriously the ideals of a social system which no longer really exists. At the same time, however, we come to feel the loss of the baron's peculiar qualities in the modern world. In a sense, the baron's ideals are never, in themselves, devalued – it

19

is a changed world which comes to consider them unnatural and even laughable.

In the context of this complex picture of Scottish society in 1745, Waverley's own history takes shape. His abandonment of his romantic impulses towards the Jacobite cause and towards Flora (the two are hardly separated in his mind) is not just a question of Waverley's growing older and being chastened by experience – though of course this is an important part of it. Instead, his disenchantment, both with the rebellion and with Flora's almost religious devotion of her life to it, comes to appear inevitable given that the nature of his commitment from the start was so purely romantic. In this, Waverley is strongly distinguished from the other Jacobite characters – Fergus, Flora, the baron, and the Prince himself. Whatever the contradictions in their behaviour, the class positions of these characters place them clearly on the Jacobite side of the conflict. This is not the case with Waverley, who has no real class or cultural affinities with the reactionary side, and whose chivalric attitudes are merely literary and personal fantasies. Even his awareness of the actual ideological issues at stake is practically non-existent, which makes it doubly ironic that he is condemned for carrying around (unread) his tutor's massive tomes eulogising the Stuart family and the ultra-High Church.

In fact, Waverley's hesitation throughout the novel, the 'wavering' which comes to characterise all his actions, tends to suggest that, far from being a natural course of action for him, his career in the Prince's service is at odds with his own common sense, patriotic feeling, and rational political views. Even before volunteering in the cause, Waverley is arguing with himself about the desirability of the rebellion:[24]

Whatever were the original rights of the Stuarts, calm reflection told him that, omitting the question how far James the Second could forfeit those of his posterity, he had, according to the united voice of the whole nation, justly forfeited his own. Since that period, four monarchs had reigned in peace and glory over Britain, sustaining and exalting the character of the nation abroad and its liberties at home. Reason asked, was it worth while to disturb a government so long settled and established, and to plunge

a kingdom into all the miseries of civil war, for the purpose
of replacing upon the throne the descendants of a monarch
by whom it had been wilfully forfeited?

These reflections show the gulf separating Waverley's political
opinions from Jacobite principles. His underlying assumptions
are that good government is liberal and democratic, as his
references to 'the whole nation' and 'its liberties' clearly show:
exactly the qualities which the Stuart monarchy could not
represent. More particularly, Waverley feels that to upset the
peaceful order in the country for the rights of one man might be
an act of grave irresponsibility. Altogether, these are not the
sentiments of one to whom the mere existence of the
Hanoverian political and economic order is a threat, as it is to
the leading Jacobite characters. To Waverley, the end of the
rebellion is merely the restoration of one man: to the others, the
restoration of the Stuart regime is only to be the beginning of a
cherished return to a state in which the clans and the feudal
aristocracy will again exercise power.

It is Waverley's commitment to the Prince's cause, therefore,
which eventually comes to seem criminal to him. At the battle
of Falkirk (in which, ironically, Waverley spends his entire time
trying to save his 'opponents' in the government forces), the
guilt of his involvement with the Jacobites comes home to him
in numerous painful ways: particularly in the pathetic story told
by his family's old retainer, Houghton, on his death-bed, and
in the 'upbraiding, yet sorrowful look' of his old commander,
Colonel Gardiner, as he recognises Waverley shortly before he
too expires. In addition to these personal tribulations, however,
Waverley is also overcome, for a moment, by 'culture-shock'.
As he recognises the standard of the very troop he himself used
to command, he is suddenly paralysed by his reflections:[25]

It was at that instant that, looking around him, he saw the
wild dress and appearance of his Highland associates,
heard their whispers in an uncouth and unknown
language, looked upon his own dress, so unlike that which
he had worn from his infancy, and wished to awake from
what seemed at the moment a dream strange, horrible,
and unnatural. 'Good God!' he muttered, 'am I then a
traitor to my country, a renegade to my standard, and a

foe, as that poor dying wretch expressed himself, to my native England!'

Waverley's cultural antipathy to the Jacobite side here, echoing that of his countrymen later, reinforces our sense of the complete inappropriateness of his conduct. This is, to be sure, something that Flora MacIvor has always recognised in Waverley. As she comments to Rose in a well-known passage in the novel, Waverley's proper place is 'in the quiet circle of domestic happiness, lettered indolence, and elegant enjoyments, of Waverley-Honour.'[26] Her comic description of Waverley's future life as a typical late eighteenth-century 'man of feeling' (as Donald Davie observes)[27] is a shrewd prophecy. She is quite right: Waverley's future position is not that of the feudal aristocrat – it is nearer to the way of life of Jane Austen's leisurely, upper-middle-class world.

Waverley's substitution of the domesticated Rose for the haughty Flora is a notable victory for the 'common sense' in him. Rose has continually made clear her opposition to the rebellion: situated in the midst of the turmoil, she has no enthusiasm for any of it, and hardly comprehends her father's notions of feudalism. She writes to Waverley early on:[28]

> I hope God will protect you, and that you will get safe home to England, where you used to tell me there was no military violence nor fighting among clans permitted, but everything was done according to an equal law that protected all who were harmless and innocent.

The mixture of naïveté and sense in Rose's letter here is again nicely ironic. Waverley's conversion to Rose from Flora takes place later, however; beginning conspicuously, at the Edinburgh tea-party at which Waverley and the other men join the ladies in polite conversation. Despite the rebellion going on outside, Waverley is concerned primarily with the excitement of this polite occasion – bearing out Flora's view of him. The group's tea-table discussion of *Romeo and Juliet* is germane: Evan Dhu is a brilliant reminder of the clan mentality, as he bristles over the unfairness of Mercutio's death, but to Waverley and Rose it is the nuances of the play's love-affairs, and their application to their own circumstances, which provide the real interest.

J. H. Raleigh has noted that 'the end of the novel alternates back and forth between the light and the dark.'[29] In particular, the weight of the *dénouement* of the novel falls on two contrasting scenes. On the one hand, there is the engagement of Rose and Waverley; on the other, the trial and execution of Fergus and Evan Dhu. Rose and Waverley are the survivors (as their marriage underlines) and as such they share a common quality with other 'survivors' in the novel – the ability to compromise with the inevitable. Thus Bailie MacWheeble, that man with 'a very quiet and peaceful conscience, *that never did him any harm*',[30] is adamant that he will not again be drawn into military adventures of any sort. Peace is essential, as far as MacWheeble is concerned, if he is to conduct his business regularly, with cash payment. Even the marriage between Waverley and Rose takes on real interest for MacWheeble only when Waverley's inheritance is made comprehensible to him in financial arithmetic as 'ten thousand a year – the least penny'.[31] In this he serves to emphasise to the reader, indirectly, that Waverley's living is liable to be comfortable. The survivors also share the ability to forget: MacWheeble's ostentatious and comical efforts to erase his memory of the Forty-Five by dyeing his tartan nightcap black, possibly satirise Waverley's own mental processes of extrication from the past during the thoroughly orthodox business of his engagement to Rose.

Scott moves directly from the scene of happy domesticity at the engagement party to the grim news of Fergus's impending doom at the hands of an English court. The Hanoverian government may be persuaded to pardon someone like Waverley, who, as Colonel Talbot argues with the king, has no real interests opposed to the established power, but to Fergus MacIvor, a dangerous man driven irresistibly into opposition by his class position, it cannot afford to show leniency. Talbot himself attempts to justify the cruel sentence heaped upon Fergus, when he refuses to plead on his behalf. Scott comments: 'Such was the reasoning of those times, held even by brave and humane men towards a vanquished enemy.'[32] Talbot is an Augustan Englishman, the representative of reasonable, 'civilised' society, yet his peculiar enmity towards Fergus leaves little room for humanity. As with his (very Johnsonian) prejudices against the Scots as a race, this incident reinforces the suggestion that Augustan humanism was itself limited by social and cultural antipathies which it could not transcend.

In the final extremity of trial and execution, Fergus's opportunist attitude disappears. By fulfilling his traditional role as the uncompromising and unrepentant chief of Clan Ivor, he finally justifies Evan Dhu's unlimited loyalty to him. The scene of their condemnation is a bitter comment on the limitations of Waverley's England's 'equal law' applied to men from a culture with different conceptions of justice and morality. Even Evan Dhu's tragic offer to fetch six other Highlanders who would, with himself, undergo execution to save the chief, is interpreted as a laughable attempt to save his own neck: Evan is completely right when he says that the English jury 'ken neither the heart of a Highlander, nor the honour of a gentleman'. Patronisingly, the judge pities Evan and his 'unhappy ideas of clanship', and offers him leniency if he pleads for mercy – but mercy is unthinkable to Evan if his chief is to have none. His spirited reply to the offer settles the matter:[33]

> the only favour I would accept of you is – to bid them loose
> my hands and gie me my claymore, and bide you just a
> minute sitting where you are.

In the end, Fergus kindly spares Waverley the sight of his execution by forbidding him to watch it: instead, he heartily congratulates him on his forthcoming marriage. Fergus realises that for someone like Waverley, who is destined to survive and participate in the new Scotland, the sight of his execution can only pointlessly undermine his future stability and happiness.

Interestingly, Scott does not have the Baron of Bradwardine share Fergus's fate. Although disinherited and at first proscribed, his purely 'ideological' Jacobitism, practically divorced from real-life considerations, presents no threat to the modern world. Pardoned by King George, the baron is returned to his estate which Talbot and Waverley have purchased on the open market. It is no accident that, although the baron continues to occupy Tully-Veolan, he does so by right of purchase and no longer, even theoretically, as a feudal baron. Tully-Veolan's transition from the status of feudal tenure to that of a bought freehold destroys the last figment of legality in the baron's feudal ideas. If Fergus's execution symbolises the end of the political and military power of the clans, the purchase of Tully-Veolan represents the end of the feudal system.

Considering *Waverley* as a whole, a common movement can be seen in both the 'private' and 'public' histories which the novel narrates. On the private scale, Edward Waverley's youthful romanticism and idealism is progressively destroyed by the rationalism and common sense necessary for survival in the 'civilised' society to which he finds he ultimately belongs. On the public scale, the heroic culture of clanship and of the feudal aristocracy comes to appear, through the events of the rebellion, hopelessly unrealistic and inopportune when confronted by the new order in Lowland Scotland and England, to which it finally gives way. The movement in both plots is to some extent analogous, provoking the same, contradictory responses from the reader, and this is largely the reason for the formal unity and cohesion of the novel.

That Scott has some such underlying thematic movement in mind throughout *Waverley* is interestingly reinforced by his use of one particular reiterated image throughout the novel. Its first appearance comes in the passage immediately preceding Waverley's approach to the 'pass of peril' – a notable crisis in his history. Although it can obviously be taken as part of Waverley's romantic interest in the scenic, the passage nevertheless strikes the reader as curiously analytic:[34]

In a spot, about a quarter of a mile from the castle, two brooks, which formed the little river, had their junction. The larger of the two came down the long bare valley, which extended, apparently without any change or elevation of character, as far as the hills which formed its boundary permitted the eye to reach. But the other stream, which had its source among the mountains on the left hand of the strath, seemed to issue from a very narrow and dark opening betwixt two large rocks. These streams were different also in character. The larger was placid, and even sullen in its course, wheeling in deep eddies, or sleeping in dark blue pools; but the motions of the lesser brook were rapid and furious, issuing from between precipices, like a maniac from his confinement, all foam and uproar.

Not only the nature of the scenery described here (which is in fact unusual for a Highland location) but Scott's almost pedantic emphasis that 'these streams were also different in character', suggest that his intention is not merely picturesque. D. D. Devlin has commented on this passage:[35]

> It is not possible to miss the identification of the 'rapid and furious' brook with rebellion that is about to burst from the mountains, nor the larger stream, 'placid and sleeping' with the House of Hanover; and in the expression 'like a maniac' Scott suggests . . . that militant Jacobitism is madness.

The more closely the passage is examined, the more obvious it is that Scott intends the reader to make this identification. The lesser brook rushes down from the mountains, as the clans do in the rebellion itself; it is the last expression of the dammed-up frustration of those regions. The main stream, with its measured, steady course towards the horizon, obviously represents civilised, undramatic, Augustan society. Yet the streams can also be applied to the two currents in Waverley's life – his romantic impulses, on the one hand; the influence of common sense and reason, on the other. It is no coincidence that it is up the course of the smaller brook that Waverley is led to his romantic meeting with Flora at the waterfall.

The same image appears again, notably, just before Waverley's other 'seduction', into the service of the Prince. After Charles's emotional appeal to Waverley's loyalty, we are told that the hero's thoughts 'rushed through his mind like a torrent, sweeping before them every consideration of an opposite tendency.'[36] This implicit reference back allows Scott to link Waverley's espousal of the Jacobite cause with his infatuation for Flora, as essentially an act of romanticism. Finally, the image of a river crops up again in Scott's 'Postscript' to the novel, where he attempts to summarise the nature of the change in Scotland since 1745. Here he writes that[37]

the change, though steadily and rapidly progressive, has
nevertheless been gradual; and like those who drift down
the stream of a deep and smooth river, we are not aware of
the progress we have made until we fix our eye on the now
distant point from which we have been drifted.

This final reference emphasises the inevitability of the victory of
the slow, steady, main stream of development (and by his
previous mention of Selkirk, it is clear Scott saw this as an
economic development) over the more spectacular effects of the
brook. For all its aesthetic attractiveness, the brook's physical
power in relation to that of the river is non-existent: despite the
influx of the brook, the main river in the earlier passage
continues on its course unaffected. The effect of Waverley's
early involvement with Flora and with the Jacobite rebellion on
the later course of his life, or of the Forty-Five on the historical
development of the eighteenth century is hardly any greater:
from the satiric viewpoint, both are merely 'foam and uproar'.

Scott's great originality in *Waverley* lies not only in his
intuition that an individual's life is fundamentally affected by
the age in which he lives, but also in a complementary intuition
that the most significant manifestation of the forces at work in
society at any one time will be in the lives of ordinary
individuals. *Waverley* is thus a brilliant evocation of an
historical situation, in which Scott attempts to illuminate the
underlying movements common to the lives of individuals and
in society as a whole at that particular period. It is this conscious
grasp of a concrete historical moment that is the common factor
of all the greatest of Scott's novels, and this which makes
Waverley the first really 'historical' novel, even if it is not the
first novel set in the past.

Waverley was in a way Scott's prentice-work as a novelist,
however, and it is only right to criticise the novel's weakness in
some respects. Most obvious is Scott's continual reliance on his
reading to supply both his irony and his narrative style. The
mock-Spenserian overtones, for example, eventually become
tiresome, and the Shakespearian allusions (though usually
well-handled) make the work overly self-conscious at points.
Maria Edgeworth quite properly took exception to the rather
uneasy authorial addresses to the reader that Scott inserted in

Waverley: 'They are like Fielding: but for that reason we cannot bear that an author of such high powers, of such original genius, should for a moment stoop to imitation.'[38] Sterne's influence in this respect is also apparent.[39] In all these cases, Scott is leaning too heavily on other writers – not an unusual fault in a first novel, and one which he subsequently avoided in his best work.

More important was Jeffrey's criticism of the novel in the *Edinburgh Review*:[40]

> The worst part of the book by far is that portion of the first volume which contains the history of the hero's residence in England – and next to it is the laborious, tardy, and obscure explanation of some puzzling occurences in the story . . . The passages in which the author speaks in his own person are also considerably below mediocrity—and form a strange and humiliating contrast with the force and freedom of his manner when engaged in those dramatic or picturesque representations to which his genius so decidedly inclines.

Jeffrey points out here the crucial superiority of the dramatic mode of presentation in *Waverley*. Even Scott's use of the 'two streams' image as a way of unifying the novel appears arbitrary and artificial in comparison with the brilliant portrayal of character evoked naturally in the dramatic scenes in the novel. Two years after Jeffrey's review, Scott himself, writing anonymously in the *Quarterly Review* on 'Tales of My Landlord', concurred in the opinion that his characters were effective principally because of their dramatic presentation:[41]

> their characteristic features are brought to the reader's eye, not by description or enumeration, but by compelling him, as in real life, to observe their effect when forced into contact with the peculiarities of others.

This dramatic strength of Scott's does not exist in isolation from the power of his historical imagination. The dramatic scenes in *Waverley* are of a peculiar kind: we can almost say that the novel proceeds, not by episodes, but by encounters. Some of these – Waverley's meeting with Flora at the waterfall, his first interview with Charles Edward, the meeting between the Baron of Bradwardine and Evan Dhu, Waverley's revealing conversation with Jinker, and Evan Dhu's confrontation by the English court – have been recalled at some length. It is in just these encounters that the characters reveal themselves: their backgrounds, their conflicting personalities and prejudices. In all these situations dramatic conflict is essential because it reveals more clearly (in Scott's hands) than any narrative the historical forces acting upon the characters. The drama of the court scene, for example, is not only of opposed characters: it is also a symbolic showdown between the opposed forces of the clans and English society. It shows that the British government possesses both the physical power and the moral rectitude, in the eyes of its citizens, to suppress the Highlanders without any sympathy or even understanding of their predicament. It is because the historical forces have their showdown in the English courtroom that Scott does not need to depict the heroic stand of the Highlanders or their merciless slaughter at the battle of Culloden.

To compare the conception of such a scene as that of the trial with that of the early chapters of the novel, as Jeffrey does, is to show clearly the source of Scott's weakness in that part of *Waverley* written in 1805. For in these early scenes, Scott does not seem impelled by the same conviction that the history of individuals and that of society are closely inter-related, nor that it is only through dramatic encounter that men's historical relationships become manifest. The narrative of Waverley's early personal life is a lengthy précis, lacking any concrete situation – Sir Everard's house and Waverley's upbringing in it have an almost *Rasselas*-like vagueness of place and time about them. Of course, Waverley's childhood is important from the point of view of his later actions, but this is the only reason it interests us at all. The first six chapters do little more than prepare the character of Waverley for the seventh, when the novel proper begins and Waverley becomes a character in the dramatic sense, forced into contact with the historical forces of his age.

Not only in *Waverley*, but in the subsequent novels, it is essential to distinguish between the fruits of Scott's original genius as an 'historical' novelist (in the sense described in this chapter) and those elements in his work which are not central to his subject, and often obscure the real interest of the novels.

Very often, as in *Waverley*, the inferior parts of the novels are those in which Scott falls back on derivative literary modes; modes which, though obviously popular with his contemporary audience, become hackneyed in his hands, or are actually inconsistent with the temper of his own imagination. It is with this lesson from *Waverley* that we should approach Scott's second novel, *Guy Mannering*.

2

Guy Mannering

Guy Mannering is not one of Scott's greatest novels. As a follow-up to his initial success in *Waverley*, it is a disappointing performance in many respects. It is quite arguable that *Guy Mannering*, unlike *Waverley*, is not primarily an historical novel at all; so much of it belongs to the world of the Gothic Romance. The return of a wandering hero, his 'quest', and his eventual restoration to his estate after evil has been defeated, are all traditional archetypal elements of romance, and Scott's manipulation of them in the novel is competent but not compelling. It is tempting to discard the whole of the 'lost heir' plot and settle merely for what Robert Gordon calls the 'items of social history'[1] – the vignettes of Pleydell's 'high jinks' in Edinburgh, or the Dinmonts' domestic life in Liddesdale. Yet it is possible to see a serious historical approach behind the romantic melodrama in *Guy Mannering* which incorporates more of the novel than Gordon allows, and which shows at work an original genius of the same order at least as that which produced *Waverley*, even if its expression is inferior.

In *Waverley*, Scott's 'Romanticism' is perfectly integrated into the novel, both through the hero's character, and through the depiction of the heroic culture of the Highland clans. In *Guy Mannering*, however, it remains largely unassimilated. This is particularly the case with the supernatural dimension Scott introduces into the latter novel. In *Waverley*, Scott's treatment of Highland superstition is acceptable, because although he shows it to be an essential part of clan life, unreasonable demands as to its credibility are never made on the reader. A good example is the incident of the appearance of the 'Bodach Glas' (the traditional apparition of doom) to Fergus MacIvor on the night before he is captured by the troops. Uncanny as the experience Fergus relates may be, the narrative does not commit the reader to accepting Fergus's version of events as final. The incident affects our view of Fergus – his experience signifies his mystical acceptance back into the clan from which he has so long been alienated – but like Waverley and Colonel Talbot, we are not convinced of the ghost's existence outside the chief's imagination. The supernatural, in other words, is given a *relative* credence. In *Guy Mannering*, Scott goes too far, by demanding our absolute credence.

Scott's purpose in introducing the supernatural into *Guy Mannering* may have been similar to that which he later claimed was Horace Walpole's in *The Castle of Otranto*:[2]

> to draw such a picture of domestic life and manners, during the feudal times, as might actually have existed, and to paint it chequered and agitated by the action of supernatural machinery, such as the superstition of the period received as matter of devout credulity.

Yet instead of relating the supernatural strictly to the historical position of the characters in the novel (as with Fergus in *Waverley*,) Scott gambles with the reader's credulity by having the actions of the novel bear out Mannering's astrological prediction and Meg's prophecy concerning the future of Harry Bertram. Robert Gordon is right to point out that Scott's apology for the presence of the astrological element in the novel (contained in the Introduction to the 1829 edition) is really inadequate.[3] Scott's explanation is in any case extremely superficial: the claim that hasty revision is to blame for traces of a 'discarded' plot is suspiciously facile. In particular, as Gordon notes, Scott fails to explain why the element of prophecy was 'actually reinforced' in the later chapters through the ambiguous figure of Meg Merrilies.

Though remaining the most celebrated Romance character in the Waverley Novels, Meg no longer appears to dominate the novel in the way she did for Scott's contemporary readership.

The fulsomeness of the *Augustan Review's* praise of her is surprising:[4]

> Meg Merrilies is, however, the great agent – the genius of the author shines forth in every line she utters and every scene in which she appears. There is a wild sublimity about her, a magnanimity in her revenge, a devotedness in her attachment to the family who have injured her tribe, and a heroism in her death, which form an object at once original and exalted. The speech she makes to the old Laird of Ellangowan immediately after the explusion of the gypsies from their dwellings, is filled with wild pathos. . . .

This is partly a 'Gothic' response to the marvellous (the 'wild sublimity about her'); partly a more critically controlled response to Meg as a human being, driven to extremity by circumstances of a peculiar, though comprehensible, nature. The modern reader is unlikely to share the first of these responses: yet the latter appreciation of Meg remains relevant. Her celebrated malediction on the House of Ellangowan: 'Ride your ways, Ellangowan. Our bairns are hinging at our weary backs; look that your braw cradle at home be the fairer spread up . . .'[5] retains its power, but as a human outburst against her fate and that of her tribe, rather than as a purely Gothic set-piece. Duncan Forbes is right to say that Meg's success is as one of Scott's 'studies in historical ecology':[6] in other words, as a character who grows naturally out of her social and cultural background. A. O. J. Cockshut has also pointed out that Scott's description of Meg's appearance at this crucial point is quite unromantic and analytical.[7] One sentence here is particularly notable:[8]

> We have noticed that there was in her general attire, or rather in her mode of adjusting it, somewhat of a foreign costume, artfully adopted perhaps for the purpose of adding to the effect of her spells and predictions, or perhaps from some traditional notions respecting the dress of her ancestors.

Both the suggested 'explanations' of Meg's costume here are those of a rationalist: either it is consciously assumed to impress the ignorant, or else Meg herself superstitiously respects her dress out of idiosyncratic 'notions' concerning her ancestors. The sceptical tone of the whole is close to Samuel Johnson's, but informed by Scott's characteristic sociological interest. The 'Romantic' Meg is held firmly on the ground here by Scott's simultaneous insistence on her as a credible historical character.

The question may be asked to what extent, if any, Scott succeeded in anchoring the Romantic 'lost heir' plot of the novel to an historic context. To answer this it is necessary to look in some detail at the social transitions in *Guy Mannering* against which the wanderings of Harry Bertram are set.

The period of *Guy Mannering* is not specifically defined by Scott: actual dates (at the beginnings of Chapters I and XII, for example) are deliberately left blank, and no great public event intrudes on the private action in such a way as to fix the date.[9] This does not necessarily mean that *Guy Mannering* is less of an historical novel than *Waverley*. The Jacobite rebellion in Scott's first novel is, after all, presented not as an inexplicable and unexpected phenomenon, but as an inevitable result of social and economic trends affecting the Highland clans and the feudal estates over a long period of time. The apparent vagueness of date in *Guy Mannering* has the effect of universalising the private history of the Bertrams into a typical history of an aristocratic family of the eighteenth century: making it more obvious that it is broad historical changes, rather than isolated occurrences, which Scott is concerned with portraying through the events at Ellangowan.

Near the beginning of the novel, Scott briefly recounts the history of the Bertrams, once the Mac-Dingawaies, lords of Galloway.[10] From the peak of their power as feudal lords of the district (when the family assumed its Norman name), the Bertrams have slowly declined in influence, undergoing particularly unfortunate experiences in the seventeenth century, when their family was ruined successively by its loyalty to Charles I in the Civil War, and then by adherence to Argyle's revolt against Charles II. In a style reminiscent of *Castle Rackrent*, Scott follows the line of descent through the drunken and degenerate Donohue (shot by a Cameronian in 1689), to the more prudent Lewis, whose participation nevertheless in the Fifteen forces him to sell part of the estate and to abandon the castle, until finally the indolent Godfrey Bertram finds he has succeeded 'to a long pedigree and a short rent-roll, like many lairds of that period.'[11] The history, despite its peculiarities, is a typical one, and establishes a pattern of decline which the events of Godfrey Bertram's lifetime only help to complete.

Against this long-established line of the Bertrams is set Gilbert Glossin, a crafty parvenu who rises from total obscurity (according to Meg, 'his mother wasna muckle better than mysell')[12] to ownership of the ancient Ellangowan estate. The agency of Glossin's rise over his employer, Godfrey Bertram, is the law: very notably, all the ploys Glossin uses to effect acquisition, however morally reprehensible, are within the bounds of the law. The problem of the meaning of 'justice' during the period portrayed is in fact one of Scott's major undertakings in the novel. On the one hand, there is the traditional justice based on feudal right, which seems to uphold the Bertrams' ancient claim to the estate, and which the country tenants and even the gypsies respect. On the other hand, there is the modern codification of 'justice', the law itself, which Scott sees existing under the Hanoverian regime as an instrument used by social climbers like Glossin to win themselves power, and 'legitimise' it in social terms. The historical action of the novel, which is the battle between the aristocratic Bertrams and the middle-class Glossins of the time, is largely fought out through the medium of the law.

The spokesman for traditional justice in *Guy Mannering* is Counsellor Pleydell, who supports the Bertrams in distress and is deeply inimical to Glossin's turn 'for the roguish part of the profession.'[13] In line with his old fashioned tastes, Pleydell sees the law primarily as a conservative force – both for seeking out the truth (as his meticulous investigation of Kennedy's death shows) and for preserving order in society. He tells Mannering: 'In civilised society law is the chimney through which all that smoke discharges itself that used to circulate through the whole house, and put every one's eyes out. . . .'[14] Pleydell's respect for traditional ways is most clearly seen in his advice to Dandie Dinmont to settle his dispute in the old Border fashion, with cudgels if necessary, rather than commit the case to a lengthy process in Edinburgh in which neither he nor his neighbour will gain anything.[15] The law is not to be applied lightly to traditional ways which have proved their worth over a long period of time.

Pitched in opposition to this deeply conservative conception of justice, however, we find not only Glossin but also, in a furore of misplaced enthusiasm, Godfrey Bertram himself. The Laird's attempts to appear a 'new broom' when he is finally appointed a J.P. (after a political manoeuvre), his thoughtless zeal for the 'progressive' and the 'lawful', are explicitly the cause of his later family catastrophe, in that he pushes the gypsies and the smugglers whom he previously encouraged into implacable hostility towards him. Yet he is also guilty, implicitly, of destroying those traditional ties stemming from feudal society from which the Bertram family ultimately derives its legitimacy. His 'improvements', culminating in the expulsion of the gypsies, are indeed 'Persecution according to law', as the mis-spelt notice has it.[16] Godfrey Bertram is oblivious to the fact that the nuisance created by the gypsies has traditionally been balanced by their loyalty to his family:[17]

> They had been such long occupants that they were considered in some degree as proprietors of the wretched shealings which they inhabited. This protection they were said anciently to have repaid by service to the Laird in war, or, more frequently, by infesting or plundering the lands of those neighbouring barons with whom he chanced to be at feud. Latterly their services were of a more pacific nature. The women spun mittens for the lady, and knitted boot-hose for the Laird, which were annually presented at Christmas with great form.

This passage brings out the fact that the justice which the gypsies have come to expect from the Bertrams is, as Robin Mayhead says, 'of a feudal nature:'[18] they are protected by the Laird in return for their loyalty and service. In setting fire to their homes, and expelling women and children with nowhere to go, Godfrey Bertram's progressive justice, based on strict legality, appears to them a kind of treachery.[19]

In a similar way, the Laird alienates his entire tenantry, by brutally doing away with any links with tradition in the village. Thus[20]

The 'daft' Jock, who, half knave, half idiot, had been the sport of each succeeding race of village children for a good part of a century, was remitted to the county bridewell, where, secluded from free air and sunshine, the only advantages he was capable of enjoying, he pined and died in the course of six months.

In his zeal to be an agent of Benthamite 'utility' and progress, Godfrey Bertram is blinded to the human suffering he causes for the sake of social tidiness. Yet he is acting in accordance with the spirit of the age. It is just these social changes, portrayed by Scott here as the acts of one individual, which took place all over rural areas in Scotland during the eighteenth century: the same disruption of the traditional balance of village society lamented by Wordsworth in *The Old Cumberland Beggar*. The irony of the situation in *Guy Mannering* is that Godfrey Bertram is acting entirely against his family's interest as the pinnacle of the traditional, feudal society of Ellangowan. In a way, there is an unwitting complicity on the part of the Laird in his own eventual expropriation by Glossin; for this is also effected by legal means and carried out without regard for traditional associations or feelings. It is more than just poetic justice that Godfrey Bertram himself is finally expelled from Ellangowan. His eviction of the gypsies, and his own eviction by Glossin, are both part of the historical process: the 'progression' from the ancient unwritten values of the feudal system, to the cold, businesslike concern with the letter of the law that characterises the rising classes.

Against this background, Harry Bertram's fate takes on a new relevance. In the identity of Vanbeest Brown he is effectively alienated from his past and his true identity. His plebeian name and his adoption by a Dutch burgher pre-empt his claims to a good family to the extent that not only Mannering but Julia herself revolts against his supposed background.[21] Yet Brown is not entirely divorced from the past: vague memories of his youth linger on to torment his reason. In his letter to his friend Delaserre, Brown recalls his feeling of familiarity, rather than astonishment, at travelling through the Indian mountains. He is, however, unable to recall the (Scottish) mountains of his own childhood: 'my memory rather dwells upon the blank which my youthful mind experienced in gazing on the levels of the isle of Zealand, than on anything which preceded that feeling. . . .'[22] Shortly afterwards, Meg recognises him at the inn at Mump's Ha' but conscious recollection again eludes him:[23]

> On his part, he was surprised to find that he could not look upon this singular figure without some emotion. 'Have I dreamed of such a figure?' he said to himself, 'or does this wild and singular looking woman recall to my recollection some of the strange figures I have seen in our Indian pagodas?'

Brown's psychological confusion is nicely rendered here. Despite the feeling of familiarity, which he naturally associates with memory, he is utterly unable to remember the real origin of the memory, and clutches at mental straws to cover his bewilderment.

Brown's alienation from his past is most explicit in the scene which follows his coach being forced to a standstill in the vicinity of Ellangowan. His pursuit of an elusive light among the trees, through pitch darkness and swirling snow, symbolises his quest for the truth about himself.[24] He is, from the beginning, 'heavily encumbered' by his clothes as he gropes his way towards the distant glimmer. Quite abruptly, the terrain over which he is walking becomes broken and almost impossible to negotiate: very much as his conscious attempts to recall his past have been thwarted by unseen mental obstacles. As he moves along 'what had once been a pathway' to what are, in fact, the remains of the gypsies' village ruined by his father, Brown is moving along a difficult track into the forgotten past: the path itself, last used by the gypsies, is like his memory almost obscured. The climax of both his actual and his mental journeys on this occasion is his glimpse through the window of the Kaim of Derncleugh of a dying man and his woman companion. Nowhere is Brown's amnesia more ironic than at this moment, when the two main agents in his personal history, Meg Merrilies and the smuggler Brown (who has given him his name) appear in front of him as complete strangers. Moreover, Brown's isolation from his past here is emphasised by his physical isolation from the scene. Looking in on them from the outside, he appears as a passive observer of events he can neither understand nor control.

As in *Waverley* a parallel can be drawn between the personal history of the hero, Harry Bertram/Brown, and the broader social developments portrayed in the novel. The hero's amnesia, his lost relationship with the past, is paralleled by the loss of the Bertrams' traditional relationship with feudal Ellangowan, through Godfrey Bertram's misguided actions. Glossin's acquisition of the estate violates traditional feudal ties in the same way that Brown's commercial upbringing in Holland violates his natural right to gentility. In both cases, past associations are buried and the Bertrams as a family suffer eclipse.

Brown's amnesia is seen to enmesh with the historical theme of expropriation when he returns eventually to the Auld Place of Ellangowan in Chapter XLI. Having landed at Warroch Point, Brown's associations with the place become so strong that he is forced to suggest '*déjà vu*' as an explanation of the familiarity he feels towards the old castle. His speculations on the ruins ironically touch upon his own position, and his alienated heritage:[25]

'And the powerful barons who owned this blazonry,' thought Bertram, pursuing the usual train of ideas which flows upon the mind at such scenes – 'do their posterity continue to possess the lands which they had laboured to fortify so strongly? or are they wanderers, ignorant perhaps even of the fame or power of their forefathers, while their hereditary possessions are held by a race of strangers?'

Brown's meeting with Glossin, which follows immediately, is the most intensely ironic and dramatic incident in the novel. Glossin's first words, which Brown overhears before he sees him, are in complete contrast with his own warm associations with the Auld Place:[26]

'Yes, sir, as I have often said before to you, the Old Place is a perfect quarry of hewn stone, and it would be better for the estate if it were all down, since it is only a den for smugglers.'

The contempt for tradition, the desire for self-aggrandisement (he intends using the stone for a new, larger house), the purely commercial view of the castle as a quarry – all masquerading as a desire for social 'improvement' of the area (very ironic, considering Glossin's connection with Hatteraick) – this defines Glossin characteristically as the middle-class *arriviste*, in every way opposed to the traditional interests of the Bertram family. The confrontation between Brown and Glossin is a classic 'encounter' in the manner of those in *Waverley*: its nuances are subtly suggestive of their opposition to each other both personally and socially.

Thus their face-to-face meeting itself upsets Glossin, who recognises in Brown's looks the features of his former employer whom he has ruined: tradition in the form of hereditary resemblance obstinately refuses to disappear. Having enquired about Glossin's name, Brown is puzzled by its lack of resonance: Scott suggests, in fact, that there is a quality peculiar to an established aristocratic name which Glossin's palpably lacks. Glossin, meanwhile, scrupulously avoids mentioning the name of Bertram which he fears will supply the missing association. Most ironically, Glossin informs Brown that he intends replacing the Bertrams' traditional family motto, 'Our Right makes our Might', graven on the ruins, with his own, blatantly opportunist sentiment, 'He who takes it, makes it.'[27] The ironically opposed mottoes nicely encapsulate the attitudes of the protagonists.

At this point it appears that it is Glossin's motto which in fact describes the reality of the situation: he seems securely in possession both of Ellangowan and of the secret of Brown's past. When Brown remembers a catch of Meg's traditional song about the Bertrams sung to him as a child, he cannot recall enough of the words to make the vital connection which would provide the clue to his identity. Suddenly, however, the traditional power of the Bertrams is displayed. As Brown plays the tune on his flageolet in an unavailing attempt to jog his memory, a country girl takes up the song.[28]

Against such a spontaneous proof of the ancient rights of the Bertrams, deeply engrained in the very folk-lore of the local people, Glossin has but one trump card to play. His two ruffians arrest Brown with a warrant signed by Glossin himself. Again the law appears as a potent weapon in Glossin's hands to use against the Bertrams' feudal rights. Underlining the fact that the establishment of a limited Hanoverian monarch was a defeat for the feudal aristocracy, Glossin now arrests Brown 'in the king's name.'[29] It is a highly dramatic inversion of the feudal 'justice' which affirms Brown's right to Ellangowan – emphasising that political power now lies in the hands of the Glossins of the nation. At the same time, Brown's discovery of his true identity is further postponed. Once again, the suppression of the Bertram family's rights is paralleled by the repression of Brown's knowledge of his past.

The scene as a whole, emphasising Brown's alienation from his past, his subconscious memories, his groping towards a rediscovery of his identity, and the reader's own realisation of Brown's relationship with the Bertrams, shows how successfully Scott could sometimes combine the Romance mode with historical realism. The 'machinery' of Romance – the hereditary resemblance, the girl singing a ballad, the coincidences, all serve here to evoke the lost feudal world. Even the ancient ballad in question:

> The dark shall be light,
> And the wrong made right,
> When Bertram's right and Bertram's might
> Shall meet on Ellangowan's height.

makes an obvious reference to the inversion of the traditional social order implied by Glossin's usurpation of the estate.

To this extent, the analogy between Brown's alienated condition and the Bertrams' social decline in the modern world works well. The artificiality of the design only becomes obvious with the conclusion of the novel. Of itself, the restoration of Brown to his true identity and his reunion with his family would be credible enough. Yet Scott also attempts to stretch his analogy by working a similar change on the Bertrams' condition and restoring to them their ancient heritage. At this point, Scott's own social realism contradicts his efforts, for the whole weight of the historical movement in *Guy Mannering* is with Glossin, against the Bertrams. A good example is the fine dialogue between Charles Hazlewood and his father Sir Robert,

the pompous baronet from the neighbouring estate to
Ellangowan:[30]

> [Sir Robert:] '. . . it concerns the country, sir, and the
> county, sir, and the public, sir, and the kingdom of
> Scotland, sir, in so far as the interest of the Hazlewood
> family, sir, is committed and interested and put in peril
> in, by and through you, sir. And the fellow [Brown] is in
> safe custody, and Mr. Glossin thinks – '
> 'Mr. Glossin, sir?'
> 'Yes, sir, the gentleman who has purchased Ellangowan;
> you know who I mean I suppose?'
> 'Yes, sir,' answered the young man; 'but I should
> hardly have expected to hear you quote such authority.
> Why, this fellow – all the world knows him to be sordid,
> mean, tricking, and I suspect him to be worse. And you
> yourself, my dear sir, when did you call such a person a
> gentleman in your life before?'
> 'Why, Charles, I did not mean gentleman in the precise
> sense and meaning, and restricted and proper use to
> which, no doubt, the phrase ought legitimately to be
> confined; but I meant to use it relatively, as marking
> something of that state to which he had elevated and
> raised himself: as designing, in short, a decent and wealthy
> and estimable sort of person.'

This is a very ironic exchange: bitterly ironic, because it shows
how easily Sir Robert is imposed upon by Glossin. Scott is
emphasising how simple it is for Glossin to take in the baronet
with a show of concern for his family and a deferential attitude
towards him personally. Sir Robert's words also indicate the way
in which Glossin can come to appear a 'gentleman' after his
purchase of Ellangowan, and the way in which the very meaning
of the word has changed because of social changes. All Sir
Robert's blustering about the honour of his family and the
kingdom of Scotland is subtly undermined by the fact that he
has, in practice, absorbed the bourgeois definition of a
'gentleman' as someone who, like Glossin, observes certain
proprieties and has money – money itself being now a sufficient
cause for esteem. Nor can we believe that it is the foolish Sir
Robert alone who is deceived: the baronet is only too obviously

repeating the opinions of the modern world in his definition of gentility.

This scene, like that of Brown's arrest, strikes the reader as both significant and authentic. It is a pessimistic view of historical change, however, which finds expression in these episodes in *Guy Mannering*. It is true to say that Scott's portrayal of the Bertrams' fate in the novel is, by implication, tragic: the most powerful stage of the novel is reached when Brown seems destined to remain alienated from his heritage, and his family stands expropriated and powerless as their surviving aristocratic neighbour welcomes Glossin to his new estate. The problem with the conclusion to *Guy Mannering* is that Scott abandons this pessimistic, but consistent and socially realistic portrayal in favour of a conventional happy ending, in which Harry Bertram returns in triumph, and Glossin is defeated and disgraced.

The restoration of Ellangowan to the Bertrams is a sharp reversal of the inexorable decline of the aristocratic family delineated in the novel: the action contradicts all the historical processes in the novel of which the expropriation of the estate has been a symbol. Scott's uneasiness about his resolution of the plot is manifest in the shaky method by which he returns Ellangowan to Harry Bertram, through an unlikely entailment of the estate – a device which 'explains' the return only technically and melodramatically. Scott does nothing really to convince the reader that historical tendencies can be reversed in this way. In other areas of the novel, conservatism is not victorious. Dandie Dinmont remains wedded to the idea of pursuing a lawsuit against his neighbour, despite Pleydell's conservative advice to the contrary. The power of modern law is extending itself even to the traditionally lawless Border. Economic forces are at work too, directed against the Bertrams' semi-feudal ownership of property. One of the reasons given for the sale of the estate to Glossin is in order 'to substitute the interest of money instead of the ill-paid and precarious rents of an unimproved estate'.[31] Although this is actually a cover-up for the real reason in this case, it establishes the economic characteristics of the period: the buoyancy of capital, the leaden weight of the rented estate. Glossin's rise to success is representative of the general rise of the middle classes, just as the Bertrams' decline represents the decay of the feudal system and its ruling class; and to this extent Harry Bertram's defeat of Glossin at the end of the novel is definitely 'unhistorical.'

The atmosphere of melodrama thickens over the closing pages, as the historical realism thins. Gilbert Glossin, for example, has previously been viewed by the author, if not with actual sympathy (as Gordon and Mayhead suggest),[32] at least with an intriguing intimacy (his feelings during his visit to Sir Robert Hazlewood, for instance, are conveyed with great satiric acumen). Yet in order to achieve his ending, Scott flattens Glossin into a stage villain, even providing him with a suitably grisly death. Glossin's historical significance, in other words, is deliberately denied. Instead, as befits a melodrama, Scott descends to a moralistic argument whereby the Bertrams are 'good,' and 'good' triumphs over Glossin's 'villainy.'

The falseness of the ending of *Guy Mannering* is apparent not only in the broader social context of the Bertrams' 'unhistorical' victory over Glossin, but also in the private history of Harry Bertram's return to his family. Having established an analogy between Harry Bertram's personal situation and the social crisis of his family, the lack of realism in the 'social' plot spills over and robs the other situation of its credibility. The lost heir plot is denied seriousness by association with the unreal restoration of the Bertrams to their estate. Scott himself accepts the triteness of the novel's reconciliation scene, as both Alexander Welsh and Cockshut point out, by affixing a tag from *The Critic* to the head of Chapter L which belittles its importance.[33] The final failure of the character of Meg is also symptomatic. Meg, through her revelations about Kennedy's death, is supposedly the key to Harry Bertram's rediscovery of his past and his return to his family: broadly speaking, she is the saviour of the situation. Yet the social situation of the novel, from the viewpoint of the Bertram family, can have no 'saviour': it is beyond even Meg's power to reverse the tide of history. The result is that as far as we take Meg's actions at the end seriously they have no real historical moment, and she declines into a Gothic, melodramatic figure. As a socially realistic character, a remnant of the 'old' order of tribal society, Meg in death might have been expected to carry a tragic resonance in accordance with the underlying, pessimistic tone of the novel: in fact the context of her death forces it too into a melodramatic mould.

Robin Mayhead is probably right to claim that the critic should not aim at 'comprehensivenes' in a discussion of *Guy Mannering*.[34] There is a basic conflict in the novel between Gothic Romance (degenerating into melodrama in the conclusion) and historical realism: the novel does not form a unified whole, to which all the parts relate, as *Waverley* does. Nevertheless, *Guy Mannering* is more similar to Scott's first novel than is at first obvious. As in *Waverley*, Scott is dealing with a real historical situation, rendered in terms of individual fates and their connection with historical forces in society. The effect is partly achieved, as it is in *Waverley*, by paralleling the individual history of the hero with the fate of a changing society. To some extent, also, *Guy Mannering* actually extends the techniques of its predecessor: Scott pursues a more personalised approach here than he does in *Waverley*, with its broad vistas and public events. The confrontation between Harry Bertram and Glossin at the Auld Place is arguably more intense than any similar dramatic encounter in the first novel: in their opposition, the two men become symbolic representatives of their respective classes, and epitomise the social conflict in the novel as a whole. Whereas conflict appears in *Waverley* as overt, political struggle, in *Guy Mannering* it is domesticated and finds its expression chiefly through the attitudes, antipathies and prejudices of the individual characters.

Despite its lesser stature, *Guy Mannering* is also important for an understanding of Scott's development as an artist. In its pessimistic, conservative attitude to social change, the novel looks forward, as Gordon suggests, to a 'far more stark and forbidding' vision in *The Bride of Lammermoor*.[35] The latter novel shows a strength of tragic purpose and a confidence of tone that probably could not have come about had not Scott studied closely and learned the lessons of his partial failure in this earlier novel. The conclusion of *Guy Mannering* is also illustrative of the manner in which Scott sometimes abandons his hold on historical realism in favour of a conventional plot resolution which does little justice to the novel as a whole, however it may have flattered the prejudices of the contemporary reader, or even those of the author himself. In this negative respect, *Guy Mannering* anticipates the flaws in two of Scott's greatest works, *Old Mortality* and *The Heart of Midlothian*.

3

The Antiquary

The defects of *The Antiquary*, Scott's third novel, are on the surface, and easy to see. David Daiches's judgment is final: 'The external plot . . . is . . . not to be taken seriously.'[1] Lovel is as slight a hero, his love-affair as slight a romantic interest, and the missing heir business as slight a plot-line as Scott could possibly have manufactured without his production ceasing altogether to be a novel. His admission in the Introduction is telling:[2]

> I have been more solicitous to describe manners minutely than to arrange in any case an artificial and combined narrative, and have but to regret that I felt myself unable to unite these two requisites of a good Novel.

It is ironic that with the change in meaning of critical jargon (which itself reflects the change in critical expectations) the modern reader might well describe the plot of *The Antiquary*, fabricated without any real relevance to the novel as a whole, and basically a mish-mash of all the 'illegitimacy' plots prevalent in the novel from *Tom Jones* to *Guy Mannering*, as both 'artificial' and 'combined'. However, mulling over the deficiencies of the plot to the point where they eclipse the real artistic merits of the novel is a pointless activity.[3] The unity of *The Antiquary* is not on the level of plot. In fact, unlike *Guy Mannering*, *The Antiquary* can survive its insidious elements of 'Romance' precisely because the romantic plot is only an external shell, not intended to bear any weight of seriousness or moment.

Similarly Scott's toying with the supernatural, which does much to damage the credibility of his second novel, obtrudes only once or twice onto the otherwise realistic tone of *The Antiquary*. J. W. Croker, reviewing the novel in 1816, suggested that to begin with the author might well have had more artistically dangerous intentions:[4]

> there are two or three marvellous dreams and apparitions, upon which, we suspect, the author intended to ground some important parts of his denouement, but his taste luckily took fright, the apparitions do not contribute to the catastrophe. . . .

In fact, through Oldbuck's 'explanation' of Lovel's mysterious dream in terms of the Hartleian psychology of unconscious associations, Scott goes a long way towards reconciling the main supernatural incident in the novel with the prevailing rational tone of the work.

The great unity and originality of *The Antiquary* is to be found, as Scott himself suggests, in the novel's portrait of 'manners' in the modern age.[5] The nature of the modern age and its relationship with the past are the real subjects of the novel. Moreover, the fact that Scott deals not only with the notions that his contemporary age entertains for the past (the antiquarianism reflected in the novel's title), but also with the real human significance of the past for men living in the present, makes *The Antiquary* an 'historical' novel in a new, more conscious sense than either of its predecessors. Indeed, it is the contrast between the theoretical ideas about history held by the antiquaries, and the actual past as it is felt and remembered by those who have experienced it, which provides the source of much of the novel's irony and satire.

The real hero of the novel is the antiquary himself, Jonathan Oldbuck, who dominates the other characters in the novel (including the nominal hero, Lovel) just as the middle class to which he belongs securely controls the town of Fairport and its environs. His pride in his descent from his ancestor Oldenbuck (= 'old book'), a man instrumental, through his profession as an early printer in the Reformation, in the dissemination of

Protestantism, places Oldbuck in his own eyes far above the status of hereditary aristocracy. His argument with Sir Arthur Wardour over an historical 'source' makes this clear:[6]

'Permit me, Mr. Oldbuck; he was a gentleman, of high family and ancient descent, and therefore – – '

'The descendant of a Westphalian printer should speak of him with deference? Such may be your opinion, Sir Arthur; it is not mine. I conceive that my descent from that painful and industrious typographer, Wolfbrand Oldenbuck, who in the month of December 1493, under the patronage, as the colophon tells us, of Sebaldus Scheyter and Sebastian Kammermaister, accomplished the printing of the great *Chronicle of Nuremberg* – I conceive, I say, that my descent from that great restorer of learning is more creditable to me as a man of letters than if I had numbered in my genealogy all the brawling, bullet-headed, iron-fisted old Gothic barons since the days of Crentheminachryme, not one of whom, I suppose, could write his own name.'

The story of another Oldenbuck's wooing of his future wife in the face of more 'gentle' suitors, and the trial of skill on her father's printing press with which he finally makes himself known to her, is an echo of Ulysses's actions with Penelope – an epic parallel which serves to emphasise that Oldbuck's ancestor was, in his way, a 'hero' of his emergent class.[7] Oldbuck's family history shows a continuity through the years down to his own inheritance of their small estate, originally acquired on the dissolution of the monastery there (itself a consequence of the Reformation) by one of the family fleeing from persecution for his Protestantism. During the Jacobite rebellions, the family has been a bulwark of resistance to the rebels; Oldbuck's father, 'a frugal, careful man', as provost of Fairport in 1745, personally led the burghers out against the neighbouring Jacobite gentry.[8] Even Oldbuck, with his sarcastic estimation of the tastes of the Fairport shopkeepers, and his own 'strange mixture of frugality and industry and negligent indolence', is really only a leisured member of the middle class, living carefully (as he is always making clear) on his father's invested wealth, and with the time to devote himself to his intellectual pursuits.

Against Oldbuck is posed Sir Arthur Wardour, his friend and fellow antiquary, but a haughty member of the country nobility who was actually imprisoned during the Forty-Five by Provost Oldbuck and the Whig town council on account of his father's Jacobite sympathies. Sir Arthur's opinions and his actions, however, have come to have less and less to do with each other. Continuing his father's purely notional line of Jacobite politics (which itself consisted entirely of intrigue without action), Sir Arthur's opinions are of a still more theoretical strain. In contrast with his continuing prayers for the return of his 'rightful sovereign', ceremonially conducted with great seriousness by his private Episcopalian minister, Sir Arthur accepts *de facto* the Hanoverian succession by 'gulping down the oaths of abjuration and allegiance' when an election to parliament occurs in which he is interested.[9] Even the extinction of the Stuart line is not calculated to affect notions with such a slender foundation in political reality, and Sir Arthur continues to pray for the non-existent Royal Family's return, despite being 'in all actual service and practical exertion a most zealous and devoted subject of George III'. Moreover, as his estate of Knockwinnock sinks further into debt, the material basis of Sir Arthur's position as a landed gentleman is slowly eroded. The speculative mines he sinks with Douterswivel are intended to redress his financial balance; but this only emphasises a sort of transformation of Sir Arthur into an active (though singularly unsuccessful!) member of the bourgeoisie.

The opposition between Sir Arthur and Oldbuck is, in other words, more notional than real. The social positions of their respective families have slowly approached one another until they are almost on a par as far as their life-styles, their properties, and even their mutual interest in antiquity is concerned.

Each man, admittedly, adjusts his studies to his temperament. Oldbuck's room bears witness to his fascination with anything and everything antique:[10]

A large old-fashioned oak table was covered with a profusion of papers, parchments, books, and nondescript trinkets and gewgaws, which seemed to have little to recommend them besides rust and the antiquity which it indicates.

This love of sheer old age in objects is possibly Oldbuck's compensation for the comparatively recent entry of his family and his class onto the stage of history. Certainly, Oldbuck's sense of identification with the ancient Caledonians, which leads him 'patriotically' to proclaim their victory in spite of Tacitus in the nonsensical *Caledoniad*, is utterly whimsical. The theory of the Germanic origin of the Picts, on which Oldbuck bases his allegiance, however, was a real source of antiquarian controversy of the time, as both James Anderson and P. D. Garside have pointed out.[11] Scott in fact has Oldbuck adopt the Whig antiquarian position of Pinkerton both in his championship of the Goths, and in his belief that Mary, Queen of Scots, was guilty of the murder of Darnley.[12] Sir Arthur, in contrast, deeply resents Oldbuck's antiquarian method (as Lawrence Poston notes[13]), complaining that Oldbuck has 'a sort of pettifogging intimacy with dates, names, and trifling matters of fact' and 'a frivolous accuracy of memory which is entirely owing to his mechanical descent'.[14] Sir Arthur's very Tory predilections are for old tomes containing lists of ancient dynasties; not only can he recite the full role of mythical Scottish kings from Crentheminachryme (the date of whose reign he concedes is somewhat uncertain) – he also defends their existence absolutely, sensing that the rights of inheritance themselves are in some way undermined by Oldbuck's objectionable scepticism on this subject.

Yet antiquarianism in the modern age fulfils an even greater need for both Oldbuck and Sir Arthur, merely by providing matter for argument. The two men 'fight old battles in modern dress', as Robert Gordon says.[15] In their contemporary world, politics as the expression of real social conflict has practically ceased to exist. Any real basis for Jacobitism has been eroded beyond even argument, while the political factions in Fairport, centred on 'clubs', are represented by Scott as basically frivolous, whether they be the 'Royal True Blues' or the 'Friends of the People'. When we remember that 'Royal' here refers to a Hanoverian monarch, and 'People' to the Fairport middle classes, their differences indeed seem unimportant or even irrelevant. Typically, both clubs entertain hostile (and mutually exclusive) ideas about Oldbuck, while Lovel makes it clear that he cannot be bothered with either of them.[16] In such circumstances, only 'history' is left as an arena for argument, and it is openly exploited as such by Oldbuck and Sir Arthur in their antiquarian controversies.

The fellow antiquaries' approach to their subject is the opposite to that of the scientific historian: instead of looking for material evidence and deducing hypotheses from it, Oldbuck and Sir Arthur marshall whatever theories and half-evidence is at their command in order to support their respective sides of the argument. The less evidence is available on a subject, the more they are attracted to it, because the greater is the scope for argumentative and fanciful theorising. Their most potent argument is therefore over the origin of the Picts, which they conduct via discussion of the sole remaining Pictish word. Lovel in vain attempts to point out that the argument is spurious: Oldbuck welcomes the lack of evidence, claiming that 'men fight best in a narrow ring: an inch is as good as a mile for a home-thrust'.[17] It might well be said of the two adversaries that[18]

> in their historical speculation they seize upon this 'prehistory' with especial eagerness because they imagine themselves safe there from interference on the part of 'crude facts,' and, at the same time, because they can give full rein to their speculative impulse and set up and knock down hypotheses by the thousand.

Marx's satire of the German Idealists here exactly parallels Scott's satire of antiquarianism.

Marx's use of puns ('speculative', etc.) to suggest a basic kinship between the theorists and the entrepreneurs who dominate 'modern' society is also germane, for antiquities do indeed allow Oldbuck to indulge in a form of property speculation. His ardent desire to show the world that the Kaim of Kinprunes is an historic 'site' – a theory he 'proves' to Lovel with a thoroughly fallacious but marvellously fanciful use of his sources – is not entirely unconnected with the fact that he has already acquired the site for himself at the lunatic price of an exchange, acre-for-acre, with good cornland.[19] Bargaining over antiques is a delight to him: 'How often have I stood, haggling upon a halfpenny, lest by a too ready acquiescence in the dealer's first price, he should be led to suspect the value I set upon the article!' Nor is the joy of possession unknown to Oldbuck:[20]

> Then to dazzle the eyes of our wealthier and emulous rivals by showing them such a treasure as this (displaying a little black smoked book about the size of a primer), to enjoy their surprise and envy, shrouding meanwhile under a veil of mysterious consciousness our own superior knowledge and dexterity. . . .

The excitement, uncertainty, and rewards that are usually associated with entrepreneurial activity are all present for Oldbuck in his hobby.

Yet the effect of this 'reification' of history, this conversion of the past into objects or 'antiques', is inevitably to dehumanise history. The real men and women whose experience makes up history are lost sight of among the 'praetoria' and the antiquaries' arguments about the gentility (Sir Arthur) or literacy (Oldbuck) of their respective sources. When confronted with a genuine, first-hand experience of the past, as Oldbuck is with Edie Ochiltree's revelation of the true origin of his 'praetorium', the antiquary is annoyed and confounded:[21]

> 'What is it that you say, Edie?' said Oldbuck, hoping, perhaps, that his ears had betrayed their duty; 'what were you speaking about?'
> 'About this bit bourock, your honour,' answered the undaunted Edie; 'I mind the bigging o't.'
> 'The devil you do! Why, you old fool, it was here before you were born, and will be after you are hanged, man!'
> 'Hanged or drowned, here or awa, dead or alive, I mind the bigging o't.'
> 'You – you – you,' said the Antiquary, stammering between confusion and anger – 'you strolling old vaga-bond, what the devil do you know about it?'

With the opposite instinct to the true historian, Oldbuck would have preferred to remain in ignorance here. His intricate hypotheses based on a lack of evidence are far more pleasing to him than the down-to-earth facts – just as the gossips gathered in the Mailsetters' kitchen find examining the envelopes of correspondence more flattering to their preconceived prejudices than a real knowledge of the contents would be.

The gossips' cruel treatment of Jenny Caxton in the post office similarly parallels the way in which antiquarianism is incompatible with a real, human concern for the past in the form of its survivors. Thus, when Douterswivel produces his first 'find' of old coins in a horn, Oldbuck shows it to Edie who affirms that the horn was once his own snuff-box. Edie continues:[22]

> But I reckon ye'll be gaun to make an antic o't, as ye hae dune wi' mony an orra thing besides. Odd, I wish ony body wad make an antic o'me; but mony ane will find worth in rousted bits o' capper and horn and airn, that care unco' little about an auld carle o' their ain country and kind.

Joan Elbers says of this passage that Edie 'with his usual perspicacity, sums up the dangers of this collector's interest in the past to a proper concern with human beings in the present'.[23] If anything, Edie's speech is still more pointed: Edie is actually a living survival from the past, yet his experience is discounted by the very men who spend so much of their time investigating history. It is the antiquaries' alienation from the human implications of the past which Edie's speech sarcastically highlights.[24]

Edie himself is both a human survivor and, as a mendicant, a social survivor of a village life which has all but disappeared. Modern 'civilised' society, with its growing emphasis on utility and its condemnation of beggars as idlers, has erected the workhouse for the likes of Edie. Despite his legal status as a Blue-Gown, a creation of the old Scottish monarchy, Edie confesses to Isabella that he feels safe only because the local Justices of the Peace, Oldbuck and Sir Arthur (through Isabella's influence) continue to tell the constables to 'owerlook' him.[25] Lovel points out that the more 'advanced' English society would not be so tolerant:[26]

> 'In England,' said Lovel, 'such a mendicant would get a speedy check.'
> 'Yes, your churchwardens and dog-whips would make

slender allowance for his vein of humour! But here, curse him, he is a sort of privileged nuisance – one of the last specimens of the old-fashioned Scottish mendicant, who kept his rounds within a particular space, and was the news-carrier, the minstrel, and sometimes the historian of the district. That rascal, now, knows more old ballads and traditions than any other man in this and the four next parishes. And after all,' continued he, softening as he went on describing Edie's good gifts, 'the dog has some good-humour. He has borne his hard fate with unbroken spirits, and it's cruel to deny him the comfort of a laugh at his betters.'

Oldbuck's feelings here are a strange mixture of human sympathy and a shrewd suspicion that the old man has an important 'antiquarian' value.

Edie survives, however, not only because of the tolerance of his 'betters', but because in spite of his lack of learning, he understands the implications of historical change in a way Oldbuck never will. He perfectly understands, for example, that his wandering life is an integral part of the traditional Scottish society which has all but passed away, and that to abandon the old ways, in any form, would only be to hasten the demise of his already threatened way of life. Thus he refuses the gold offered to him at different times by Oldbuck, Isabella and Lovel in gratitude for his services. He shrewdly explains to Isabella:[27]

> Were the like o' me ever to change a note, wha the deil d'ye think wad be sic fules as to gie me charity after that? It wad flee through the country like wild-fire that auld Edie suld hae done siccan a like thing, and then I'se warrant I might grane my heart out or ony body wad gie me either a bane or a bodle.

His strongly traditional reliance on the general wealth of the country people, rather than on an 'easy living' through the support of a single patron (such as the pension Isabella offers him) is at odds with the prevailing commercial ethics of society, and requires in Edie an adherence to strong principles such as the refusal of gold. It is therefore ironic when the author comments: 'Upon these whims, which he imagined intimately connected with the honour of his vagabond profession, Edie was flint and adamant, not to be moved by rhetoric or entreaty.'[28] Here Scott is using the depreciatory tones of a 'modern' man to describe Edie; in fact, he has already established that Edie's conservatism is absolutely essential for his survival.

As he rigorously maintains the traditional 'honour of his profession' against the modern encroachments of the workhouse and the overgrateful, Edie displays an historical tension in his life which is very apparently missing from the lives of the other, modern characters. The lack of conflict as a whole in *The Antiquary*, when compared with the other Scottish Waverley Novels, is even more notable. David Daiches has commented on *The Antiquary*: 'It is essentially a static novel . . . The characteristic tension of Scott's novels is scarcely perceptible.'[29] Yet this static quality of the novel itself reflects the nature of the society depicted: social conflict itself has practically been eliminated by the changes in the aristocracy epitomised by Sir Arthur Wardour's approach to the life-style and social status of the middle classes, whose respectability is in turn epitomised by Oldbuck. Only the shadows of the great religious and political issues which formerly divided Scottish society remain in *The Antiquary*, and these never seem as contentious to Oldbuck and Sir Arthur as does their insubstantial argument about the origin of the Picts.

The two centuries of religious prejudice, intolerance, and often bloody conflict in Scotland seem, in particular, as distant to most of the characters in the novel as Oldbuck's favourite war between the Romans and the ancient Caledonians. The religious tendencies of the eighteenth century are shown to have reached completion: the moderate Presbyterian kirk has expanded to the extent that the Catholic and Episcopalian opposition is completely subdued; yet at the same time, society has become secularised, and Presbyterianism itself has become more of a nominal creed than a deeply felt faith. The strongest asseveration of Presbyterianism in the novel is Edie Ochiltree's declaration to Glenallan: 'I thank Heaven I am a good Protestant', and here the motive force is stated by Scott to be Edie's memory of the unequal distribution of the dole in the earl's household according to the recipient's religion, which has been to his previous disadvantage.[30] The most powerful indication of the decline of religious feeling in the modern world of *The Antiquary*, however, occurs during the funeral of the drowned fisherman's son, Steenie Mucklebackit, when Steenie's parents notably refuse to take religious consolation from the Presbyterian minister:[31]

> 'Yes, sir, yes! Ye're very gude! ye're very gude! Nae doubt, nae doubt! It's our duty to submit! But, O dear, my poor Steenie, the pride o' my very heart, that was sae handsome and comely, and a help to his family, and a comfort to us a', and a pleasure to all that lookit on him! O my bairn, my bairn, my bairn! What for is thou lying there, and eh! what for am I left to greet for ye?'

Against this powerful and natural human grief, the Presbyterian doctrinal refusal to admit mourning is simply powerless. Scott as narrator, explicitly criticises the kirk's doctrinaire antipathy to any sort of burial service:[32]

> With a spirit of contradiction which we may be pardoned for esteeming narrow-minded, the fathers of the Scottish Kirk rejected, even on this most solemn occasion, the form of an address to the Divinity, lest they should be thought to give countenance to the rituals of Rome or of England. With much better and more liberal judgement, it is the present practice of most of the Scottish clergymen to seize this opportunity of offering a prayer and exhortation suitable to make an impression upon the living, while they are yet in the very presence of the relics of him whom they have but lately seen such as they themselves, and who now is such as they must in their time become.

The force of Scott's criticism here is that it is delivered from the point of view of the modern Scot. In contrast with the original kirk's strict, Calvinist view that an intercession with God for the deceased could do no good, the modern, liberal, quasi-secular intention of the clergyman is to aim the service at the funeral attendants so as to effect a moral resolution in their minds: as such, the kirk's original, narrow qualms are indeed irrelevant.

Toleration of the other, minority churches is shown to be universal. The Episcopal Church is aptly represented in the novel by Sir Arthur Wardour, an adherent to old loyalties in religion as in politics. Sir Arthur's belief is a quiet and private one; not so different, in its moderation, from Presbyterianism in its modern form. Most striking, however, is the change in attitude towards the Catholic Church. Mrs Mucklebackit's views are telling:[33]

> Ye maun ken the papists make a great point o' eating fish; it's nae bad part o' their religion that, whatever the rest is. I could aye sell the best o' fish at the best o' prices for the Countess's ain table, grace be wi' her! especially on a Friday.

The comedy of this is that the fisherwoman has no very clear idea what 'the rest' of the Catholics' religion is at all, though she would herself claim to be a loyal member of the kirk. There is also a serious insight into her tolerance, however: most important to her is the Catholic habit of eating fish regularly, a habit which, as she considers it apart from any doctrinal significance, seems a trait she would rather see emulated than eliminated. The fisherwoman's attitudes are typical of the modern age: the burial of the Countess (which prompts these remarks) takes place at night, but through custom only – not because there is any longer a fear of persecution. To old Elspeth, the change in attitudes is incomprehensible: she says of the Glenallans' Catholicism:

> they aye stickit by it; and the mair in the latter times, because in the night-time they had mair freedom to perform their popish ceremonies by darkness and in secrecy than in the daylight; at least that was the case in my time. They wad hae been disturbed in the day-time baith by the law and the commons of Fairport. They may be owerlooked now, as I have heard; the warld's changed; I whiles hardly ken whether I am standing or sitting, or dead or living.

Old Elspeth and the atrophied Catholic Lord Glenallan are the only decrepit remains of feudal society left in the present. The Glenallan story which links them, for all its futility and its air of anachronism, still carries enough of the atmosphere of Catholic absolutism and feudal loyalty – almost savagery – to make the contrast with the modern world obvious and horrific.

Robert Gordon points out Elspeth's key death-bed declaration that 'Nae man parted frae his chief for love of gold or of gain, or of right or of wrong.'[34] Elspeth makes no excuse for her atrocious actions in the past other than the fact that they were the will of her mistress, the Countess. Glenallan himself, a pathetic victim of ingrowing Catholic guilt, is only the shadow of a man, notably lacking the heart to defend the moribund social order to which he belongs. Having made the mistake of accepting Oldbuck's invitation to dinner, the earl is mortified to find not only that his host feels it quite in order to advise him against his fasting diet, but also that he himself is expected to take part in the democratic conversation at table about the French Revolution. To Oldbuck's provoking comments that 'There were many men in the first Constituent Assembly who held sound Whiggish doctrines' and that the latter stages of the Revolution might be linked to a hurricane, 'which does great damage in its passage, yet sweeps away stagnant and unwholesome vapours' – to this, Glenallan declines to reply.[35] The earl's political beliefs, based on his hereditary aristocratic ideas about the social order, are not a subject for discussion at a middle-class dinner-table. Yet the impression left with the reader is that Oldbuck's view remains unrefuted, and this too is significant in terms of the middle-class supremacy which Scott is concerned to depict in the novel.

Thus both the main political and religious conflicts of the past appear to have been resolved in the world of *The Antiquary*. In the economic sphere too, the pursuit of money has replaced the traditional ties between master and servant. The Mailsetters' attempt to extort half-a-guinea in an express charge for despatching little Davie on a horse to Monkbarns may be an extreme example of profiteering, but it is more the norm than Edie's later acceptance of sixpence to see that the job is actually carried out. 'Value' to Edie is true worth: to him, the journey to Fairport is 'not out of his way'; to the Mailsetters, the 'value' of their service is the maximum price they can extort. Again, for Sir Arthur Wardour, to whom mere discussion of his debts is painful, his servant's suggestion in a heated moment that he would leave the baronet if he thought Sir Arthur could pay his wages up to date is a terrible blow to his illusion that a man might be attached to him for reasons other than mere

monetary gain.[36] As with the Bertrams in *Guy Mannering*, Sir
Arthur's ancient estate is subjugated to the bourgeois world in
the shape of debts and loans, but here ruin is hastened by the
Baronet's own very unaristocratic speculative mining ventures.
The full sense of family ruin comes home to him when he is
committed to a debtor's prison:[37]

> 'When I was sent to the Tower with my late father, in the
> year 1745, it was upon a charge becoming our birth – upon
> an accusation of high treason, Mr. Oldbuck. We were
> escorted from Highgate by a troop of life-guards, and
> committed upon a secretary of state's warrant; and now,
> here I am, in my old age, dragged from my household by a
> miserable creature like that (pointing to the messenger)
> and for a paltry concern of pounds, shillings, and pence.'

Even here, though, Oldbuck's suggestion that there is
consolation in his own and Isabella's presence, 'even without
the certainty that there can be no hanging, drawing, or
quartering on the present occasion' denies Sir Arthur tragic
status. Sir Arthur's lament is too obviously maudlin in its tone.

Sentimentality is, indeed, the fate which overcomes the
modern characters whenever they attempt to come to terms with
the emotional heritage of the past. Oldbuck's nephew, Hector
McIntyre, tries to live up to what he supposes to have been his
Highland ancestors' virtues, yet the defeat of the clans, the
suppression of their way of life and their subsequent dispersal
have in reality destroyed the continuity of Highland culture.
Hector, as his name suggests, is an egotist puffed up with the
importance of his heritage and the Highland name which he
dogmatically throws in the face of any man he considers his
inferior – almost everyone, in fact. His lack of any true
clan-feeling is revealed when he throws off Edie's claim on him
as a follower of his father's, and by his complete lack of
deference, or even of respect, for the Earl of Glenallan, a fellow
aristocrat. Of his behaviour on this latter occasion, Scott
comments that Hector 'cared no more for an earl than he did for
a foreigner', strongly implying that the source of his excessive
pride is indeed egotism rather than feudal hauteur.[38]

If Hector shows his real ignorance of Highland culture
whenever it comes to bear materially upon his conduct, he

nevertheless prides himself in defending what he imagines that culture to be. Here, the battle is primarily in the field of literary remains: the debate revolving around the truth or falsity of Macpherson's 'Ossian'. The irony of course is that, by the time of *The Antiquary's* publication, the fictitiousness of Macpherson's verses had been exposed beyond all doubt: Hector, arguing at the time of the great uncertainty about Ossian's authenticity, is known by the reader to be on the wrong side. None the less,[39]

> like many a sturdy Celt, he imagined the honour of his country and native language connected with the authenticity of these popular poems, and would have fought knee-deep, or forfeited life and land, rather than have given up a line of them.

The metaphors here are somewhat ironic. Hector's only feat of arms occurs when, in the middle of the above argument, he spots the seal which puts up such a celebrated resistance to his attack. Though he enters the assault 'with the eagerness of a young sportsman', when he shamefacedly returns he excuses himself by pleading 'that a Highlander could never pass a deer, a seal, or a salmon where there was a possibility of having a trial of skill with them.'[40] This is a ludicrous travesty of the martial courage of his Highland ancestors.

In reality, Hector is a typical man of his profession and time. His military occupation, with the officers' 'code of honour', enables him to carry off his pretensions well enough, but to a true aristocrat like Glenallan, Hector's manners 'savoured much more of the camp than of the court'.[41]

When Glenallan's offer of two excellent horses makes Hector liable to become the envy of his fellow officers, such a small detail as the traditional contempt of Highlanders for cavalry is immediately forgotten. Only Oldbuck intervenes:[42]

> 'My lord – my lord – much obliged – much obliged. But Hector is a pedestrian, and never mounts on horseback in battle. He is a Highland soldier, moreover, and his dress ill adapted for cavalry service. Even Macpherson never mounted his ancestors on horseback. . . .'

Hector's behaviour only confirms the insidious suggestions in the novel that the past is quite dead to the modern characters.

In *The Antiquary* as a whole Scott indeed seems to be expressing his pessimism about the very possibility of understanding the past in any way but the superficial inquiries of the antiquaries or the fake partiality of Hector. On rare occasions, this pessimism surfaces and becomes explicit. Early in the novel, when Oldbuck shows Lovel 'the Green Room', his former associations (which we only later come to understand) prompt him to meditate on age and the effects of the passing of time. At this moment when Oldbuck reveals a thoughtfulness and sensitivity usually hidden behind his confident, crusty exterior, he voices his doubts about the possibility of men even understanding their past selves:[43]

> 'The same objects are before us – those inanimate things which we have gazed on in wayward infancy and impetuous youth, in anxious and scheming manhood – they are permanent and the same; but when we look upon them in cold unfeeling old age, can we, changed in our temper, our pursuits, our feelings – changed in our form, our limbs, and our strength – can we be ourselves called the same? or do we not rather look back with a sort of wonder upon our former selves, as beings separate and distinct from what we now are?'

This soliloquy goes beyond the immediate circumstances of which Oldbuck is thinking, though it gains pathos from them. It reflects, among other things, upon the very possibility of history, for the modern age is to the past as Oldbuck's old age is to the earlier periods of his life: the human paradox Oldbuck describes is also the dilemma of the true historian. For a moment, Oldbuck seems on the threshold of understanding that his antiquarianism represents only the historical understanding of old men, and that the 'temper, pursuits and feelings' of the real inhabitants of the past must remain a closed book to such inquiry.

The novel's interest in the subject of 'history' is obvious to any reader. In Chapter XVII Scott parodies the 'modern' polite interest in local history when the characters make a picnic inspection of the ruins of the monastery of St Ruth's. Here they specifically discuss the vagaries of historical knowledge. The Presbyterian clergyman euphemistically considers that 'his parishioners were too deeply impressed with the true Presbyterian doctrine to preserve any records concerning the papistical cumberers of the land'.[44] Lovel, in contrast, sees the question of the monks' anonymity resolved by considering the events which most deeply impress the lower classes:

> 'These,' he contended, 'were not such as resemble the gradual progress of a fertilising river, but the headlong and precipitous fury of some portentous flood. The eras by which the vulgar compute time have always reference to some period of fear and tribulation, and they date by a tempest, an earthquake, or burst of civil commotion.'

This is an interesting re-working of the river-flood image noted in *Waverley*. Joan Elbers sees the novel as odd 'not because it has no structure but because its structure is peculiarly static for a book so deeply concerned with time.'[45] Yet this comment misses the point which is that, unlike most of Scott's novels, *The Antiquary* is not concerned with time or history in an immediate way, but at a second remove, through the characters' own obsession with history as a subject. The attraction of the past for them is actually a result of the lack of historical change or conflict in society in their own age, a quality of modern society which in turn determines the 'static' quality of the novel. On the whole, Scott finds the contemporary world stabler and more rational, but intrinsically less interesting than the times which have given birth to it. Even feelings seemed to have cooled: Oldbuck is amazed at the equanimity with which Hector accepts Lovel's engagement to Isabella:[46]

> 'Sir,' answered the young man, 'you would not have me desperately in love with a woman that does not care about me?'
> 'Well, nephew,' said the Antiquary, more seriously, 'there is doubtless much sense in what you say; yet I would have given a great deal, some twenty or twenty-five years since, to have been able to think as you do.'
> 'Anybody, I suppose, may think as they please on such subjects,' said Hector.

'Not according to the old school,' said Oldbuck; 'but as I said before, the practice of the modern seems in this case the most prudential, though I think scarcely the most interesting.'

Oldbuck's comment really says it all.

It is perhaps questionable whether we can really call *The Antiquary* an 'historical' novel in the same sense in which we use the term of the other Scotch novels: not because Scott is attempting to portray his own age here, but because the historical understanding of society and social change which Scott brings to the other novels has little material to work on in an age which the author finds essentially stable and therefore static. Edie Ochiltree, old Elspeth and Lord Glenallan are there to remind us of the past and the changes which have taken place, but the Glenallan episode itself is explicitly distanced, and both Elspeth and Glenallan have such a fragile hold on the present that they can hardly be called 'living' characters at all.

The lesser stature of *The Antiquary* – Croker's judgment that it belongs to a rank below that of *Waverley* but above that of *Guy Mannering* still seems to hold[47] – is due more to this fundamental lack of historical tension in the novel than to thematic excrescences like the Douterswivel episodes. These are indeed a blot on the novel, despite Scott's attempt, in one or two places, to make the thin melodrama relevant by exploiting the difference between past and present attitudes to magic.[48] The lack of historical tension in the novel as a whole is nevertheless more important, because it robs the novel both of narrative moment and of dramatic 'encounters' in the manner of the previous novels: the insubstantial arguments between Oldbuck and Sir Arthur hardly count, despite their humour. Edgar Johnson, who does not distinguish *The Antiquary* from its predecessors in any basic way, singles out two passages in particular of 'colloquial poetry' in the novel: the scene of Edie with Sir Arthur Wardour as the tide closes in on them, and that of Saunders Mucklebackit with Oldbuck on the day of Steenie's funeral.[49] Yet he does not point out that these scenes stand out partly because, as dialogues of dramatic and social conflict, they are almost unique in the novel. The irony of the first scene is that Sir Arthur, offering Edie a fortune to extricate him and his daughter from their peril, fails to see that the mendicant is in the same situation himself: events have socially levelled them.[50] The other incident is even more interesting and has in a way no parallel elsewhere in Scott's work, as we shall see.

The one 'public' event which occurs in *The Antiquary*, the alarm over the French invasion, only manifests the absence of social tensions in the country and the unity of the people in the face of foreign domination. The citizens' militia, the British army and the remnants of Glenallan's body of retainers gather alongside each other,[51] while even Edie Ochiltree prepares himself to fight for 'the bits o' weans'.[52] The spirit of nationalism – British, not Scottish nationalism – is supreme, though given sound economic foundations by Scott:[53]

> 'Let us,' said Bailie Littlejohn, 'take the horses into our warehouses and the men into our parlours, share our supper with the one and our forage with the other. We have made ourselves wealthy under a free and paternal government, and now is the time to show we know its value.'

The alarm makes clear the commercial prosperity which is being defended: the burghers of Fairport have reason to consider the country 'their' country now. It is perhaps fitting that the enemy should in the end turn out to be illusory: in the unified society Scott depicts there is, indeed, no real opposition.

There is another, final reason for disappointment with *The Antiquary*. Despite its pretensions, the novel does not quite represent Scott's contemporary world: the slight backdating of twenty years or so tends to avoid those very issues in Scott's contemporary society which might challenge the view expressed in the novel of the stability and stasis of modern, civilised, middle-class society. Lukács notes: 'Scott very seldom speaks of the present. He does not raise the social questions of contemporary England [sic] in his novels, the class struggle between bourgeoisie and proletariat which was then beginning to sharpen.'[54] By turning the clock back twenty years, Scott seems to evade just those social questions which were, at the time of writing, rearing their heads. The one exception to this is the dialogue between Oldbuck and Saunders Mucklebackit already mentioned:[55]

When he came in front of the fisherman's hut, he
observed a man working intently, as if to repair a shattered
boat which lay upon the beach, and, going up to him, was
surprised to find it was Mucklebackit himself. 'I am glad,'
he said, in a tone of sympathy – 'I am glad, Saunders, that
you feel able to make this exertion.'

'And what would you have me to do,' answered the
fisher, gruffly, 'unless I wanted to see four children starve,
because ane is drowned? It's weel wi' you gentles, that can
sit in the house wi' handkerchers at your een when ye lose
a friend, but the like o' us maun to our wark again, if our
hearts were beating as hard as my hammer.'

W. M. Parker calls this, with reason, 'the one and only
democratic view Scott ever expressed in his fiction.'[56] It is,
indeed, the only indication in *The Antiquary* that the new
social order in Scotland does not give uniform cause for
satisfaction. To Mucklebackit, Oldbuck is as much of a 'gentle'
as Sir Arthur: the vital distinction is between those living a
leisured existence, and those who must work for their living
even on the day of their son's funeral. The actual dialogue is
one of the most poignant interchanges in Scott. There is just a
hint of superiority in Oldbuck's greeting – the antiquary is
rather shocked to see that Mucklebackit's feelings allow him to
work that day. Yet in his reply, hiding his sorrow in angry
sarcasm, Mucklebackit bitingly rebuts this implication of
insensitivity, and instead shows up the unconscious class
prejudice behind Oldbuck's assumption. Mucklebackit himself
is not a proletarian, but the circumstances of the fishing trade
put him in a similar social position, and his defence of the
sensibilities of 'the like o' us' in the face of the harsh necessities
of life makes him, in a way, the only spokesman for the incipient
working classes in Scott's work.[57]

On the whole, however, Lukács's analysis of Scott's response
to contemporary social issues is true: he says of Scott that 'As far
as he is able to answer these questions for himself, he does so in
the indirect way of embodying the most important stages of the
whole of English [sic] history in his writing.'[58] The tension that
we feel *The Antiquary* lacks in comparison with the best of
Scott's work is the novel's own final criticism. In other novels,

Scott's insight into society in its historical dimension is dynamic, and this fact inevitably undermines by implication his static portrayal of modern society in *The Antiquary*. The stability, even boredom, of life for the modern characters of the novel, subtly and humorously depicted though it is, results in a lack of the sense of the pressure of the times on typical individuals conveyed in Scott's greatest work. To this extent, Lukács is right to say that Scott answered questions about historical development (including, implicitly, the development of his own society) better indirectly, in the novels about the Scottish past written with an understanding of the long-term historical transformations which had taken place, than when he attempted directly, as in *The Antiquary*, to analyse the character of the modern age.

4

Old Mortality

The Antiquary is a novel about what was to Scott 'modern' Scotland: as we have seen, it depicts a society lacking any real basis for internal conflict, whether political, religious or economic. *Old Mortality* is in complete contrast: set in Lowland Scotland during the latter years of Charles II's reign, it is a highly dynamic portrait of a society convulsed by internal contradictions, by implacable antagonism, persecution and revolt. It is not surprising to find that Karl Marx greatly admired *Old Mortality*:[1] in it 'the motley feudal ties that bound man to his "natural superiors"' are indeed visibly torn asunder.[2] In other words, Scott passes directly from his most lackadaisical novel to one of his most intensely dramatic works – a movement which seems to defy attempts to find any logical development from one novel to the other.[3]

Nevertheless, one central theme of *The Antiquary* does show itself in *Old Mortality*, in the 'introductory' chapter which opens the novel. This chapter is strictly unnecessary from the point of view of the novel's action, and considered merely as an opening, is certainly inferior to Chapter II.[4] It can best be understood as a reference back to the scepticism Scott expressed in *The Antiquary* about the very possibility of historical enquiry in the modern age. It serves to show the reader that *Old Mortality* is not conceived in the manner of Oldbuck's *Caledoniad*, as a merely antiquarian study of the dead past. Even though, as Hugh Trevor-Roper points out, in *Old*

Mortality Scott 'passed beyond the barrier of mere living memory', and had to rely exclusively on written evidence of the period, he clearly felt the lasting human and historical significance of the age in Scottish history he was portraying.[5] By fictitiously citing Old Mortality as the inspiration for the novel, Scott establishes for the reader the essential, human link with the past.

Thus the novel opens in the near-present, with the narrative of Peter Pattieson, a schoolmaster. His mind dulled by the boredom and repetition of his job, Pattieson seems the least likely source of historical imagination: even the impression on him of the old graveyard he retreats to is notably muted: 'Death has indeed been here, and its traces are before us; but they are softened and deprived of their horror by our distance from the period when they have been first impressed.'[6] This feeling of distance from the buried dead remains unchanged as Pattieson notices the monuments in the cemetery which 'to an antiquary' are the most interesting: the ornate tombs of 'a doughty knight' and 'a nameless bishop'. It is not on these that he finds Old Mortality working, however, but on the almost nameless graves of the Presbyterian martyrs of the previous century. Pattieson's interest immediately quickens when he hears the passionate reverence with which the old man talks of his heroes' exploits:[7]

> One would almost have supposed he must have been their contemporary, and have actually beheld the passages which he related, so much had he identified his feelings and opinions with theirs, and so much had his narratives the circumstantiality of an eye-witness.

The change of tone from Pattieson's quiet, uninvolved meditation on the gravestones to Old Mortality's impassioned defence of 'the only true Whigs' is significant. The directness of the old man's narrative here is Scott's imaginative model for the rest of the novel.

For its encapsulation of an entire period with all its leading features and contradictions in one descriptive scene, the occasion of the 'wappenschaw' which opens the novel proper was probably never surpassed by Scott in his later work. Here, in the gathered array of crown vassals, and the reaction of the local tenants, Scottish society of the period stands symbolically displayed. The wappenschaw is intended to manifest the feudal order of Scotland under the Stuarts; in theory, it is a gathering of the aristocratic hierarchy, supported by their retainers and vassals in the lower orders. Yet as the scene progresses it becomes clear that the assembly is actually a monumental façade, a ceremony reintroduced by the Stuart government long after any significance it has had as an actual expression of feudal relationships has disappeared, for the express purpose of intimidating the discontented, and impressing on them that the traditional order and authority are still in existence.

The wappenschaw makes clear the intimate relationship between religion and politics in the minds of the participants and the spectators: though it seems, as Lars Hartveit says, 'harmless and religiously neutral',[8] it becomes a focal point for Presbyterian opposition. The extreme Presbyterians object to the whole edifice of the episcopal church, feudal authority, and monarchical absolutism represented by the Stuart government: in such circumstances, to absent themselves from the ceremony is to challenge at once both the political and the religious authority of their rulers. Among the more numerous Presbyterian tenants who do turn up to watch the day's sport, rebelliousness takes the more moderate form of the championship of Henry Morton against Lord Evandale in the popinjay contest: a form of dissent which is equally galling to the Royalist gentry.

Guse Gibbie's unfortunate loss of control over his horse – the incident which finally makes a laughing stock of the wappenschaw – is merely the culmination of events. The idiot boy is only drafted into the Bellendens' body of 'vassals' because mass absenteeism has already necessitated the conscription of[9]

> the fowler and the falconer, the footman and the ploughman, at the home farm, with an old drunken Cavaliering butler, who had served with the late Sir Richard under Montrose, and stunned the family nightly with his exploits at Kilsyth and Tippermuir, and who was the only man in the party that had the smallest zeal for the work in hand.

Typically, Scott provides strong, economic reasons for the

steward's unwillingness to call in the troops to punish the refractory tenants:[10]

> 'For,' said Harrison to himself, 'the carles have little enough gear at ony rate, and if I call in the redcoats and take away what little they have, how is my worshipful lady to get her rents paid at Candlemas, which is but a difficult matter to bring round even in the best of times?'

The precarious economic position of Lady Margaret's estate has, as its inevitable consequence, the weakening of her effective feudal authority: nor can her pompous parade of the forms of feudalism reverse this underlying weakness. In this situation, Cuddie Headrigg's absence from the ranks merely precipitates the crisis which Harrison has been trying to stave off. As a result, Guse Gibbie's disastrous flight, instead of being a fancifully unique accident, gathers about it an air of inevitability: the reader feels that it was only a matter of time before the whole charade of the wappenschaw must have been exposed.

Harrison's defensive position over the disobedient tenants on the Bellendens' estate is constantly paralleled by the defensive posture assumed by the authorities in the early stages of the novel. The battle at Loudon Hill, for example, is lost primarily because Claverhouse, against Major Allan's military judgment, feels committed to an engagement with the rebels: even a tactical retreat would, he feels, be politically impossible.[11] Scott's distortion of actual events in the battle seems intended to emphasise this point: the changes he makes in the landscape of the battle noted by Kay Mathias[12] make the Lifeguards' attack more reckless militarily than it was in real life, while the council of war called by Claverhouse, at which the officers declare their differing views on the situation, is also an invention of Scott's to make the political reasons for the attack clear.[13] Claverhouse's fear of a general insurrection is substantiated by the universal antipathy of the local tenantry to the Government: something we see a little later, when even Major Bellenden's strenuous efforts can find only nine men prepared to help defend Tillietudlem.[14] By the time the Privy Council gets round to calling out 'the feudal array of crown vassals' – for which the wappenschaws have supposedly been the preparation – we are not in the least surprised to find that 'the summons was very slackly obeyed'.[15]

To begin with, however, Lady Margaret is able to restore some of the pride shattered by Guse Gibbie's undignified exit by evicting Mause and Cuddie from her estate – the standard penalty for religious dissent in the period.[16] The scene of Lady Margaret's confrontation with old Mause brilliantly displays the links between Presbyterianism as a religious movement, and its appeal to the Scottish peasant's aspirations for political and economic emancipation. Just as the wappenschaw visually assembled Scottish society in the mass, so the scene of Mause's defiance of her landlady portrays the same social tensions on an individual level, sharpened into some of the best of Scott's circumstantial dialogue. Mause's embarrassment as she finds herself torn between her former, deferential friendship with Lady Margaret, and the independence of her mistress which she now feels called upon to exert, is marvellously and subtly portrayed. Having declared timidly, to her Ladyship's horror, that she finds 'nae warrant' for the wappenschaws, Mause continues:[17]

> 'ane canna serve twa maisters; and if the truth maun e'en come out, there's Ane abune whase commands I maun obey before your leddyship's. I am sure I would put neither king's nor kaiser's nor ony earthly creature's afore them.'
> 'How mean ye by that, ye auld fule woman? D'ye think that I order onything against conscience?'

Lady Margaret misunderstands Mause to be implying that she is acting in bad faith herself, a telling misapprehension which shows that she still conceives of a naturally ordered universe with the chain of command running from God, through the king, the aristocracy, and the gentry, down to the tenantry at the base of the social pyramid. It is the same world-view that makes her incredulous of Mause's claim to find 'nae warrant' for the wappenschaw when the warrant comes from the king's own person. Yet, as in the scene of the wappenschaw, it is this 'natural' order which is under attack. Mause's reply makes this clear:

> 'I dinna pretend to say that, my leddy, in regard o' your

leddyship's conscience, which has been brought up, as it were, wi' prelatic principles; but ilka ane maun walk by the light o' their ain, and mine,' said Mause, waxing bolder as the conference became animated, 'tells me that I suld leave a' – cot, kaleyard, and cow's grass – and suffer a', rather than that I or mine should put on harness in an unlawfu' cause.'

Mause's egalitarian reasoning is anathema to Lady Margaret's ears: like Glenallan at Oldbuck's dinner-table, she is both unwilling and unable to conduct an argument with Mause on the basis of the equality of conscience Mause asserts. To the old woman's revolutionary interpretation of the good book – 'there was ance a king in Scripture they ca'd Nebuchadnezzar' – Lady Margaret has no reply. Instead, she shows her contempt for such discussion:

'I see which way the wind blaws,' she exclaimed, after a pause of astonishment; 'the evil spirit of the year 1642 is at wark again as merrily as ever, and ilka auld wife in the chimney-neuk will be for knapping doctrine wi' doctors o' divinity and the godly fathers of the church.'

Lady Margaret's view of religious doctrine as a subject reserved for the learned episcopal hierarchy is, of course, perfectly in keeping with her class perspective and her respect for authority in all matters. Mause will not let such a remark pass. Her reply – 'If your leddyship means the bishops and curates, I'm sure they hae been but stepfathers to the Kirk o' Scotland' – returns the reader to the central political and religious issue of the day, an issue which has been given immediate relevance through the murder of Archbishop Sharpe which has just taken place. Scott shows his characters' argument here naturally proceeding from their own particular circumstances to the main ideological controversies of the day: in this way, he shows the controversies themselves to be deeply rooted in the social life of the people, and in no way to be purely theoretical disputes.

Scott makes every effort in this scene to treat his characters 'fairly', showing both the positive and negative aspects of their respective causes. The legal eviction of the Headriggs, for example, is seen to be entirely lacking in justice. Lady Margaret sets up her own 'solemn court of justice' in the absence of both Cuddie and Mause, and at which the only participants other than herself are Harrison and the butler, who attend 'partly on the footing of witnesses, partly as assessors' – in other words, as both prosecution and jury.[18] Scott lays on the irony by concluding: 'The charge being fully made out and substantiated, Lady Margaret resolved to reprimand the culprits in person, and, if she found them impenitent, to extend the censure into a sentence of expulsion from the barony.' The quasi-legal language here is in strong contrast with the injustice of the proceedings: yet Scott is doing no more than record the actual practice in the Scottish 'baron courts' of the period.[19] On the other hand, Mause's rebellion against Lady Margaret is satirised by the tendency of her protest to turn into sermonising and cant, and by the ludicrous argument she appends to her complaints, concerning the iniquity of the estate's newly acquired winnowing machine. Here, Scott appears to be opening himself to the charge of caricature of the Presbyterians levelled at him originally by Thomas McCrie, and more recently by David Craig.[20] Yet the Covenanting style of speech used by Scott for Mause and the other extreme Presbyterian characters has been praised by the latest surveyor of the historical sources of the novel, James Anderson, as 'certainly not parody, it is hardly fair even to call it pastiche . . . Scott speaks the language [of the Covenanters] like a native'.[21] Similarly, Mause's claim that Tillietudlem's winnowing machine is 'impiously thwarting the will of Divine Providence by raising wind for your leddyship's ain particular use by human art, instead of soliciting it by prayer . . .'[22] seems exaggeratedly ridiculous, but in fact it satirises the dogmatism and rigidity of the Covenanting character, as well as Mause's reliance on 'the Calvinistic conception of individual, God-inspired judgement – so-called "inner light"', as Hartveit puts it.[23] Mause has applied the determinist philosophy of Calvinism, taken to its logical extreme.

George Goodin puts Scott's 'impartiality' in *Old Mortality* down to his use of a dramatic form, arguing that this necessitates an ironic approach, essentially lacking in political commitment.[24] However, it can be claimed that Scott shows a 'centrist' commitment in the novel: D. A. Cameron, for example, sees an expression of Scott's own moderation 'in the care with which [he] makes the reader see the horrors of fanaticism, its warping and distortion of character, its dehydration of the faculties of human sympathy. . . .'[25] This is partly a result of Scott's setting the character of Henry Morton in the middle of the novel. At the beginning of the story, Morton is conceived of by Scott, rather like Waverley, as the victim of events, rather than their arbiter. Like Waverley, Morton is committed by his family history to equivocation: his father, we learn, was a moderate in the Civil War, sustaining an upright but difficult course through the vicissitudes of that period. Even here, however, Morton is a more active figure than Waverley: it is his actions – his success with the popinjay, and with Edith Bellenden (both of which anger the Royalists at the wappen-schaw), his protection of Cuddie and Mause, and his sheltering of Burley – which, although unwitting, tend to commit him in the ensuing conflict. Morton visibly changes, moreover, as he takes part in political events, until by the time of his brief return to Milnwood he is presented as a fully mature character.[26] Our respect for Morton, and our identification with his predicament, come to depend to a large extent on our agreement with his principles, and our sympathy for his position as 'the humane, intelligent liberal in a world of extremists.'[27] In Cameron's words, Morton has 'a normative function.'[28]

One danger of this attitude to Morton is that he may seem an anachronism, an eighteenth-century liberal shoe-horned into a seventeenth-century context. Nevertheless, for most of the novel Scott succeeds in situating Morton convincingly in the period. In particular, Scott uses the peculiar historical compromise of 'Indulged' Presbyterianism to characterise the instability of Morton's position – open as it is to accusations of 'erastianism' from the Cameronians, and to the suspicion that it is merely disguised sedition from Royalists such as Bothwell. This is in fact a subtle manipulation of historical fact by Scott: as far as is known, no 'Indulged' Presbyterians took part in the 1679 revolt.[29] The uneasy compromise represented by the Indulgence nevertheless aptly describes Morton's predicament: Scott's distortion of history here is completely functional.

Morton is compelled into action by a number of factors. There is his disgust with the 'neutrality' of figures like Neil

Blane, the innkeeper, and his own miserly uncle, Milnwood.
Blane's object in life is solely self-interest, playing off one side
against another to his own advantage, and quite prepared to
turn a blind eye to injustice if there is a profit to be made from
it.[30] Milnwood's neutrality, on the other hand, is equally
contemptible, proceeding as it does from personal cowardice:
his debasing servitude during the dragoons' forced entrance to
his house appals his nephew.[31] Morton is also sickened by the
constant atmosphere of authoritarian persecution, by the troops
who 'do whatever they like through the haill country wi' man
and woman, beast and body',[32] and who, according to Jenny,
string up 'the puir Whig bodies that they catch in the muirs like
straps o' onions'[33] – when persecution can be described by so
commonplace a metaphor we feel Morton is right to rebel. Yet
Alexander Welsh is correct to point out that Morton's final
resolution to join the Covenanters is due to quite personal
motives: his despair of winning Edith. Welsh concludes:[34]

> In *Old Mortality* Scott even argues a connection between
> love and politics. Interpretations that would reduce the
> Waverley Novels to historical dialectics or the hero to a
> 'symbolic observer' must balk at [Morton's] soliloquies
> [over Edith] . . .

This is to take a narrow view of the meaning of 'historical
dialectics': in fact, Morton's relationship with Edith is one of
the most successful romantic affairs in the Waverley Novels
specifically because politics, in the shape of the class differences
between the two lovers, provides a realistic and interesting
obstacle to any conventional, romantic resolution. At the
point in the novel to which Welsh refers, the obstacles to
Morton's union with Edith appear absolute: the hero
mistakenly believes that Edith is favouring her socially
acceptable suitor, Lord Evandale. It is no coincidence that at this
moment Morton should commit himself fully to a cause which
has as part of its rationale a revolt against the prevailing social
order and an espousal of the egalitarian view of man. Morton
himself sees the connection between his stymied love for Edith
and the authoritarian political situation only too clearly:[35]

'And to what do I owe it,' he said, 'that I cannot stand up

like a man and plead my interest in her ere I am thus
cheated out of it? to what but to the all-pervading and
accursed tyranny which afflicts at once our bodies, souls,
estates, and affections? And is it to one of the pensioned
cut-throats of this oppressive government that I must yield
my pretensions to Edith Bellenden? I will not, by Heaven!
It is a just punishment on me for being dead to public
wrongs that they have visited me with their injuries in a
point where they can least be brooked or borne.'

This, as the reader knows, is hardly fair to Evandale: the point
is, however, that Morton's anger at his rival is partly on account
of Evandale's superior social qualification (in the eyes of the
Bellendens) to woo Edith. If it is true to claim, as Welsh does,
that Morton's romantic frustration prompts him to turn to civil
rebellion, it is also true that class antagonism has been the cause
of his frustration in the first place. It is this sort of interaction
between the hero's private and public life, after all, which
might properly be called 'dialectical'.

One continuing irony of the different class backgrounds of
the lovers is that Edith is quite unable to equate Morton's part
in the revolt with any sort of moral principle. Hearing that
Morton is with the rebels besieging Tillietudlem, Edith's first
reaction is of utter disbelief:[36]

'Henry Morton is incapable of such treachery to his king
and country, such cruelty to me – to – to all the innocent
and defenceless victims, I mean – who must suffer in a civil
war; I tell you he is utterly incapable of it, in every sense.'

Not unnaturally, Edith interprets Morton's rebellion as a
personal treachery, a view apparently confirmed when Morton
has to lead a firing party against the Tillietudlem garrison and
Major Bellenden. Jeanie's repulsion of Cuddie with the hot
'brose' at this point serves to parody Edith's feelings towards
Morton. Edith is also notably hostile later on, when Morton
finds an opportunity to speak to her as his party is escorting the
family out of Burley's hands into safety. As Edith sees it:[37]

'Treason, murder by the sword and by gibbet, the
oppression of a private family such as ours, who were only
in arms for the defence of the established government and

77

of our own property, are actions which must needs sully all that have accession to them, by whatever specious terms they may be gilded over.'

This is an excellent revelation of Edith's opinions: the sanctity of the 'established government' and of the Bellendens' property figure high on her scale of values, to the virtual exclusion of any awareness of the injustices which have prompted Morton to rebel, or of the part he has played in the family's protection. Irresistibly the lovers are forced apart by events and their own prejudices: in the end, Scott has to resort to unlikely means (Evandale's 'chivalric' unselfishness, for example) in order to restore Edith's opinion of Morton.

Morton's relationship with Edith is subject to the same pressures of polarisation which affect all the other characters in the novel, Covenanters and Royalists alike. Again these pressures seem to arise inevitably, like the strains on the lovers, from the social differences between the characters typical of the time portrayed.

The Royalist characters, for example, exemplify the degenerate nature of feudalism in the period. The fascinating, contradictory character Scott assigns to Claverhouse is an example. On the one hand, Claverhouse aspires to the courtly ideal of nobility – his features, for example, 'form such a countenance as limners love to paint and ladies to look upon.'[38] On the other hand, he is prepared to resort to the most cruel and rapacious methods in order to keep the masses of the vulgar in their naturally subservient place: to this extent, he is shown to deserve the inherited Presbyterian view of him as a diabolical character. In his anonymous review of 'Tales of My Landlord', Scott says of Claverhouse: 'Few men have left to posterity a character so strikingly varied. It is not shaded – it is not even chequered – it is on the one side purely heroic, on the other, cruel, savage and sanguinary.'[39] In fact, as Kay Mathias has pointed out, and in contradiction to McCrie's accusations, Scott seems to have exaggerated the real cruelty of Claverhouse's conduct (and also to have invested Burley with extreme religious enthusiasm) 'to suit his fictional purposes and make them appropriate representatives of the Royalist party and Covenanting party respectively.'[40] As drawn by Scott, Claverhouse epitomises the two-faced nature of Royalism in 1679: the heroic ideal and the bloody practice.

Other Royalist figures give similar insights into the degeneracy of the aristocratic order. Sergeant Bothwell represents the social downfall of lineage based on birth: his remarkable ancestry, contrasting with his degraded rank, poses a personal dilemma for him which is also a general dilemma of the nobility. Even so profound an admirer of the blood royal as Lady Bellenden is unable to cope with the situation:[41]

> 'Well, Mr. Stewart,' rejoined the lady, '. . . I heartily wish you good evening, and commit you to the care of my steward, Harrison. I would ask you to keep ourselves company, but a-a-a-'
>
> 'O, madam, it requires no apology; I am sensible the coarse red coat of King Charles II does and ought to annihilate the privileges of the red blood of King James V.'
>
> 'Not with me, I do assure you, Mr. Stewart; you do me injustice if you think so. I will speak to your officer to-morrow; and I trust you shall soon find yourself in a rank where there shall be no anomalies to be reconciled.'
>
> 'I believe, madam,' said Bothwell, 'your goodness will find itself deceived; but I am obliged to you for your intention, and, at all events, I will have a merry night with Mr. Harrison.'

Lady Margaret's embarrassment, at which Bothwell's sensitive feelings immediately catch, reveals her own hypocrisy. For all her tiresome mouthing of her respect for royalty, she is not prepared to take a scion of the Stuart royal family into her dining-room unless he has the added 'respectability' of being a commissioned officer. Like Sir Robert Hazlewood in *Guy Mannering*, Lady Margaret's conception of a 'gentleman' has undergone a subtle revision which tends to undermine the Royalist hierarchy of birth itself. Bothwell himself sardonically accepts the steward's company that night, but the butler's manoeuvres to bring himself up to physical (and social) equality with the sergeant at the table emphasise the depth of Bothwell's degradation. Morton's discovery of Bothwell's pocket-book after the sergeant's death at Loudon Hill adds a tragic, 'noble' dimension to his character – again the 'dual' nature of Royalism in the period is seen. Moreover, the history of degeneracy which is peculiarly Bothwell's contributes to the atmosphere of decadence on the Royalist side as a whole. Respect for birth *per se* has gone: even Charles II, during the infamous *disjune* at Tillietudlem, pays as much attention to the serving maids as he does to Lady Margaret herself.[42]

The Covenanters are similarly characterised by Scott in terms that clearly relate to their social background, expressed through their religious and political ideas. Immediately after their victory at Loudon Hill, Scott draws attention to the outstanding feature of their 'army' – its fatal lack of discipline:[43]

> It followed from this state of disorganisation that the whole army appeared at once to resolve itself into a general committee for considering what steps were to be taken in consequence of their success, and no opinion could be started so wild that it had not some favourers and advocates.

This behaviour, which Cameron rightly describes as 'something approaching anarchism',[44] is quite consistent with the Presbyterian emphasis on the supremacy of the individual conscience which Mause Headrigg has already displayed at work. It is also consistent with the social composition of the 'army' as Scott describes it: we are told that 'the towns, the villages, the farm-houses, the properties of small heritors, sent forth numerous recruits to the Presbyterian interest'.[45] The Covenanters, in other words, are drawn predominantly from the peasantry and the petit-bourgeois class in the towns and villages: their army is an amalgam of individual interests. In their fragmentation by individualism, and their fatal lack of any perspective of class unity in the face of the government forces at Bothwell Bridge, the Covenanters may well be said to make up an 'army' 'by simple addition of homologous magnitudes, much as potatoes in a sack form a sack of potatoes', as Marx said of the French peasants in 1848.[46] The fanaticism of the large part of the Covenanters, typefied brilliantly by the apocalyptic preachers Kettledrummle, Macbriar, and Habbakuk Mucklewrath, panders precisely to their followers' parochialism and individualism, their lack of political realism, and their private, sectarian grievances. Here again charges of exaggeration levelled at Scott – by Craig, for example, who finds Mucklewrath 'against all credibility'[47] – are vitiated by the discovery of historical prototypes for the preachers.[48]

Where there is exaggeration, as in Scott's investment of the historical Burley with extreme religious fanaticism, his aim is only to clarify the issues by presenting traits that historically did exist in a principal personage of the novel.[49] Thus, Burley is intended to display the Presbyterian characteristic of 'inner light' taken to its logical extreme: his dedication to becoming the hand of God's vengeance may instead he interpreted as an extreme of egotistical mania. The stronger the sense of individual righteousness, the less is the concern for the opinions of others, however. Burley's contempt for the understanding of the mass of the Covenanters is obvious in one incident, notable for being one of Scott's 'elaborations', he kills Cornet Grahame under a flag of truce rather than allow him to address the ranks of the Covenanters directly.[50] Even more cynically, he uses Kettledrummle's fervent orations to occupy the masses while he himself and a few other leaders hold 'a private council of war, undisturbed by the discordant opinions or senseless clamour of the general body'.[51] The disparaging terms here used by Scott are undoubtedly those in which Burley thinks of his own followers. Burley's regard for Morton, despite his own former comradeship with the hero's father, is no more sincere: he is quite prepared to use 'moderate' arguments to win Morton over even though he himself is contemptuous of such liberal scruples.[52] Yet Scott shows Burley's very ruthlessness of action to achieve his ends by whatever means as taking an inevitable toll on his psychological state. His hallucinatory struggles with the Devil, for instance, are all too obviously an agony of self-doubt:[53]

The perspiration stood on his brow 'like bubbles in a late disturbed stream,' and these marks of emotion were accompanied with broken words which escaped from him at intervals – 'Thou art taken, Judas – thou art taken. Cling not to my knees – cling not to my knees; hew him down! A priest! Ay, a priest of Baal, to be bound and slain, even at the brook Kishon. Firearms will not prevail

against him. Strike – thrust with the cold iron – put him
out of pain – put him out of pain, were it but for the sake
of his grey hairs.'

Most effectively, this is the only description of the murder of
Sharpe that Scott puts in the novel. Burley's waking
rationalisation of the murder, his studied callousness in the
great 'cause', is contradicted by his daily agony in which his
unconscious mind revolts. The atmosphere of the novel here is
almost Jacobean: Burley's self-revelatory soliloquy owes its
effect to Scott's reading of Shakespeare – the quotation is
actually from *I Henry IV* – in a far deeper and more mature way
than the Shakespearian allusions in *Waverley*.

The point of the novel's action, however, is to distinguish
Morton from the extreme Covenanters in the same way that he
has cut himself off from the Royalists at the beginning of the
novel. The 'moderate' views which the hero slowly comes to set
up against both the government and the Cameronians bear
examination in some detail. His views on religion are the first to
be sharply distinguished from Burley's providential opportunism. Early on he warns Burley:[54]

'I own I should strongly doubt the origin of any inspiration
which seemed to dictate a line of conduct contrary to those
feelings of natural humanity which Heaven has assigned to
us as the general law of our conduct.'

This essentially Augustan, commonsense view of religious
morality, with its condemnation of the Covenanters' habit of
out-of-context scriptural quotations, naturally accords with
Morton's aversion to the murder of Sharpe and his horror at
Burley's justification of the deed as an act of divine retribution.
Similarly, Morton's political principles resemble neither the
absolutism of the Royalists nor the theocratic idealism of the
Cameronians. Morton's original revulsion is against the conduct
of the authorities,[55]

the misrule, license, and brutality of the soldiery, the
executions on the scaffold, the slaughters in the open
field, the free quarters and exactions imposed by military
law, which placed the lives and fortunes of a free people on
a level with Asiatic slaves.

and this conviction in the rights of 'a free people' continues to dominate his political beliefs. When his arrest by Bothwell manifests to him his own lack of freedom Morton exclaims: 'I will resist any authority on earth, that invades tyranically my chartered rights as a freeman'[56] – an interesting declaration. Welsh has said of Morton's liberal views:[57]

> Henry Morton is neither leveler [*sic*] nor libertine, but a sore-set defender of the British Constitution. By a slight anachronism, the constitution he defends is that of 1688, but even in 1679 he consistently refers to himself and his followers as 'subjects' of the king.

Morton in fact, as Welsh points out, is a constitutional monarchist: he is certainly no extreme democrat. Horrified by the near-anarchy in the ranks of the Covenanters after Loudon Hill, only Burley's announcement of the formation of a council of leaders persuades him to stay on. His belief is in 'chartered rights': rights manifested in the petition he draws up for Monmouth's consideration, so phrased as to be acceptable to moderate (that is, constitutional) Royalists and to his own followers in the Covenanting camp alike.

The question of the historical realism of Morton's political position is more complex. Welsh accuses Scott of anachronism, of 'post-dating' his hero in a way that violates the novel's historical authenticity. Here again, research seems to bear Scott out: as Kay Mathias has pointed out, a supplication similar to Morton's for freedom of worship, a free parliament and a free General Assembly of the Kirk was actually drawn up by moderate Presbyterians prior to Bothwell Bridge.[58] In other words, men like Morton, who anticipated the compromise settlement of 1688, certainly existed in Scotland ten years previously. Nor is this entirely surprising, given that the liberal principles in religion and politics which Morton professes belonged historically to the growing Scottish middle class of which Morton, as a middling laird, is a representative. His key proposal, 'that a free Parliament should be called for settling the affairs of Church and the State' epitomises the new, middle-class conception of both Church and State as separable entities, the businesses of both of which were to be settled in such a way as least to interfere with men's 'private affairs'.[59]

This is an equal distance from theocracy and from absolutism. The problem for Morton depicted by Scott in *Old Mortality* is that the middle class does not, in 1679, figure as much of a force at all in a world dominated by the conflict between the upper and lower classes of society.

Apart from their restricted numbers Morton's adherents in the camp of the Covenanters also tend to be too comfortably off, too lacking in desperation, to form a viable alternative force to the Cameronians, with whom they have little in common. Poundtext, the moderate Presbyterian minister who supports Morton, is depicted in a telling passage as far happier at home with his pipe, a jug of ale, and a theological treatise, than when taking an active part in the Covenanting body: 'when he knew the matter in hand, he gave up, with a deep groan, the prospect of spending a quiet evening in his own little parlour . . .'[60] In a well-known 'apologetic' note to the novel, Scott asks his reader's forgiveness for his drawing of Poundtext, asserting that among the moderate Presbyterians there were indeed 'many ministers whose courage was equal to their good sense and sound views of religion.'[61] Yet it is impossible not to agree with Scott's artistic judgment as expressed in the novel: the portrayal of Poundtext may not be strictly fair, but it illustrates an important truth about the social background of the moderates. The same end is achieved by having Morton and Poundtext speak English while peppering the speech of the extreme Covenanters with Scots dialect and Biblical allusions – a distinction to which Craig strongly objects.[62] As usual in the Waverley Novels, English dialect spoken by Scottish characters denotes their superior class, while the very fact that, as Hartveit puts it, 'the two factions within the Whig camp speak two entirely different languages' contributes to the atmosphere of social division among the Covenanters.[63] Craig objects to Morton's measured tones in his addresses to the Covenanters, but misses the point that the Cameronians also object to his moderate language and middle-class accent. His final exhortation to the ranks at Bothwell Bridge falls on deaf ears partly because, like Brutus in *Julius Caesar*, Morton lacks the ability to appeal to the lower orders.

Scott underlines the powerlessness of Morton and of the class to which he belongs by isolating the hero to a greater extent

than would have been the case in reality.[64] Scott presents the
embassy to Monmouth, for example, as a personal effort of
Morton's, denying him any accompaniment on his mission.[65]
The meeting with Monmouth is, indeed, vested with an almost
symbolic appositeness by Scott. As the troops line up opposite
the body of the Covenanters, the social battle-lines seem to be
drawn:[66]

> Large bodies composed of the Highland clans, having in
> language, religion and manners no connection with the
> insurgents, had been summoned to join the royal army
> under their various chieftains; and these Amorites, or
> Philistines, as the insurgents termed them, came like
> eagles to the slaughter.

This is not a purely military description: it is the social
distinction between the Highlanders and the Covenanters which
is important. As the most backward, even pre-feudal order in
the Scottish nation, the clans are the most implacable
supporters of the Stuart government against the Covenanters.
The mutual contempt of the Highlanders and the Presbyterians
for each other is nicely portrayed in the metaphors Scott uses
here, taken from the Bible on one hand to indicate the way the
Covenanters view the clans, and from nature on the other, to
indicate the predatory, savage character of the conflict as it is
seen by the Highlanders themselves. Morton's meeting with
Monmouth reflects this hardening of attitudes between the two
sides: the reasonable Duke is eclipsed by his hard-line generals,
Claverhouse and Dalzell. The latter figure is present against
history (as Scott himself pointed out in the *Quarterly Review*)
purely for the purpose of physically overbearing Monmouth and
giving the reader a further insight into the fanatical Royalism
which thwarts Morton's peace-mission. Dalzell's very appearance is astonishing: his beard grown in unforgiving memory of
Charles I's death, and his features which 'evinced age unbroken
by infirmity, and stern resolution unsoftened by humanity'[67]
make him a symbol of the Stuart monarchy in 1679, essentially
anachronistic, but persisting with a perverse energy and
tenaciously refusing to give way to compromise. The sticking
point in Morton's negotiations with Monmouth is equally
symbolic. Just as the whole theory of Stuart absolutism hangs on

the doctrine of divine right, so the king cannot agree to 'treat' with the rebels in any way. The most Monmouth can offer is to intercede with the king if the Covenanters first lay down their arms, and this, Morton sees, is not sufficient:[68]

> 'To do so, my Lord Duke,' replied Morton undauntedly, 'were to acknowledge ourselves the rebels that our enemies term us. Our swords are drawn for recovery of a birthright wrested from us; your Grace's moderation and good sense has admitted the general justice of our demand – a demand which would never have been listened to had it not been accompanied with the sound of the trumpet.'

It is this very fact that the Stuart monarchy is unable to accept: concessions may possibly be granted, but they cannot be seen to be exacted. Morton's reasonable demands come up against the essentially unreasonable ideological foundation of the whole Stuart system – divine right cannot be bargained with.

The problem with Scott's design on Morton as 'hero' of *Old Mortality* is that his failure, and the failure of his political principles, inevitably reflect on his positive status in the novel. Adolphus, in the *Letters to Richard Heber*, complained that Morton's presence, 'pardon in his hand', at the harrowing torture of Macbriar – an ordeal the enthusiast undergoes with a martyr's courage – reflects ignominiously on the hero.[69] Cameron agrees, and further suggests that just as Cuddie's actions elsewhere parody the hero's, so in the interrogation scene Cuddie's evasions and cowardice implicitly comment on Morton's own equivocation and his easy escape.[70] Certainly it is rather fortunate that, through the protection of the novel's most complacent Royalist, Morton should not even be required to swear loyalty to Charles II and so be patronised by the Privy Council in the same way that Cuddie is. The reader must already have doubts whether the moderate Presbyterians, even including Morton, are of the stuff from which martyrs are made. Daiches comments that Burley 'may have been an impossible fanatic, but he represented a kind of energy possessed by none of the wiser characters'.[71] Burley's precipitation of the conflict at Loudon Hill, and the energy he displays in his epic personal combat with Bothwell, are the natural consequences of his fanaticism, his knowledge that he has nothing to lose by his actions. The mainly middle-class moderate Presbyterians, on the other hand, have a great deal to lose from too extreme a revolution in the state, and this consideration continually qualifies the effectiveness of their participation in the revolt. Morton, leading the firing-party on Tillietudlem, is arguably more concerned with saving Major Bellenden's life than he is with taking the castle – we are continually reminded that he has interests on the other side of the siege. Goodin says of Morton that he 'represents [his supporters'] desire for political moderation – and the moderation of their desire for politics.'[72] Even Morton's actions in battle seem characteristically defensive, whether protecting his men by creeping through a copse at Tillietudlem, or taking sensible but cautious measures to hold Bothwell Bridge against the government troops. The contradiction in the novel is that, although Scott undoubtedly intended Morton and the moderates to 'point the way to the future' as Daiches puts it, in the actual world of the novel the opposite happens – the moderates are eclipsed by the polarisation of extremist forces, much to their detriment.

Scott's 'centrist' bias is most obvious in the 'last awkward chapters' of the novel, as Welsh calls them, apparently appended to the main action precisely to counteract the tendency of the moderates to be eclipsed in the bulk of the novel. The justification of the moderates, as Scott sees it, was the Revolution of 1688: the end of the novel is therefore set after that date in order to show how the reforms Morton desired had eventually come to pass. But this is how Scott attempts to cover the events of 1688 and their consequences:[73]

> Scotland had just begun to repose from the convulsion occasioned by a change of dynasty, and, through the prudent tolerance of King William, had narrowly escaped the horrors of a protracted civil war. Agriculture began to revive; and men, whose minds had been disturbed by the violent political concussions and the general change of government in church and state, had begun to recover their ordinary temper, and to give the usual attention to their private affairs in lieu of discussing those of the public.

The superficiality of this is bad enough: in its vagueness of generalisation, this passage is at the opposite pole from the brilliantly particularised scenes in the main part of *Old Mortality*. Cameron also quite rightly objects to the idea of change 'imposed by King William as *deus ex machina*';[74] a crude device which evades the real issues. The detail Scott does give is arguable, or even factually incorrect: Calder notes that, though Scott asserts that 'agriculture began to revive', William's reign actually coincided with a dearth of terrible proportions – so terrible, in fact, that the period was remembered by the peasantry as 'King William's Ill Years'.[75] The case Scott was attempting to put is clear enough: in the *Quarterly Review* article, Scott underlines the lesson of the story, as if in explication of the novel:[76]

> It is enough for our present purpose to observe that the present Church of Scotland, which comprizes so much sound doctrine and learning, and has produced so many distinguished characters, is the legitimate representative of the indulged clergy of the days of Charles II settled however upon a more comprehensive basis. That after the revolution, it should have succeeded episcopacy as the national religion, was natural and regular, because it possessed all the sense, learning and moderation fit for such a change, and because among its followers were to be found the only men of property and influence who acknowleged presbytery.

Scott's purpose, in other words, was to stress the continuity of post-Revolution society with the religious and political views avowed by Morton and the moderate Presbyterians in 1679. The last sentence actually makes a potentially interesting observation on the settlement – but the last eight chapters of *Old Mortality* fail to take this idea up.

Instead, Scott falls back, as in previous novels, on the hackneyed Romance tradition, treating the conflict of love and honour involved with Morton and Evandale's rivalry over Edith. Their chivalric respect for each other – Mathias notes that Evandale's actions at his death actually parallel *The Knight's Tale*[77] – is given little historical credibility. In this it resembles Scott's characterisation of Bessie Maclure, almost the only other force for unqualified humanism in the novel. Bessie, the old woman who appears to Morton and Burley at the fatal crossroads, has seen her husband shot 'within these three months' by the Lifeguards and her sons leave to join the Covenanters in the hills; she is 'in principle a rigid recusant'; yet she hides Evandale, an unknown Royalist officer, because he is a 'fellow-creature'.[78] Hartveit finds it suspicious that Bessie's action even takes place 'in a world of apparently universal hatred':[79] yet even if Scott does convince us with Bessie, it is only as the exception to the rule. We can rightly object that Scott gathers her christian mercy and Morton and Evandale's chivalric respect for each other into a loose design which supposedly helps to 'explain' the ultimate victory of toleration after 1688. Similarly, the scene of Cuddie and Jenny's prosperity portrayed in the final chapters is not convincing in the way it is supposed to be. If Cuddie is contented under William III, we remember that he has been equally content under Charles, except for the trouble occasioned him by his mother's outspokenness. Happiness for Cuddie, after all, consists of drinking the king's health 'when the ale's gude' without inquiring too closely about the identity of the incumbent: the interrogation scene makes this abundantly clear. In Lukács's phrase, Cuddie is a 'world-maintaining individual', essentially a supporting character rather than a protagonist in the drama of historical action: we cannot generalise from Cuddie to the state of the country as a whole, as Scott seems to intend us to do in the last chapters of the novel.

The ending of *Old Mortality* shows Scott's 'inability to envision a satisfactory synthesis after the strenuous antitheses of the Civil War' as Gordon puts it.[80] Calder suggests that it is necessary to distinguish the 'formal' victor of the novel, Morton, from the 'emotive' victors, the fanatics whose energy carries the action forward. Our interest, according to Calder, is with the Cameronian and Royalist characters, but Morton carries the 'sense' of the author as 'the man of "moderate" synthesis squeezed out of the dialectic of "extremes"'.[81] Yet even formally (apart from the last eight chapters) Morton does not appear the victor: if he is 'squeezed out' of the conflict at all, it is not out of the present into the future, but into exile, out of Scotland altogether. The ten-year hiatus after Chapter XXXVI is actually disruptive of the form of what has gone before: up to this point, the novel has been formally and emotively a whole.

In fact, the difficulties of the ending of *Old Mortality* cannot be resolved if the novel is considered purely as a battle-ground of political or religious ideals. Calder, for example, says of the novel:[82]

> Two principles are set in collision. The Cavaliers represent Loyalty, Order, Aristocracy. The extremist Covenanters rage against the King, admire the understanding of mean people, see rebellion as altogether lawful and are, in effect, republicans.

This comes dangerously close in its implications to Hegelian 'dialectics': the view of history as the meeting place of opposing Ideas. If the opposition were indeed essentially abstract, it would be by no means obvious why the extremists should win out at the expense of the moderates: indeed, we might expect the victory of the moderates as the embodiment of the 'synthesis.' However, these are not the terms in which Scott portrays the struggle in *Old Mortality*: instead, the complexities of the 1679 rebellion are grounded in the social world of the novel. Morton, along with his political, theological, and moral views, is defeated because, unlike Burley or Claverhouse, he lacks a strong social base. The small middle class, of which Morton is the chief representative among the Covenanters, is simply not capable of backing him up: it is for this reason that Morton finds himself continually isolated and frustrated in his efforts. In terms of the area covered by the novel, the Scottish Lowlands, Scott is quite right to show both the Cameronians and the Royalists as the chief forces to be reckoned with, rather than Poundtext and his ilk. As for the Glorious Revolution, Scott falls into confusion here because he tries to explain the event in the same restricted terms as the 1679 revolt. T. C. Smout makes the point that the 1688 revolution was primarily an English revolution: it could not have come about in Scotland alone.[83] To properly explain the events of 1688, a Scottish focus is not sufficient: this is Scott's fundamental difficulty in *Old Mortality*. Cameron is right to say that the final peace 'has no relation to any of the forces that have been shown as significant in the clash of Scottish religious ideas.'[84] Though the settlement of 1688 was extremely favourable to the growth of the Scottish middle class (as was the Union of 1707, to an even greater extent), it occurred for reasons outside the Scottish arena. Even in the last chapters, Scott seems unconsciously to admit this point: almost the only reason we can find for Morton's depression, even in the reformed state, is that his own actions have proved extraneous – as Hartveit says, 'his efforts had not only been fruitless but also unnecessary'.[85]

To some extent, then, the limitations of time and space in *Old Mortality* prevent the novel from conveying the wider implications of the historical development of seventeenth-century British society. Yet it is the economy with which Scott covers the events of the rebellion – preparatory events, like the murder of Sharpe, are actually moved closer to the actual uprising, in order to gain a greater sense of concentration – which results in the dramatic tension of the novel, the urgency and inevitability of the incidents of the plot. If we take the world of the novel to be bounded by the wappenschaw at the beginning, and the exile of Morton after the rebellion, we see how perfectly Scott succeeded in recreating an historical world within these limits: for symbolic or 'typical' incident, for the dramatic encapsulation of social tendencies in concrete events and characters, *Old Mortality* is more consistently brilliant even than *Waverley*. Indeed, the later development of Scottish society, the 'perspective' within which Scott too crudely seeks to place the action in the last chapters, is irrelevant to the real dramatic world of the novel: it is almost as though Scott felt obliged to reassure his reader after the completeness of Morton's failure. Daiches concludes his discussion of the novel by saying that '*Old Mortality* is a study of a society which had no place for such a character [as Morton]: it is essentially a tragedy, and one with a very modern ring'.[86] This judgment tends to under-estimate the extent to which the novel is rooted in its period, but Daiches is right to see the tragic potential of the novel. The career of Morton is set dramatically against an antipathetic formal order: not a moral order (as in Elizabethan tragedy), but a social order in the shape of the objective, historical situation of 1679. It is this 'historical' conception of tragedy which ultimately marks Scott's originality in *Old Mortality*: it is in this conception that the 'universality' of his vision is to be found.

5

Rob Roy

It is generally agreed that *Rob Roy* is a flawed novel, though it contains some of Scott's greatest writing. The problem lies in the lengthy 'preliminary' section of the book, set before the hero reaches Scotland, during which Scott appears to be going through the motions of writing a novel, creating characters which move mechanically without ever properly coming to life. Indeed, Scott's two greatest creations in the novel, Nicol Jarvie and Rob himself, do not take the centre of the stage until the novel is well over a third of the way through.

The trend of modern criticism of *Rob Roy* has nevertheless been towards a revaluation of these early scenes, with a growing emphasis on their thematic links with the more memorable episodes which follow. David Daiches was the first to suggest that the English scenes 'represent . . . a statement of the theme on which the Rob Roy scenes are a variation':[1] in other words, that the contrast between civilised London and wild Northumberland is similar to that later repeated between Jarvie's Lowland Glasgow and Rob's Highland valleys. This idea was further developed by E. M. Tillyard, who states that 'the same opposition exists simultaneously in England and Scotland through opposed pairs of characters', that Jarvie is the Scottish equivalent of Frank Osbaldistone's father, the London Puritan merchant, while Rob is the Highland version of the Northumbrian country squire, Sir Hildebrand.[2] Other critics have elaborated this thesis. D. A. Cameron claims that the conflict between 'old' and 'new' worlds (the 'subject' of the novel) begins with the opening quarrel between Frank and his father, and also notices other parallels between the English and Scottish characters, such as that Frank's father and Sir Hildebrand are brothers, while Jarvie and Rob are also (more distantly) related.[3] Attempts have also been made to salvage the Rashleigh/Die Vernon incidents from the realms of pure melodrama. Cameron suggests that Rashleigh and Die are 'the villainous and the laudable representatives of the old order', for example.[4] James Anderson notes that Rashleigh's involved plot to bring 'out' the Highlanders hinges on sound economic premises: the (historical) sale of Highland forests to English companies and the impossibility of the chiefs' paying off sudden debts.[5] Lawrence Poston even sees significance in the novel's conventional conclusion: according to him Frank's marriage to Die, a Catholic, 'signifies the growing irrelevance of religious differences in the age of commerce' – a theme we have already noted in *The Antiquary*.[6]

The question really is not whether such a parallel structure as Tillyard describes actually exists in *Rob Roy*, but rather what purpose it serves, if any, in furthering the expression of the basic vision which informs the Scottish scenes of the novel. The only answer which seems to have been given is that the structure is connected with the hero, Frank, and his 'progress' in the novel. Thus Avrom Fleishman says that Rob draws Frank 'away from the propriety of his English background towards the romance of free Highland ways' while an opposite movement can be seen as 'confirming him in his civilised prudence in the face of lawless Highlanders and Jacobites'.[7] The suggestion is that Frank learns from his Scottish experience the lessons of qualified romanticism and prudence which enable him to forge a synthesis between the alienated arms of his own family.[8] The problem here is that, despite the first person narrative, Frank remains an ineffectual figure throughout the whole novel – the classic 'passive observer', in fact. Whereas we put up with the opening chapters of *Waverley* because they are essential to our understanding of the hero's character and development, in *Rob Roy* we tire of similar preliminaries if only because we never become interested in Frank as a person: we are concerned with him only because he is our camera for observing the other characters. Alone with Rob in the most moving scene of the novel, for example, Frank is seen to be more Scott's excuse for having Rob reveal himself than an integral part of a two-way dialogue.[9] Indeed, during the Scottish scenes as a whole Frank's personal concerns (with Die Vernon and his father's money-bills) strike the reader as a tiresome diversion from the real interest of the novel. Frank's general failure to command interest on his own account detracts from any importance the English scenes might be said to have for him.

The efforts of Tillyard and of those who have followed him have succeeded, in fact, merely in establishing a marginal relevance for the English part of the novel. The whole Osbaldistone business still feels 'external' to the novel, like the plot of *The Antiquary*, and like the plot of that novel, 'not to be taken seriously'. The external paraphernalia of the conventional novel is there, but that is all: the romantic hero, a love intrigue with a suitable heroine, a melodramatic villain, a mysterious priest, and so on. We are justified in asking whether Rashleigh really strikes us as 'the villainous representative of the old order' or just as a stock villain. Even the style of the English scenes is inferior; Scott descends frequently into a sub-Fieldingesque mode when treating Sir Hildebrand and his sons, characterising them as 'sot, gamekeeper, bully, horse-jockey and fool' respectively, and remaining quite happy with this caricature.[10] Sometimes Scott's interest does seem to be engaged: that ill-yoked pair, Justice Inglewood and Clerk Jobson, relieve the tedium temporarily for example, and we catch a fleeting glimpse of real social contradictions beneath the humorous scene of the J.P. whose clerk rules him.[11]

We are left, then, with the Scottish scenes, and the disparate worlds which Scott brings together during Frank's journey from Glasgow to the MacGregors' glen. The subject here, as Mayhead observes, is, in a way, 'quintessential Scott'';[12] yet, somewhat in the manner of his later short stories, Scott simplifies the issues in *Rob Roy*. On the one hand there are the remains of the society of the Highland clans, epitomised by Rob: on the other, the culture and society of the growing Lowland commercial classes, whose peculiar qualities are marvellously represented in the character of Bailie Nicol Jarvie.

The world of the clan is nowhere better described than in *Rob*

Roy. The first mention of the Highlanders occurs in Scott's description of Glasgow, where they appear on the streets leading Highland cattle to market. We are told that:[13]

> Strangers gazed with surprise on the antique and fantastic dress, and listened to the unknown and dissonant sounds of their language, while the mountaineers, armed even while engaged in this peaceful occupation with musket and pistol, sword, dagger, and target, stared with astonishment on the articles of luxury of which they knew not the use, and with an avidity which seemed somewhat alarming on the articles which they knew and valued.

The effect which the sight of the Highlanders has on the townspeople is reminiscent of the reaction of the English during their invasion by Charles Edward's forces in *Waverley*: the gulf between Highlander and Lowland Scot is just as wide. Here though, Scott shows the other side of the coin: the Highlanders' savage ignorance of the Lowland way of life, and the directness and aggressiveness of their mien.

Throughout the novel, Scott characterises the clans as a specifically tribal form of social organisation: constant comparisons are made with other tribal societies. References to the American Indians are the most common: Frank is even said to have entered Rob's 'hospitable wigwam', and in the 1829 Introduction Scott underlines the identification by describing Rob's character as 'blending the wild virtues, the subtle policy, and unrestrained licence of an American Indian'.[14] Rob is also said to have had the ideas of morality 'of an Arab chief', and is compared in the power of his command with 'the Sultan of Delhi':[15] in both cases, pre-feudal chieftains with whom contemporary readers would have been familiar. Similarly, Rob's wife Helen is described as looking like an Israelite woman – Judith or Deborah.[16] The first real confrontation with the Highlands in *Rob Roy* incongruously takes place in Glasgow's town jail, when Frank sees the turnkey, Dougal, transported by an ecstasy of happiness at seeing Rob, his chief, once more. Again the 'tribal' image recurs:[17]

> In my experience I have met nothing so absolutely resembling my idea of a very uncouth, wild, and ugly

savage adoring the idol of his tribe. He grinned, he shivered, he laughed, he was near crying, if he did not actually cry. He had a 'Where shall I go? What can I do for you?' expression of face, the complete, surrendered, and anxious subservience and devotion of which it is difficult to describe . . .

The suggestion running through the novel is that the clan's social organisation, and the manners of its adherents, are nearer to those of other, far-flung tribal societies than they are to Jarvie's Glasgow, or indeed, to anything Scott's readers would have recognised as modern civilisation.

As the novel progresses Scott gives further insights into the clan mentality. The absolute fidelity of even distant relatives of the clan to their chief is marvellously illustrated in the incident of Rob's escape from military captivity: his call to loyalty proves stronger than the fear of army discipline for the trooper to whom he has been entrusted.[18] Similarly, it is Dougal's unshakeable loyalty to Rob, self-evident in the passage already quoted, which makes the episode in which he is supposed to have betrayed the chief so ironic. Dougal plays up perfectly to the English officer's expectation that he can be bought with money – his apparently greedy reminder to the captain of 'ta foive kuineas' convinces even Jarvie that he has given himself up to 'the filthy lucre'.[19] Both the officer and the Bailie apply the typical standards of their own society, quite mistakenly, to Dougal: in fact the clansman is utterly incapable of being bribed to such an end. It is not until a long way through the novel that it dawns on the reader how impossible Dougal's treachery would have been.

Despite the victory of the heroic life-style of the clan in this incident, however, the clans are generally seen in *Rob Roy* as doomed to destruction, physically and economically. The Highlanders at feud with the MacGregors are themselves exploited by the British government for the purpose of extirpating Rob Roy. For the clans it is purely a Highland affair, yet by helping the British government subdue the Highlands they are sealing their own fate along with Rob's in the long term. As it is, the lairds and chiefs accompanying the soldiers occasionally make clear their lack of shared political objectives with the government: when the English captain decides to arrest Jarvie and Frank, for example, on suspicion of 'treasonable practices' – in other words, as Jacobite agents – the chiefs immediately demur:[20]

> 'We'll wash our hands o' that,' said Inverashalloch. 'I came here wi' my men to fight against the red MacGregor that killed my cousin seven times removed, Duncan MacLaren in Invernenty; but I will hae nothing to do touching honest gentlemen that may be gaun through the country on their ain business.'

The Highlanders owe an instinctive allegiance to James III: Jacobitism relates strongly to their yearning for an older, simpler state of society in which the power of the clans was still unchallenged. At one point Rob exclaims:[21]

> 'I gie God's malison and mine to a' sort of magistrates, justices, bailies, sheriffs, sheriff-officers, constables, and sic-like black cattle, that hae been the plagues o' puir auld Scotland this hunder year. It was a merry warld when every man held his ain gear wi' his ain grip, and when the country-side wasna fashed wi' warrants and poindings and apprizings, and a' that cheatry craft.'

Rob's resentment at the encroachment of Lowland law and law-enforcers upon country traditionally free for the taking is exactly paralleled by the resentment of one of his Highland enemies to the economic thraldom in which the Lowlands holds him. When reminded of his 'duty to his creditors' by Jarvie, Garschattachin explodes:[22]

> 'D – n my creditors, . . . and you, if ye be ane o' them. I say there will be a new warld sune. And we shall hae nae Cawmils cocking their bonnet sae hie, and hounding their dogs where they daurna came themsells, nor protecting thieves, nor murderers and oppressors, to harry and spoil better men and mair loyal clans than themsells.'

The chief's confusion here of an end to his debts with revenge on the Campbells is particularly pathetic. It is, of course, a Jacobite revolution upon which Garschattachin is relying to bring about his 'new warld' – his dream is actually of the same golden age as Rob's 'merry warld'. This is to say that, despite their feuds, the clans have more in common with each other than they have with the forces of 'civilisation'. Jarvie shrewdly prophesies that:[23]

> 'They may quarrel among themsells, and gie ilk ither ill names, and maybe a slash wi' a claymore; but they are sure to join in the long run against a' civilised folk that wear breeks on their hinder ends and hae purses in their pouches.'

The rising of the Fifteen proves Jarvie right.

The debts run up by Garschattachin make clear one main cause of the downfall of the clan-system – the extreme economic plight of the Highlanders. Mere subsistence is impossible unless the clan derives some income from outside its own Highland homeland, as Jarvie's brilliant economic account of the Highland situation to Frank makes clear. Jarvie's figures (which Scott took from an actual manuscript in his own possession, as Anderson points out[24]) prove the existence of a huge, surplus population in the glens:[25]

> 'now . . . ye hae five hundred souls, the tae half o' the population, employed and maintained in a sort o' fashion, wi' some chance of sour-milk and crowdie; but I wad be glad to ken what the other five hunder are to do?'
>
> 'In the name of God!' said I, 'what *do* they do, Mr. Jarvie? It makes me shudder to think of their situation.'
>
> 'Sir,' replied the Bailie, 'ye wad maybe shudder mair if ye were living near-hand them. . . .'

The Bailie's sly riposte here is only too appropriate: the conditions he describes indeed mean that only the clan's traditional means of support, 'reiving' and the levying of blackmail, can possibly stave off starvation. Legal outlets, such as cattle-droving, can have only a limited value, while Jarvie's story of Rob's explusion from his home shows the problems for a clan seeking to establish itself peacefully on a Lowland basis. Yet the very desperation of the MacGregors' way of life degrades them from their ancient state: Daiches says rightly that 'they represent a confused and divided Highlands and are, after all, nothing but glorified freebooters'.[26] The withdrawal of the

chiefs' pensions by George I is, as Jarvie sees, critical for the
clans in this sort of situation: the Fifteen rebellion is the
inevitable result. Rob's own vague adherence to the House of
Hanover, a result of his protection by the Duke of Argyle and
various feuds with Jacobite clans, is revealed as mere political
opportunism: Rob is first, as Jarvie says, 'for his ain hand', and
the rebellion seems the only outlet for his frustrated energies.
When Frank regrets aloud the confusion and distress that a civil
war must inevitably cause, Rob is fatalistic:[27]

> 'Let it come, man – let it come,' answered MacGregor; 'ye
> never saw dull weather clear without a shower; and if the
> world is turned upside down, why, honest men have the
> better chance to cut bread out of it.'

Rob uses the word 'honest' here quite unambiguously:
Highland 'honesty' – which consists of taking what one wants
without the interference of legal 'cheatry' – cannot prosper
while Lowland civilisation does. Rob's resignation to the
forthcoming chaos is that of a man for whom peace has brought
only harassment and decline.

Like Rob, Bailie Nicol Jarvie typifies his class and culture: in
this case the optimistic, frugal, self-sufficient middle class
thriving on the growing commercial prosperity of Glasgow.
Daiches is right to see Jarvie as the heir of the Covenanting
tradition[28] – Jarvie himself tells us that his father was at
Bothwell Bridge[29] – but it is as the descendant of the moderate
Covenanters of *Old Mortality* that the bailie must be seen.
Jarvie's attitude to religion, indeed, is brilliantly depicted by
Scott against the broader backcloth of the Presbyterian religion
in Glasgow. Frank's first impression of Scotland is of a
Presbyterian Sabbath: the sermon Andrew Fairservice takes him
along to in the crypt of the Barony Laigh Kirk serves no other
purpose than that of acquainting the English reader with this
most important aspect of Lowland culture. Frank is struck that
evening by the quietness and restraint of the citizens returning
to their houses from evening service: he observes 'something
Judaical, yet at the same time striking and affecting, in this
mode of keeping the Sabbath holy'.[30] The traditional
Presbyterian spirit is strongly apparent here. Yet later on, when
Nicol Jarvie appears, we are given a subtle psychological analysis

of the man's religious feeling which comments implicitly on the earlier scene. Jarvie explains why he has waited till the early hours of the morning to visit Owen in jail:[31]

> 'Why, man! it's my rule never to think on warldly business on the Sabbath, and though I did a' I could to keep your note that I gat this morning out o' my head, yet I thought mair on it a' day than on the preaching. And it's my rule to gang to my bed wi' the yellow curtains preceesely at ten o' clock, unless I were eating a haddock wi' a neighbour, or a neighbour wi' me – ask the lass-quean there if it isna a fundamental rule in my household – and here hae I sitten up reading gude books, and gaping as if I wad swallow St. Enox Kirk, till it chappit twal, whilk was a lawfu' hour to gie a look at my ledger just to see how things stood between us . . .'

This, with all its scrupulousness, is the Lowland character, yet it represents a change from the Covenanting attitude to religion in the previous century. As a proof of his self-discipline, Jarvie's restraint is no doubt laudable, but as a proof of religious devotion it is hardly convincing. The enthusiasm of the Covenanters is altogether lacking: here only the outward, dogmatic form of piety is retained. Reflecting again on the citizens' behaviour as observed by Frank, our response to Glaswegian quietude becomes more suspicious: Jarvie has shown us that observance of the Sabbath in the letter does not necessarily imply observance in the spirit.

It is interesting that Jarvie's speech here shows both a frugality typical of Calvinism and an impatience with those Puritan restrictions which interfere with business. If Calvinist ethics have formerly assisted the accumulation of capital, they are now beginning to retard it.[32] This is another insight into the moderation of Scottish Presbyterianism in the eighteenth century: Jarvie, in 1715, clearly points the way to the future (moderate) developments of the kirk.

In other ways too, the bailie is a prophetic figure. The self-confidence he everywhere displays (sometimes tending to complacency), his lauding of the economic virtues such as creditworthiness, his resolute independence in business affairs – all this reflects the optimism and potential of his class in the Scotland of the day. Scott's first description of Glasgow, as Frank enters it, has not been encouraging: the town is still a town, rather than a 'city' as Andrew insists, starved of capital and geographically ill-placed for trade with Europe.[33] On the other hand, Scott hints simultaneously that these obstacles are to be overcome: we are told that Glasgow already has taken the bulk of the Western Lowlands' commerce, and reminded that the opening of markets in the West Indies and America was to give it a new advantage as a Western port. In his portrait of Nicol Jarvie, Scott is showing that exactly the right kind of man was in existence even in 1715 to take advantage of these pre-conditions for commercial prosperity. In his dinner conversation with Frank, the bailie strongly asserts Scotland's capability of achieving economic independence and equality with England:[34]

> 'Na, na, sir, we stand on our ain bottom; we pickle in our ain pock-neuk. We hae our Stirling serges, Musselburgh stuffs, Aberdeen hose, Edinburgh shalloons, and the like, for our woollen or worsted goods, and we hae linens of a' kinds better and cheaper than ye hae in Lunnon itsell; and we can buy your north o' England wares, as Manchester wares, Sheffield wares, and Newcastle earthenware, as cheap as you can in Liverpool; and we are making a fair spell at cottons and muslins. Na, na! let every herring hing by its ain head, and every sheep by its ain shank, and ye'll find, sir, us Glasgow folk no sae far ahint but what we may follow.'

Scott took the details of this passage – at points *verbatim* – from Defoe's *A Tour Thro' the Whole Island of Great Britain*, published in 1726.[35] The accusation of anachronism levelled at Scott here by James Anderson is largely unfounded: Anderson wrongly attributes Jarvie's description to a later version of the *Tour*, and thus his comment that 'such a passage could scarcely have been written earlier [than 1748]' is contradicted by the facts.[36] In so far as any slight anachronism still remains, it is possible that, by putting the words into the bailie's mouth in 1715, Scott tended to emphasise Jarvie's forward-looking optimism – in Jarvie's slight anticipation there lie the confidence and energy essential to Scotland's future economic development.

Even Jarvie's nationalism is progressive, rather than backward-looking to the days of Scotland's independence in the manner of Andrew Fairservice's grumbling sentiment. Typically, Jarvie sees the Act of Union as an opportunity rather than a national tragedy. Unlike Andrew, he refuses to mourn the extinction of Scotland as a political entity: Scotland's ancient feudal autarchy means nothing to him in comparison with the economic independence which the advantages of free trade within the Union will bring:[37]

> 'I say, "Let Glasgow flourish!" whilk is judiciously and elegantly putten round the town's arms by way of bye-word. Now, since St. Mungo catched herrings in the Clyde, what was ever like to gar us flourish like the sugar and tobacco trade? Will ony body tell me that, and grumble at the treaty that opened us a road west-awa' yonder?'

This is bourgeois nationalism at its most canny, and Andrew's sour reply: 'What wad Sir William Wallace, or auld Davie Lindsay, hae said to the Union, or them that made it?' is interesting, but hardly germane.

Andrew, a fine comic character in his own right, exists partly as an implicit comment on Jarvie's character-traits. Edgar Johnson suggests that: 'Andrew's cunning parodies Jarvie's shrewdness, his avarice Jarvie's thrift, his conceit Jarvie's self-esteem, his contempt for poetry Jarvie's practicality, his pharisaical intolerance the Bailie's staunch Presbyterianism.'[38] This could be seen as similar to the way Cuddie Headrigg parodies Morton's actions and motivations in *Old Mortality*, but whereas the Cuddie-Morton parallel is obviously parody, an artificial invention of the author's, Andrew's relationship to Jarvie has a basis in social realism: as Daiches points out, Andrew 'is the degenerate scion of the Covenanting tradition, while the Bailie is its more attractive heir'.[39] The qualities Johnson picks out above form the two extremities of the Lowland character of the period: between them, Andrew and Jarvie illustrate for the readers both the positive and negative aspects of their common culture. Even Jarvie's comically

extreme hatred of Andrew possibly arises because in Andrew the
bailie sees the very characteristics which he customarily regards
as virtues transformed into vices. In his fractiousness and
obstinacy, Andrew certainly resembles the lower orders in the
Covenanting army of *Old Mortality*, as Jarvie seems the heir of
the moderate Presbyterians. This is only consistent with
Andrew's social origins, of course: A. O. J. Cockshut comments
that 'his religious hypocrisy is strongly rooted in that good
old-fashioned peasant roguery';[40] in fact, Andrew's petit-
bourgeois roots are clearly revealed when he talks of his home
among the small towns in Fife, or as he colludes with his
kinsman, the pedlar, to make some money out of Frank.[41] If
Andrew's small dealings with Frank represent the less attractive
side of the commercial ethic, just as Jarvie's own scrupulously
honest dealings with Osbaldistone and Tresham represent
commerce's positive aspects, it is not because of any artificial
parallelism but because Scott has made Andrew a convincing,
lower middle-class analogue of Jarvie.[42]

The essential irony of the novel results from bringing together
the disparate worlds of Rob Roy and Nicol Jarvie. The initial
meeting point Scott chooses is the clachan of Aberfoil, a village
situated, significantly, on the Highland line itself. The issues
are clear-cut: on the one side are Frank, Jarvie and Andrew, on
the other the Highland 'gentlemen' occupying the only room in
the only inn in the village. From the moment they enter
Aberfoil, Frank and Jarvie are comically unconscious of the alien
traditions they unwittingly trample upon: Frank's insistence
that they enter the room occupied by the Highlanders, rather
than go without a *second* hot meal that day, strikes the landlady
as pure English madness.[43] To Frank and the bailie, of course, it
is no more than they would expect from any English or Lowland
tavern, and their attempts to treat the smoke-filled hovel filled
with Highlanders as an ordinary public house is rich comedy.
Quiet enjoyment of their own corner of the room is impossible,
however, given that to the Highlanders they are either enemies
or, after they have proven themselves, brothers: the clan-
mentality has little use for peaceful coexistence. The actual
fight, in which the bailie seizes a hot coulter to repel his
assailant when he finds his sword rusted to the scabbard, is a
very characteristic success of Scott's. On the naturalistic plane,

Jarvie's action emphasises his energy and his pragmatic ability to improvise: on a symbolic level, it represents the new confidence of the Lowlanders, repelling the clansmen through the peaceful power of the ploughshare.[44]

The murder of Morris, the 'gauger', at the hands of Rob's clan, repeats the clash of cultures at Aberfoil on the level of ethics. Morris, a cowardly petty official, embodies Lowland greed at its most despicable: his doom is sealed when he undertakes to betray Rob for money, but finds himself held hostage for the chief's safe conduct by Rob's wife. The scene of his death at the hands of the vengeful clan, hastened to his end by pathetic pleas for life that the Highlanders scorn, is memorable not only for the physical description, but for Scott's treatment of the moral gulf which separates tribal revenge from civilised justice. In their own terms, the clan are perfectly entitled to take Morris's life for his treachery – Dougal has shown that betrayal of the chief is unthinkable to them – yet the brutality of the killing overwhelms Frank and appals the bailie, with his respect for the legal process. Scott himself remains neutral in his judgment and presentation: the clansmen are 'murderers, or executioners, call them what you will,' while the tone of the narrative itself is spare, or in some cases ambiguous.[45] The incident serves to emphasise sharply the lack of any common ground between the clans and Lowland or English civilisation. 'Civilised' justice, indeed, is inapplicable to the case: Morris's 'crime' has the blessing of the legal authorities.

Other incidents too show the limitations of 'civilised' values when applied to the clans. Though Frank earlier has found Jarvie to possess a 'shrewd, observing, liberal, and, to the extent of its opportunities, a well-improved mind', despite a lack of education,[46] the limitations of the bailie's Lowland outlook become more obvious the further he and Frank pursue their journey into the Highlands. Jarvie's famous epigram: 'Honour is a homicide and a bloodspiller, that gangs about making frays in the street; but Credit is a decent honest man, that sits at hame and makes the pat play',[47] has an appositeness when cited in his house in Glasgow that it loses when he is in the Highlands, lecturing impoverished chiefs on the virtues of creditworthiness. Even the Bailie's pity for the clans' predicament is tied up with his sense of wastage, and his earnest but misguided desire that the Highlanders should 'reform' themselves.

The ironic vision of the novel, the sense of the disparity between Jarvie's world and Rob's, is naturally most apparent in the meetings between the two characters themselves. The dialogues between them are full of misunderstandings and conflicting values, symptomatic of the gulf separating their respective ways of life. The bailie's respect for his father, for example, is impressed on us by his frequent fond references to 'the worthy deacon'; but when he speaks to Rob about him the Highlander's response is comically incongruous:[48]

'he was a considerate man the deacon; he kend we had a' our frailties, and he lo'ed his friends. Ye'll no hae forgotten him, Robin?' The question was put in a softened tone, conveying as much at least of the ludicrous as the pathetic.

'Forgotten him!' replied his kinsman, 'what suld ail me to forget him? a wapping weaver he was, and wrought my first pair o' hose.'

This is certainly damning, particularly as three pages earlier Rob has congratulated Frank on his 'contempt of weavers and spinners, and sic-like mechanical persons and their pursuits'.[49] Yet given Rob's derisory view of Lowland law, it is hardly surprising that Deacon Jarvie's civic triumphs have made little impression on him.

Later, in the Highlands, Jarvie makes it clear that he in turn is no less contemptuous of the traditional way of life and attainments of the clan. He upbraids Rob about his two sons:[50]

'It's my belief they can neither read, write, nor cipher, if sic a thing could be believed o' ane's ain connexions in a Christian land.'

'If they could, kinsman,' said MacGregor, with great indifference, 'their learning must have come o' free will, for whar the deil was I to get them a teacher? Wad ye hae had me put on the gate o' your Divinity Hall at Glasgow College, ''Wanted, a tutor for Rob Roy's bairns?'''

'Na, kinsman,' replied Mr. Jarvie, 'but ye might hae

sent the lads whar they could hae learned the fear o' God
and the usages of civilised creatures. They are as ignorant
as the kyloes ye used to drive to market, or the very English
churls that ye sauld them to, and can do naething
whatever to purpose.'

'Umph!' answered Rob; 'Hamish can bring doun a
blackcock when he's on the wing wi' a single bullet, and
Rob can drive a dirk through a twa-inch board.'

'Sae muckle the waur for them, cousin – sae mackle the
waur for them baith!' answered the Glasgow merchant in a
tone of great decision; 'an they ken naething better than
that they had better no ken that neither. Tell me yoursell,
Rob, what has a' this cutting, and stabbing, and shooting,
and driving of dirks, whether through human flesh or fir
deals, dune for yoursell?'

It is arguable whether Scott ever surpassed the dramatic
intensity of this passage – a comic intensity, of course, but with
serious undertones. The attitudes of the speakers are brilliantly
suggested: the Bailie, admonitory, in a tone somewhere
between that of a kirk-sermon and a magisterial caution; Rob,
sulky, but scarcely able to suppress his innocent pride in his
sons' Highland achievements.

The apparent paradox of *Rob Roy* is that, despite the social
barriers which separate them, the two men are good friends and
even kinsmen. Possibly it is the bailie's Highland blood which
has left him with a predilection (though he depreciates it to
Frank) for the 'daft tales' of Highland heroism: it also perhaps
explains why he lapses into Celtic superstition when they enter a
particularly isolated region – another sentiment he is ashamed
of immediately they regain civilisation. Despite his strict moral
disapproval of Rob's way of life, Jarvie has some real
understanding of the circumstances which have given rise to
Rob's predicament: as he tells Frank the terrible story of the
destruction of Rob's settlement and of Helen's rape by the
raiders, Frank notes that the bailie's voice 'was broken by his
contending feelings'.[51] Similarly Rob respects Jarvie, despite his
bourgeois sentiments which Rob in turn ascribes to an
'unfortunate' upbringing:[52]

'But my cousin Jarvie,' he added, more gravely, 'has some

gentleman's bluid in his veins, although he has been unhappily bred up to a peaceful and mechanical craft, which could not but blunt any pretty man's spirit.'

The two men's friendship, and their disapproval of each other's way of life, are in strong tension. Whenever it seems that one component of this tension has triumphed, the other reappears to renew the conflict. The friends' parting offers of assistance to each other brilliantly encapsulate the contradiction: on the one hand, their professions of aid are completely sincere; on the other, the very inappropriateness of the offers once again reaffirms the distance between them:[53]

> After kissing each other very lovingly, and when they were just in the act of parting, the Bailie, in the fulness of his heart, and with a faltering voice, assured his kinsman, 'that if ever an hundred pund, or even twa hundred, would put him or his family in a settled way, he need but just send a line to the Saut Market', and Rob, grasping his basket-hilt with one hand, and shaking Mr. Jarvie's heartily with the other, protested, 'that if ever body should affront his kinsman, an he would but let him ken, he would stow his lugs out of his head, were he the best man in Glasgow.'

This paradoxical relationship between Rob and Jarvie is one of Scott's most impressive and original conceptions. It is paralleled, in a way, by the paradoxical relationship between the Lowlands and the Highlands which Scott sees in the early description of Glasgow. The picture of the Highlanders in the city closely follows the assessment of the town's commercial prosperity which has already been noted. Scott continues:[54]

> It is always with unwillingness that the Highlander quits his deserts, and at this early period it was like tearing a pine from its rock to plant him elsewhere. Yet even then the mountain glens were overpeopled, although thinned occasionally by famine or by the sword, and many of their inhabitants strayed down to Glasgow, there formed settlements, there sought and found employment, although different, indeed, from that of their native hills. This supply of a hardy and useful population was of conse-

quence to the prosperity of the place, furnished the means
of carrying on the few manufactures which the town
already boasted, and laid the foundation of its future
prosperity.

The societies of Jarvie and Rob, Scott is saying, were not isolated
worlds: the decline of the Highlands furnished the Lowlands
with the labour essential for its commercial expansion. This
same passage points out the social realism of Jarvie's distant
Highland ancestry: it also underlines the historical forces behind
Jarvie's suggestion that Rob's sons should be apprenticed to him
as weavers. Jarvie's relationship with Rob, in fact, is put in an
economic context by the passage.

It is true to say that, through the characters of Rob Roy and
Nicol Jarvie, the social and economic conflicts in Scotland come
across more strongly in *Rob Roy* than in any of the preceding
novels. This is true even though the conflict in *Rob Roy* is
personalised, and Scott does not treat great public events of
political and religious concern, as he does in *Waverley* and *Old
Mortality*. Georg Lukács, recognising this greater emphasis on
economic factors in Scott's portrait of the clans in *Rob Roy*,
concludes: Thus we have here already an element of dissolution,
the beginnings of a class-uprooting which were as yet absent
from the clan picture of *Waverley*.'[55] Unfortunately, Lukács
suggests that this development comes about because *Rob Roy* is
set 'several decades later' than *Waverley*: a silly mistake which
was noticed immediately on the English publication of *The
Historical Novel*,[56] and which has detracted from the accuracy of
Lukács's observation here. In fact, the development has a purely
artistic explanation: Scott's imagination had acquired a greater
explorative force in this direction when he came to write *Rob
Roy* than is evident in *Waverley*. In terms of actual
'dissolution', the clans in *Waverley* are actually further
decayed – the chief of the MacIvors, for example, is alienated
from his native culture in a way Rob Roy is not – but the
economic forces behind the dissolution are not so explicit as
they are in the later novel, though they are certainly latent. *Old
Mortality* may be seen as a stage in this artistic development. In
that novel, Scott appeared to be reaching from the overt, public
issues (religious and political) of the Covenanters' rebellion to

the human implications of these issues for the characters involved: implications which have more to do with material issues of social and economic status than they do with theoretical questions – the causes of Mause's break with Lady Bellenden are a fine example. Thus the conflict in *Old Mortality* is not conducted on a purely idealistic level: despite the strength and rationality of Morton's liberal views – views with which Scott evidently sympathised – the author nevertheless depicts the hero ground between the Puritan fanaticism of Burley and the authoritarian Royalism of Claverhouse, principally because it is the 'fanatics' on both sides who best represent the classes involved in the 1679 rebellion. One effect of *Old Mortality* is to make us feel that idealistic argument *per se* is irrelevant to the outcome of history, or at least that ideology is secondary, fuelled by basic social circumstances. In *Rob Roy*, Scott's lack of emphasis on explicit religious or political argument, and his concentration instead of the conflict generated by Jarvie's and Rob's opposed ways of livelihood, can be seen to follow naturally from these discoveries in the previous novel.

A stronger atmosphere of 'historical necessity', as Lukács calls it, is present in *Rob Roy* than in the earlier novels. In a painful protest against Jarvie's 'advice' to him on his future, Rob complains to Frank:[57]

> 'My cousin Nicol Jarvie means well . . . but he presses ower hard on the temper and situation of a man like me, considering what I have been – what I have been forced to become – and, above all, that which has forced me to become what I am.'

Rob's near-soliloquy in this scene hesitates between tragedy and pathos: the force of events which has brought Rob to his desperate state is inexorable, yet Scott does not quite allow Rob the stature of a tragic hero. Even in this scene, Jarvie implicitly counterbalances Rob – his willing acceptance of the future is set against Rob's nostalgia for the heroic past. In the same way, however, Rob's existence and the sympathy Scott feels for his dying culture deny Jarvie the reader's whole-hearted acquiescence in his progressive zeal. It is difficult to agree with Fleishman that 'the hero is brought to see that Jarvie's hope for economic progress, and not Rob Roy's nostalgia for primitive freedoms, is the true heroism of the modern world':[58] the effect of the novel is more complicated than this. One scene in particular acts specifically to dissociate the reader from Jarvie's values during Frank's return from the Highlands with him. Rowing back across Loch Lomond, Frank is absorbed with the beauty of the lake's scenery, a beauty which, combined with the low, Gaelic chant of the oarsmen, epitomises the romance of the Highland way of life. The bailie's thoughts, however, are entirely taken over with utilitarian projects for the commercial improvement of the Highlands, involving the reclamation of the loch 'from whilk no man could get earthly gude e'enow'. Frank continues:[59]

> Amidst a long discussion, which he 'crammed into mine ear against the stomach of my sense,' I can only remember that it was part of his project to preserve a portion of the lake just deep enough for the purposes of water-carriage, so that coal-barges and gabbards should pass as easily between Dumbarton and Glenfalloch as between Glasgow and Greenock.

There is obviously comic exaggeration here, but Scott could expect his readers, who would have shared Frank's passion for the romantic picturesque, to be repelled by Jarvie's plan to turn the whole of Scotland, in the name of economic progress and commercial enterprise, into a replica of his favourite hive of industry, the Gorbals.

Possibly the character of the hero was intended by Scott to effect a synthesis of both the opposed traditions in the novel: if this was the case, Frank fails to carry out his task. Any desire to have 'the best of both worlds' is contradicted by the very realism with which Scott imbues the characters of Rob and Jarvie in the novel. The men's friendship – which itself represents a sort of synthesis – is too historically inauspicious: too many obstacles of attitude, values and interests attached to their respective class positions lie between them. The historical themes Scott treats in the novel are not, in fact, ostensibly comic, despite the comic mode he adopts. There is rather in *Rob Roy* a growing emphasis on the complexity of the personal and social issues involved in his subject, an emphasis which defeats any attempt of the author's to mould his material into a conventional 'artistic' form.

There is a development in Scott's historical realism: historical forces appear more implacable, as Lukács observes, but at the same time Scott's sympathy for the human beings involved in the drama of history deepens. The best of *Rob Roy* results from Scott's abandonment of artificial form in favour of greater truth in reflecting basic historical reality as he saw it, and Scott follows a similar intuition in the novels succeeding *Rob Roy*: in *The Heart of Midlothian*, and most particularly in *The Bride of Lammermoor*.

6

The Heart of Midlothian

Robin Mayhead has recently claimed that 'a large proportion, perhaps a majority, of those who admire Scott today, rate *The Heart of Midlothian* as his best novel.'[1] In fact the opposite seems to be true: it is usually those critics who put no great store by Scott's work as a whole who are ready to agree, though only as a concession, that this novel is the best of a bad lot. F. R. Leavis is typical – in the damning footnote he allots Scott in *The Great Tradition*, he allows only that 'Of his books, *The Heart of Midlothian* comes the nearest to being a great novel, but hardly *is* that: too many allowances and deductions have to be made.'[2] Like many of Leavis's curt dismissals, this is opinionated rather than critical: the author prefers quasi-Johnsonian pithiness to a serious elaboration of the actual merits and faults of the novel as he sees them. Nevertheless, an exemplary case-study of the novels in the Leavisite tradition exists in an earlier article of Mayhead's – '*The Heart of Midlothian*; Scott as Artist'[3] – which makes clear the attitude behind Leavis's own, enigmatic judgment.

Applying the canons of the Cambridge School directly to the novel, Mayhead claims at least half of it for salvage:[4]

the real distinction of the first half stems from something quite different, something unique in Scott. For once he is mastered by a theme, a theme that he approaches with real seriousness and integrity. Crudely to indicate the nature of this theme, it is as though Scott were asking 'What does human justice amount to?'

The key 'Great Tradition' word here (apart from 'seriousness' and 'integrity') is 'theme'. While it is arguable that *Waverley* and *Old Mortality*, for example, also have a thematic unity and seriousness, this is to use the word in a different and broader sense than that which Mayhead intends. For Mayhead, the 'theme' of *The Heart of Midlothian* is Scott's treatment of the concepts of justice and the law in such a way as to achieve universal, 'moral' significance. Scott is judged on the originality and power of his answer to Mayhead's question, and for this reason Mayhead finds that the novel after Effie's trial is thematically irrelevant. He adds to this a formal criticism: Scott eschews the potentially tragic form for which he is heading, when he sets Jeanie on the road to London for a pardon. Mayhead concludes his appraisal by admitting that he has neglected the 'historical' aspect of the novel, but justifies his neglect on the grounds that this aspect is merely part of the background, a 'sense of the past' which only affects the novel's richness of interest. It does not affect the novel's 'theme': 'The historical setting has its own interest, but the central question would be the same whatever the period and whatever the particular manifestations of justice shown.'[5] Such are the preconceptions of the school of criticism typified by Mayhead here that Scott's claim to originality specifically as an *historical* novelist does not receive attention. Only an examination of the novel can prove whether Mayhead's critique does it justice, and whether or not Mayhead has even asked the right question in his search for an all-embracing ethical concern.

To begin with, Mayhead is obviously right to point out that the interest in Scott's description of the Porteous riots depends more on the issues seen to be arising from the disturbances than on the actual description of events. It is difficult to agree with E. M. Tillyard that Scott is writing in 'his most intense and exalted style':[6] much of the action is recounted rather than directly dramatised, and Scott's narrative style is certainly inferior in intensity to the style of his great dialogue scenes in, say, *Rob Roy*.[7] The interest lies in the conflicting interpretations of the riots which Scott gives us, and the insight into the very different motivations of those who take part in them. Scott controls the turns and checks in the reader's sympathies and emotions here with an almost Augustan subtlety of irony: frustratingly, however, he refuses to accept a consistent direction for the point of the irony, and continually contradicts the emotional reaction he has just evoked. Taking the single act of Porteous ordering the City Guard to open fire on the crowds attending Wilson's execution, we see Scott hedging round the incident with enormous individual, political, and moral complexities. There is the character of Porteous himself: the cruelty revealed in his shackling Wilson with undersize handcuffs, his paranoic personal hatred of the mob, but also his proud determination to fulfil his duty, and the fact that he is the only man upon whom the magistrates can rely. Wilson, on the other hand, is a hardened, unregenerate criminal; yet his loyalty to his partner, Robertson, and the popular nature of his original offence, smuggling (only resorted to of necessity since the Union with England), claim our sympathy. Later, personal considerations of any kind are seen to be largely irrelevant, as the incident becomes subsumed in the long-standing feud between the Edinburgh populace and the City Guard: the veteran Highlanders who make up the sole instrument of authority in the city are culturally antipathetic to the urban mob, and vice versa. Lars Hartveit sees class issues at stake in the conflict:[8] certainly the accusations of class-discrimination levelled against Porteous weigh heavily with the mob:[9]

> It was averred, in order to increase the odium against Porteous, that, while he repressed with the utmost severity the slightest excesses of the poor, he not only overlooked the licence of the young nobles and gentry, but was very willing to lend them the countenance of his official authority in execution of such loose pranks as it was chiefly his duty to have restrained. This suspicion, which was perhaps much exaggerated, made a deep impression on the minds of the populace.

The care with which Scott treats these allegations is typical: at first it seems a deliberate fabrication of the mob's, but the rumour is related with an energy that gives it the ring of truth. When Scott ends by saying the claims were 'perhaps much exaggerated' the 'perhaps' effectively contradicts the allegation of exaggeration and our response is further confused. The actual events of the day are themselves in question, with witnesses contradicting each other even over the question of whether Porteous himself gave the fatal order. Scott concludes: 'The verdict of the jury sufficiently shows how the evidence preponderated in their minds'. [10] but his tone is ironic, for in the previous paragraph he has pointed out that Porteous's trial took place 'ere men's tempers had time to cool'.

These contradictory views of the situation culminate in the highly ambiguous scene of Porteous's death. The aesthetic beauty of the mob's organisation and its restraint in carrying out a sentence which has certainly been commuted for political reasons is countered by Butler's final, horrific glimpse back at Porteous, when he sees him being cruelly strung up and mutilated in the most bestial manner. One problem with which Scott is faced by the riots is, as Mayhead sees, that of finding some ethical basis for judging what has occurred. The alternatives seem hardly satisfactory. The Edinburgh citizens are uniformly callous, selfish and prejudiced in their attitudes, while the legal authorities are socially insecure, and apparently happy to demote justice to an instrument of political manipulation of the Scots. The Procurator-Fiscal's conversation with Ratcliffe, a petty villain, leaves the impression that there is nothing to choose between the two sides of the law: [11]

> They sate for five minutes silent, on opposite sides of a small table, and looked fixedly at each other, with a sharp, knowing, and alert cast of countenance, not unmingled with an inclination to laugh, and resembled more than anything else two dogs. . . .

Belief in the law itself, as an impartial legal form, is also made impossible when Scott embodies it in the character of Bartoline Saddletree, who reduces matters of life and death for the defendant to legalistic quibbles. Saddletree's very interest in the legal details makes him insensitive to the human beings in the case: as a result, as Crawford notes, the impartiality of the law is seen to be invested with Saddletree's representative human weakness. [12] We are left only with the conflicting opinions of individual characters, resulting from their own personal or class

115

interests. Robert Gordon sums up the atmosphere of the novel at this point when he says that 'the opening chapters of *The Heart of Midlothian* offer a definitive portrait of a world in which Truth is dead'.[13]

Thus created, this world of ethical confusion serves, as Mayhead says, as the context for Effie's 'crime'. Mayhead neglects the fact, however, that the Porteous riots are also seen by Scott in an historical dimension, and particularly in terms of the anti-English feeling which followed the Act of Union. Old Peter Plumdamas is grieved 'to see the grit folk at Lunnon set their face against law and gospel';[14] telling his neighbour that 'this reprieve wadna stand gude in the auld Scots law, when the kingdom *was* a kingdom'. The rising is a matter of Scottish national pride: 'I'll tell ye what it is, neighbours,' said Mrs. Howden, 'I'll ne'er believe Scotland is Scotland ony mair, if our kindly Scots sit doun with the affront they hae gien us this day.'[15] David Daiches sees this clearly, suggesting that Scott is asking whether a Scottish identity in 1736 was only to be found in robbery, murder, and mob violence.[16] The story of the Deans is set not only against a moral confusion but also against this historical predicament. Historical considerations are integral to Effie's case just as they are to the riots: sometimes obviously – as in the English government's denial to Effie of the pardon it had granted to Porteous in an obviously less deserving case; sometimes much less obviously, through the character traits of the protagonists themselves.

Ostensibly, Davie Dean's rigid Presbyterian principles are the moral alternative to the world in which 'Truth is dead', yet Davie's views have ossified in the mould of the strict Calvinism of the hard-working peasant tradition of the previous century. Always judging the present by the standards of an idealised past – the heroic stand of the Covenanters during the persecution of the 1680s – Davie's condemnation of the 'national defections' is never qualified by an understanding that times have changed:[17]

> 'out upon your General Assembly, and the back of my hand to your Court o' Session! What is the tane but a waefu' bunch o' cauldrife professors and ministers, that sate bien and warm when the persecuted remnant were

warstling wi' hunger, and cauld, and fear of death, and
danger of fire and sword, upon wet brae-sides, peat-hags,
and flow-mosses, and that now creep out of their holes,
like bluebottle flees in a blink of sunshine, to take the
pu'pits and places of better folk – of them that witnessed,
and testified, and fought, and endured pit, prison-house,
and transportation beyond seas? A bonny bike there's o'
them!'

Only if we remember that Davie is talking about events which
occurred fifty years previously does the injustice of his
accusations and the extent of his fixation become apparent. To
Davie the few years of the persecution have expanded to fill his
memory: the half a century which has followed them is
contracted in his mind into 'a blink of sunshine'. Other events
too impress us with the outdatedness of Davie's ideas. A
favourite story of Davie's concerns the abandonment of a man
to drown by Covenanters convinced he was the Devil Incarnate.
The enthusiasm with which Davie concludes his story – 'and he
went adown the water screeching and bullering like a Bull of
Bashan, as he's ca'd in Scripture' – is unwittingly ironic in the
context of 1736; the distance of half a century makes the
Covenanters' fanaticism so gruesome as to be barely credible.[18]
Most significantly, at a time in which Davie is wrestling with his
conscience over the matter of Jeanie's testifying for Effie, his
mind instinctively returns to the Covenanters' discussion of the
issue of bearing witness in a secular court, at their council at
Talla Lins, in 1682 – a scene observed by Davie as a young man,
and which has deeply affected his subsequent life. Scott uses the
setting of the Covenanters' meeting, its isolation in a mountain
wilderness, to comment ironically on the unworldliness of
Cameronian dogma: the leaders, hardened by persecution in
the rigidity of their beliefs, argue 'with a turbulence which the
noise of the stream could not drown, points of controversy as
empty and unsubstantial as its foam'.[19] This is the realm
Davie's imagination still inhabits fifty-four years later. His
complete detachment even from the religious controversies of
the modern world is revealed when Bailie Middleburgh
discovers that Davie has had no contact with the Cameronian
faction since the settlement of 1688; he is a 'Deanite' or in his

own view, the only inhabitant of modern Scotland to have held to the 'middle and straight path' in the light of the Presbyterian martyrs.

Davie's failure to cope with the real moral issues arising out of his daughter Effie's conduct and Jeanie's crisis of conscience can only be understood if we see that Davie is not, morally, a hypocrite: his failure is that his principles are utterly anachronistic. Davie exemplifies Puritan fortitude in his reaction to his wife's death: natural affection contends with his affected stoicism in an agonising fashion, and the incongruity of his behaviour is noted but not criticised by Scott. When it comes to the issue of guiding his daughter, however, Davie's strict fidelity to his codified principles is seen to be insufficient to protect Effie, an inhabitant of a changed world. Davie is unable even to distinguish the real issue at stake – the danger of Effie's sexual temptation – from the Puritanical pseudo-issues of the seventeenth century. As David Craig has noted, Davie's launching into a lecture on the evils of dancing immediately he hears the word used in his house prevents Effie confiding in Jeanie:[20] it also shows Davie's inability to communicate with his daughters. Craig gives another good example of the 'propensity of Davie's . . . to avert his gaze' in the advice Davie gives Effie when she leaves to work for Saddletree in Edinburgh. Passing up a real opportunity to warn her of the dangers that may lie in wait for her in the big city, he worries her only with the need to avoid the 'legalised formalism' of her employer and the Erastian heresies of the kirk.[21] The blind incomprehension with which Davie receives the knowledge of Effie's condition, and his unwillingness even to recognise her as his daughter 'if her gude name be gane' are not admirable reactions: when the real world impinges on him, Davie retreats behind his Calvinistic attitudes and abandons his daughter to a fate that is partly of his own making. He repeats his mistakes with Jeanie, though less fatally: when his elder daughter seeks his support he is unable even to understand the moral dilemma with which she is faced – he sees no farther than the Puritan doctrinal issue involved in testifying before a secular court. Davie's non-comprehension at this point becomes comic: we no longer take him seriously, even though the advice he gives Jeanie in this case is almost soberingly inappropriate in its effect.

Davie's inability to come to terms with the real world in this way – his total immersion in the memories, ideals, and points of dogma which fill his head – bequeaths to Jeanie the crucial moral responsibility for action. Again, however, Scott's treatment of his heroine cannot be properly understood purely in 'moral' terms, as Mayhead leads us to believe. The question of moral and historical relativity is crucial to the novel. It is Scott's success in situating Jeanie and her battle with her conscience firmly in the context of Lowland Scottish life in 1736 that gives conviction to the moral drama here. This is why George Bernard Shaw's comment in 'The Quintessence of Ibsenism' that 'Jeanie Deans sacrificing her sister's life on the scaffold is far more horrible than the sacrifice in *Rosmersholm*'[22] strikes us as so inappropriate; he is criticising a Lowland Scottish peasant girl of 1736 from the point of view of Shavian morality. Indeed, Shaw shows his disregard of the historical nature of the novel when he begins by saying: 'There is a tale by a famous Scotch story-teller which would have suited Ibsen exactly if he had hit on it first': clearly, Shaw imagines he is faced with a universal moral dilemma (a 'theme' in Mayhead's sense) which Scott merely happens to have used first. The setting of Scott's novel is never mentioned by Shaw – implicitly, he updates it to 1891 to make the contrast with Ibsen's and his own moral radicalism viable. Scott on the other hand sees that an identical dilemma may take on different moral aspects in different ages and cultures, and this is essential to his delineation of Jeanie's battle with her conscience. The historical context of *The Heart of Midlothian* is more than Mayhead's 'sense of the past:' it is integral to the central actions of the heroine.[23]

Scott makes Jeanie's moral crisis convincingly real in terms of her history and upbringing. He emphasises that Jeanie has been imbued from childhood with her father's moral rectitude:[24]

Douce Davie knew better things, and so schooled and trained the young minion, as he called her, that from the time she could walk, upwards, she was daily employed in some task or other suitable to her age and capacity; a circumstance which, added to her father's daily instructions and lectures, tended to give her mind, even when a child, a grave, serious, firm, and reflecting cast.

This is in strong contrast to Effie's spoilt childhood.[25] Jeanie shows very strongly the effects of her upbringing in a strict Presbyterian tradition: it is manifest in what Alexander Welsh calls her 'scrupulousness',[26] in the supersitition she feels at Muschat's Cairn, and, most significantly, in the very weight Jeanie places on the reliability of her individual conscience in testifying for Effie. Her peculiar pride in the Presbyterian faith is also seen later, when she feels called upon to defend the merits of the Scottish kirk to the Anglican Rev. Staunton. Her decision not to lie to save Effie's life can only be understood through the particular concept of honesty Jeanie owes to her religion, which presupposes a personal contract between the individual and her Maker. Jeanie does not accept the utilitarian premises of Robertson's argument to her that she should lie to save Effie's life: 'It is not man I fear,' said Jeanie, looking upward; 'the God, whose name I must call on to witness the truth of what I say, He will know the falsehood.'[27]

Unlike her father's frozen dogma, however, Jeanie's moral principles are in touch with reality: her morality is a living thing. The theological minutiae which occupy her father's brain leave Jeanie cold – she hardly even understands his lectures on past religious controversies. Instead, illustrating in her own way the tendency of Presbyterianism in the eighteenth century to value practice above fanatical theory, Jeanie has converted the Presbyterian philosophy on which she has been raised into her own highly practical way of life. Her honesty, for example, has become instinctive. Earlier than the trial scene, Jeanie's sincerity is put to the test by her fiancé, Reuben Butler, who is concerned about her secret meeting with Robertson. Jeanie's discretion over Effie's plight forces her to reply to Butler merely by giving him her 'word' that there is nothing for him to be jealous about: this is enough for Reuben because the example of Jeanie's life is such that she has a right to be believed when she gives her word. To lie later in court would be to bring the honesty of her entire life into question, to deny one of the foundations of her personality – her integrity. When Ratcliffe ventures to upbraid Jeanie over her refusal to lie under oath, he unwittingly underlines this point:[28]

'I must needs say,' interposed Ratcliffe, 'that it's d – d

hard, when three words of your mouth would give the girl
the chance to nick Moll Blood, that you make such
scrupling about rapping to them. D – n me, if they would
take me, if I would not rap to all Whatd'yecallum's –
Hyssop's Fables – for her life. I am used to't, b – t me, for
less matters. Why I have smacked calf-skin fifty times in
England for a keg of brandy.

For Ratcliffe, lying is nothing, because dishonesty is his way of
life: comically, such is the force of habit that swearing on
Aesop's Fables seems weightier to him – because more unusual – than taking an oath on the Bible. For Jeanie, on the
other hand, her integrity is a practical expression of her life-long
faith and trust in God.

This confluence of cultural and personal influences on
Jeanie's character underlines the historical aspect to Scott's
characterisation of his heroine. Yet these influences are not to
be understood as merely 'external' to Jeanie, as the instruction
she received from her father might have been. If this were the
case, Jeanie would surely hesitate when Davie appears to be
condoning a lie the night before Effie's trial. In fact, although
her father's apparent defection from his principles is a
tremendous blow to Jeanie, she never wavers in her resolution.
Scott perfectly understands the 'internalising' influence of
education, culture, and religious belief on human beings:
through her own life and her moral struggle, Jeanie gives these
influences an independent status of her own. Lukács writes of
Jeanie:[29]

> The story of these inner battles and of this struggle to save
> her sister show the rich humanity and simple heroism of a
> really great human being. Yet Scott's picture of his
> heroine never for a moment obscures her narrow Puritan
> and Scottish peasant traits, indeed it is they which again
> and again form the specific character of the naïve and
> grand heroism of this popular figure.

By neglecting the historical dimension, Mayhead loses the rich
particularity of circumstance which controls the ethical problems posed in the novel, and also the complex relationship
between the historical setting of the novel and the religious

background of Jeanie's character which W. H. Marshall has detected in *The Heart of Midlothian*. In a perceptive reading of the novel, Marshall suggests that while the historical setting tends to make Jeanie a 'pawn', her religion gives her an independent motivation and integrity.[30] The dialectical relationship between historical setting and individual morality which Scott has created here might properly be described as having a universal human importance.

Mayhead's other, formal criticism of *The Heart of Midlothian* – that the novel never realises its tragic potential – is similarly invalid, because it fails to understand Jeanie's historical character. From the first reference to a pardon at the trial, Jeanie's mind is working on journeying to London: her practical, providential view of life precludes the possibility of tragic inaction. To end the novel after the trial scene would be to force the book into the mould of 'tragedy' by violating the historical realism with which the central character is portrayed. Jeanie's struggle to save her sister is as much a part of the drama as her earlier struggle with her conscience: both actions reflect the peculiar characteristics of Jeanie's nature.

A possible objection remains that the queen's granting of the pardon is too unlikely: a '*deus ex machina* expedient', as Shaw calls it, which destroys the realism of the novel. The novel's proven connections with *Measure for Measure* tend rather to reinforce this criticism: it has even been suggested that Scott got the idea of the Duke of Argyle's part from Shakespeare's duke, who certainly plays the part of *deus ex machina* in the play.[31] The point to make here, however, is not merely the fact that Scott's source bears out the action – that is to say, that the Duke of Argyle did procure a pardon for Helen Walker – but that Scott avoids any tendency to a sentimental solution in his brilliantly ambiguous presentation of Jeanie's interview with the queen.

Any feeling of sentimentality in the scene of the interview can only come about if the reader 'reads results from Jeanie's point of view', as W. J. Hyde says.[32] Yet Scott determines that we should not see events exclusively from this angle. The ground is prepared by showing the limitations of Jeanie's horizon when she first discusses her journey with Butler: her naïveté in taking government ministers first for clergymen, and then for servants to be won over by 'siller', puts Jeanie in a comic light, showing the simplicity of her peasant-girl's imagination. Chapter XXXVII, in which the royal interview takes place, is full of significant mistakes on Jeanie's part. She notices the duke's plain dress, but draws exactly the wrong inference from it:[33]

> this circumstance helped to shake an opinion which Jeanie began to entertain, that perhaps he intended she should plead her cause in the presence of royalty itself. 'But, surely,' said she to herself, 'he wad hae putten on his braw star and garter, an he had thought o' coming before the face of Majesty; and after a' this is mair like a gentleman's policy than a royal palace.'

Jeanie's reasoning shows, as Scott explicitly notes, her ignorance both of court manners and of the political circumstances which affect the duke's position at that time. Similarly, the queen's exchange with Argyle over his interest in Jeanie takes place unknown to her:[34]

> 'She does not seem (and she scanned Jeanie, as she said this, with the eye of a connoisseur) much qualified to alarm my friend the Duchess's jealousy.'
> 'I think your Majesty,' replied the Duke, smiling in his turn, 'will allow my taste may be a pledge for me on that score.'

This is in a quite different, cynical tone, from the duke's previous speech with Jeanie: we are in the sophisticated world of court amours of which Jeanie knows nothing. Again, the very innocence with which Jeanie almost wrecks her chances by unwittingly touching on unmentionable scandals verges on the farcical. When, finally, Jeanie has made her moving plea for her sister, the queen's reply (as many critics have noticed) seems detached, and almost inappropriate: 'This is eloquence'. Though obviously impressed, the queen seems to respond as though she had been listening to a piece of finely pitched rhetoric on the stage. The pardon is granted, but the pages Scott has devoted to explaining the duke's position at court, and the queen's known desire for a political reconciliation with her powerful subject, allow an alternative explanation to Jeanie's providential justice. It is certainly doubtful whether the moral lesson on christian mercy would affect the queen in such a direct manner as it appears to Jeanie to do. Previously, Jeanie has told the duke that her only 'friends' at court are 'God and your Grace'. The duke replies: 'Alas . . . I could almost say with old Ormond, that there could not be any whose influence was smaller with kings and ministers.'[35] This is a wry comment on Jeanie's faith that christian charity may motivate her rulers as it does herself.

Nevertheless, the scene is ambivalent in its effect: Scott provides us with political considerations which mean nothing to Jeanie, and which seem to show, in Cockshut's phrase, that Jeanie's plea has been 'granted in the letter and denied in the spirit',[36] but nothing occurs to shake Jeanie's own belief that God's providence has willed Effie's pardon. The ambiguities of the pardon-scene unfortunately show up the remainder of the novel as distressingly simplistic. Scott succumbs to a sort of favouritism towards his heroine, just as he succumbs to a conservative favouritism in *Guy Mannering*: in both cases, the realism of the novel suffers as Scott withdraws from objectivity. Jeanie's subjective world-view expands to take over the action: the pastoral idyll on Roseneath can only have as its aim 'bearing out what Jeanie has believed from the beginning, that on this earth justice finally prevails', as Marshall puts it.[37] As Marshall sees too, the weakness of the last third of the novel lies in the fact that incidents reinforce Jeanie's view of affairs even when she is not present: in other words, Scott takes over the view himself. Jeanie gets her reward in the form of a Utopian existence in the mild climate of Roseneath, with Reuben and her father; Effie is punished by having to live a high life with a guilty conscience, or at least with a constant fear of discovery. The melodramatic ending, in which poetic justice is meted out in the most heavy-handed way by having Staunton murdered by his ferocious animal-son, is so extravagant that any intended 'moral' significance is completely lost, while the concluding moral to the story looks as though it had been written by a Presbyterian divine. Real life was not so generous to Helen Walker: as Scott's Introduction shows, the 'real' Jeanie ended her life as she began it, a peasant struggling to exist.

It is true that the last third of *The Heart of Midlothian* is not altogether lacking in interest, but the interesting features have little to do with the previous plot or the themes raised by Scott therein. The Highland–Lowland satire of the Captain of Knockdunder episodes is amusing and to a certain extent original: Scott used the same, paradoxical situation of patriarchal and feudal rule continuing under a Presbyterian chief in *A Legend of Montrose*, but to better effect. The other interesting feature of the last part is the continuing argument between Davie Deans and Reuben Butler over the latter's conduct of the parish's affairs. This can perhaps be related to the earlier action thematically: the growing moderation of the Presbyterian religion in the eighteenth century is Scott's subject here, and to some extent the practical morality Jeanie has shown in comparison with Davie's dogmatic, seventeenth-century fanaticism exhibits the same tendency. Similarly, the extension of Davie's life does serve to make clearer the implicit criticism with which Scott has faced him earlier in the novel; Davie's eccentricity, 'the congealing effect of remaining in old traditions', as Cockshut calls it,[38] becomes more obvious, though it is less sympathetically handled.

In Reuben Butler, Scott portrays with some nicety a 'modern,' moderate Presbyterian minister, notably cool on the subjects of witch-hunting and sexual transgression,[39] and with no qualms about taking the oath of allegiance which was for Davie one of the dreaded 'national defections'.[40] In contrast with even Jeanie's superstitiousness, Butler is a rational, eighteenth-century man. When, near the end of the novel, Robertson/Staunton suggests that a storm seems to be holding off for some event in the world below, Butler replies:[41]

> 'what are we, that the laws of nature should correspond in their march with our ephemeral deeds or sufferings? The clouds will burst when surcharged with electric fluid, whether a goat is falling at that instant from the cliffs of Arran or a hero expiring on the field of battle he has won.'

Butler gives the modern, scientific explanation of Nature here – in strong contrast to the Covenanters' former regard to natural omens. His speech also reflects the ending of the Scottish kirk's isolation from contemporary intellectual currents in the eighteenth century; a movement Scott links here with the decline of introspective Calvinism.[42] At the same time, Butler's social class has obviously changed: his university education and his comfortable living – the novel closes with his purchase of a neighbouring farm – have naturally cut him off from his peasant origins and from the characteristic religious extremism of the peasants of *Old Mortality*. Unfortunately Scott's treatment is again only sketchy: any serious treatment of Butler's rationalism would need to be implicitly critical of Jeanie's providential outlook, but Scott shies away from any such conflict in the last chapters of the book.

The same lack of serious interest is seen in the minor characters of the novel: Robertson/Staunton, Meg Murdockson, Madge Wildfire and Effie in later life. These melodramatic figures are inferior inventions for Scott: in previous novels minor characters have been delineated firmly, and occasionally brilliantly. Madge Wildfire is the only character here who seems to have serious potential at least, in that Scott seems to have intended to use her plight to parallel Effie's. Like Effie, Madge is the daughter of an upright Cameronian; like her, she has an innocent love-affair (with the same man, Robertson); the consequences are in both cases the same; both girls have their babies murdered by Meg Murdockson. The significant difference between the girls can be considered as functional: Effie is new to her state of guilt, while Madge shows a later stage of self-recrimination in which insanity has overcome her mind. Madge's pathetic obsession with her dead child and her lost childhood, obscured by her snatches of bawdy ballads and her outrageous behaviour, is successful after a fashion, but the parallel with Effie becomes too strained to be credible, and Madge dies to little effect. Scott strains our credibility equally, of course, by taking Effie herself into an unrealistic future: the real problem of assessing Effie's behaviour is not satisfactorily tackled at all.

These are the obvious 'allowances and deductions' that any reader of *The Heart of Midlothian* has to make: yet the problem posed by the novel when it is considered as part of Scott's corpus of work is deeper than this. The whole novel seems loosely bound rather than closely integrated by its historical theme: Daiches is right, for example, to point out that the Laird of Dumbiedikes shows the degeneracy of the landed gentry,[43] but this alone is not sufficient: Dumbiedikes remains isolated from the real action of the novel, and so any historical significance in his portrait seems incidental (*Guy Mannering* is the contrast here). A worse criticism is that the Porteous riots section of the novel and the section involving the Deans family are connected only mechanically – through unimportant intermediary characters like Robertson and Butler. As Hartveit says, 'detachment rather than connection exists between the two communities' (of Edinburgh and Leonards' Crags, where the Deanses live).[44] Avrom Fleishman, aware of this criticism, can say only that the 'public' and 'private' plots were linked in Scott's mind: that the later abolition of the Tolbooth and the abolition of the statue under which Effie is condemned were both regarded by Scott as part of his country's 'destiny'.[45] Even if this is true, the reader can legitimately complain that Scott has not made this connection comprehensible in the novel itself. The peasant life of the Deanses and the urban unrest of the Edinburgh citizens in 1736 are not connected in the way that Rob Roy's and Nicol Jarvie's worlds are connected in *Rob Roy* – differing, even opposed as those worlds may be. This in turn is a result of Scott's failure to present Edinburgh as a full-bodied society: only a few snatches of conversation dramatically embody the tensions manifest in the riots and relate attitudes to the citizens' way of life. Meticulously though Scott chronicles the events of the riots, he fails to 'explain' them as he 'explains' the Jacobite rebellions in *Waverley* and *Rob Roy*, or the Covenanters' rebellion in *Old Mortality*. As we have already remarked about *Guy Mannering*, Scott's historical realism does not consist in merely treating 'public' historical events: in *The Heart of Midlothian* the public event remains unrelated to its social origins through significant characters, and the result is that – as far as the Porteous riots are concerned – the novel feels only superficially 'historical'.

The strength of *The Heart of Midlothian* is seen in Scott's treatment of Jeanie and Davie Deans. Scott succeeds with Jeanie marvellously because he shows that his heroine, and her moral principles, are historically relative – as in the Court scene when she is only part of the picture – but he manages to convey this relativity without devaluing the human importance of Jeanie's heroic struggle to carry out what she sees as her duty. This is the essential tension in the novel. When Scott gives in to Jeanie's point of view, in the last third of the novel, this tension dissolves: Scott becomes 'moralistic' to use an expression of Leavis's at precisely the point that he ceases to put his heroine into social and historical perspective. Paradoxically, Jeanie's morality only appears forceful to the reader as long as Scott is portraying her principles as essentially limited in scope by time and space. As soon as he universalises from them, as he does in the Roseneath scenes, we feel a loss of reality. For this reason, any treatment of the novel which like Mayhead's sees its 'theme' in terms of universal moral questions inevitably misses the point.

It follows from this appreciation that it is difficult to agree that *The Heart of Midlothian* stands out from the rest of the Scottish Waverley Novels in the way that some critics have suggested. It may be true that it is the one novel which stands up to 'ahistorical' criticism to a point, but this is to miss the real quality of the novel. Moreover, the novel's strength does relate to the best of Scott's other work: as studies in historical realism Jeanie and Davie Deans are excellent, but not unique in Scott. The development from the earlier novels can be seen clearly enough: like Nicol Jarvie for example, Jeanie is imbued with a specific social reality; her character epitomises traits that belong to her particular culture and class, and we see these traits both in their admirable aspect and in their limiting capacity. To this extent, *The Heart of Midlothian* partakes of Scott's character-istic originality. Yet Mayhead's revised judgment on the novel's relative status seems correct: '*Waverley* . . . is a more completely satisfying achievement overall'.[46] Like *Rob Roy, The Heart of Midlothian* contains in it the makings of a great novel, but too much of the book is either altogether inferior, or contains only minor rewards for the reader. On the other hand, it is true to say that at their best these later works have a depth of characterisation and social insight that *Waverley* itself lacks. For the formal unity and integrity of *Waverley*, combined with the maturity of style and outlook of these later novels, we have to look further on to Scott's dark masterpiece, *The Bride of Lammermoor*.

7

The Bride of Lammermoor

The Bride of Lammermoor exhibits Scott's art at its most mature. In comparison with *The Heart of Midlothian*, Scott's broadest canvas, it may appear limited in scope, but the whole novel is characterised by a cohesion, a unity, and an intensity within these limits nowhere equalled in the Waverley Novels. It has been held against Scott that his sympathies in *The Bride* are also limited; that the balance and objectivity for which *Rob Roy* is so notable are hardly in evidence. Robert Gordon's controversial reading of the novel, '*The Bride of Lammermoor* – A Novel of Tory Pessimism,' reached the conclusion that Scott's personal views at the time of writing had become more conservative and pessimistic:[1] but there is little evidence for this. Gordon is right, nevertheless, to point out a certain 'imbalance' in the novel: the death of the traditional feudal world in the novel is not felt to be validated by the emergence of a new one, with its own values and sympathetically 'modern' attitudes, as in *Rob Roy* Nicol Jarvie's ascent 'balances' Rob's decline. On the other hand, critics since Gordon have been at pains to stress some of the ways in which Scott subjects feudal values and attitudes to criticism in *The Bride*, showing the novel to be a far subtler imaginative composition than Gordon understood it to be.[2] It is my objective here to show that Scott's tone in *The Bride* can best be understood if we consider the novel in relation to the other Scottish novels, as a further essay in historical realism. The peculiarity of *The Bride*, including its

uniquely tragic form, can be seen as the result of Scott following his intuitions with respect to the historical situation and
his chosen dramatic point of view more rigorously and determinedly than ever before.

The source of *The Bride* – in an imaginative rather than a
literal sense – is in the same material that Scott had worked
years before in *Guy Mannering*: the decline of an ancient
family, and its expropriation by an upstart bourgeois antagonist.[3] Like Bertram/Brown in the earlier novel, Edgar
Ravenswood's personal history is set against the decline of his
family over the centuries: in many ways the two cases are
parallel. We are told that the Ravenswoods' line, like the
Bertrams', 'extended to a remote period of antiquity', having
intermarried in its day with the greatest feudal families in
Scotland. Like the Bertrams too, the Ravenswoods' chief decline
comes in the seventeenth century: significantly, the old laird's
expulsion from Ravenswood castle, his hereditary domain, takes
place at the same time as his espousal of the lost cause of James
II in 1688 – the eclipse of Stuart absolutism thus coincides with
the eclipse of the family's feudal power.[4]

Ravenswood himself, however, is a far more realistic character
than Brown. Scott does not romanticise his plight as he does
Brown's: if Edgar is a 'lost heir' it is in a wholly realistic,
historical sense: he is heir to his family's lost inheritance, the
possessor only of an empty courtesy title and the cheerless
retreat of the castle of Wolf's Crag. Edgar's alienation from the
world is conditioned by his knowledge of the decline of his
family – the 'trauma' which corresponds to Harry Bertram's
abduction is the harrowing funeral of his father, hounded
literally to the grave by his Whig enemies. If Edgar sometimes
wishes later that he could forget his historical position, some
incident always serves to recall these painful memories to his
mind. Moulded by his family's experience, Edgar is, by instinct,
a feudal aristocrat: this is clearly seen in his proud honesty and
antipathy to political manoeuvre, his chivalric protection of
Bucklaw at the risk of his own life, his distaste for
mock-gentility, and, often, in the way anger irrepressibly wells
up in him when he is faced by the degradation of the ancient
order. Towards the end of the novel, in the belief that Wolf's
Crag has caught fire, Edgar goes to watch the final ruin of his

only remaining property. Instinctively he is disgusted at the attitude of the boys from the village who also run to watch the spectacle:[5]

> As they ran one by one past the Master, calling to each other to 'Come and see the auld tower blaw up in the lift like the peelings of an ingan,' he could not but feel himself moved with indignation. 'And these are the sons of my father's vassals,' he said – 'of men bound, both by law and gratitude, to follow our steps through battle, and fire, and flood; and now the destruction of their liege lord's house is but a holiday sight to them!'

This extreme conservatism, verging on reaction, is Edgar's emotional heritage – the passage typifies the way Edgar struggles in vain to accept the changed circumstances of his family with equanimity.

Edgar's antagonist, Sir William Ashton, is similarly a more convincing and realistic character than Gilbert Glossin in the earlier novel. Like Glossin, Ashton epitomises the usurping middle classes, but Scott goes one better than in *Guy Mannering*, where Glossin manipulates the law, and makes Ashton Lord Keeper of Scotland, the arbiter of the law itself. As the early scene of barely concealed corruption in the Scottish Privy Council shows, the reins of government are now in the hands of profiteering lawyers, like Ashton, and Whiggish aristocrats like Lord Turntippet who are only too anxious to learn the tricks of legal spoliation.[6] Scott also excels himself in the novel with his acid satire of Ashton, a dissection of bourgeois manners which is deeply revealing. Early on, in a fine scene between Ashton and the old forester of the Ravenswood estate Scott harps on the Lord Keeper's utter inability to play the part of laird on the lands he has acquired by purchase. Ashton's indifference to a deer-hunt prompts the forester into reflections which his new employer can hardly welcome:[7]

> 'It was not so, he had heard, in Lord Ravenswood's time: when a buck was killed, man and mothers son ran to see, and when the deer fell, the knife was always presented to the knight, and he never gave less than a dollar for the compliment.'

Ashton's immediate, typically bourgeois reaction is to give the man money to buy his goodwill: he fails to understand that the old man values the 'dollar' merely as part of the feudal service formerly performed as a traditional duty. Such money was an 'earnest' rather than the devalued, purely commercial payment Ashton makes and the man shows his contempt for Ashton while taking the money:[8]

> The fellow received it as the waiter of a fashionable hotel receives double his proper fee from the hands of a country gentleman – that is, with a smile, in which pleasure at the gift is mingled with contempt for the ignorance of the donor.

Ashton even tries to joke about sueing the man if he misses the buck, lowering himself still further in the old man's estimation. The whole episode is memorable, not only because it establishes Ashton's weakness and his acute social discomfort in his new role, but because Scott characterises so concisely the change in relationship between master and servant which accompanies the estate's change of hands. The ancient, feudal wood-fee is transformed into a mere tip.

Other scenes similarly satirise Ashton, particularly his attempts to make an impact by putting on a more grandiose display in every respect than the feudal proprietor he has displaced – attempts which his lack of taste and finesse continually betray. Ravenswood castle is not so large that he cannot make 'large additions to it in the style of the 17th century' – an incongruity of architectural styles which marks his philistinism.[9] This is despite the fact that Ashton is evidently unequal to the castle even as he has inherited it: to fill the empty spaces in the hall left by the removal of the Ravenswood family portraits, he has to put up portraits of William and Mary – symbols themselves of the 'new' order – as well as those of 'two distinguished Scottish lawyers'. Even the pictures belonging to Ashton's limited ancestry are an embarrassment:[10]

> The pictures of the Lord Keeper's father and mother were also to be seen; the latter, sour, shrewish, and solemn, in her black hood and close pinners, with a book of devotion in her hand; the former, exhibiting beneath a black silk

Geneva cowl, or skull-cap, which sate as close to the head as if it had been shaven, a pinched, peevish, Puritanical set of features, terminating in a hungry, reddish, peaked beard, forming on the whole a countenance in the expression of which the hypocrite seemed to contend with the miser and knave. 'And it is to make room for such scarecrows as these,' thought Ravenswood, 'that my ancestors have been torn down from the walls which they erected!'

This is very obviously a biased description ('hungry', used of the beard, is both descriptive and indisputably prejudiced) – we are looking through Edgar's eyes here – but there is enough objective realism about the features of Ashton's parents, so effectively satirised here, to make them recognisable types of the Puritan *nouveau-riche* rapidly advanced through the wheelings and dealings of the Civil War.

The resemblance between *Guy Mannering* and *The Bride of Lammermoor* lies not only in the social position of the protagonists. Also strangely reminiscent of the earlier novel are the apparently irreconcilable modes of *The Bride*: extremely realistic social analysis and portrayal on the one hand; on the other hand, Gothic supernatural elements that seem to belong to another genre entirely. From the beginning of the novel we are made aware of the legends and prophecies which surround the ancient house of Ravenswood. As narrator, Scott relates the ominous story of Malise Ravenswood (presumably pronounced 'malice', and so a pun on the vindictiveness of Edgar's feudal forebears) and his bloody revenge on a previous usurper of the estate: a legend which more than once has consequences in the novel's action. There is also the legend of Mermaiden's Fountain, which bears directly on the love-affair of Edgar and Lucy Ashton,[11] and later, Caleb superstitiously relates Thomas the Rhymer's prophecy of the fall of his master's house[12] – a prophecy which is fulfilled in the closing pages of the novel. All these legends bear upon the realistic action in *The Bride*: they appear to the reader, as Edgar Johnson says, 'dark mists swirling through a solid world'.[13] Apparently coincidental occurrences are also invested with a mysterious significance. Touring his new estate with his daughter, for example, Sir William Ashton is attacked by a bull – Edgar interferes by shooting the animal, when we suspect he had intended shooting the Lord Keeper, an incident which has far-reaching repercussions for his history. Yet the episode does not take place solely on a realistic level: Scott's rational explanation of the bull's behaviour in terms of Lucy's scarlet mantle and the capricious temper of wild animals in general is not adequate to the incident's symbolic effect in its context. In an apparently incidental description, Scott has already told the reader that the preservation of wild cattle was 'a point of state . . . of the Scottish nobility' – in other words, that the cattle are to be specifically associated with the old owners. Of the herd Ashton and Lucy come across, Scott comments that although 'they had degenerated from the ancient race in size and strength . . . they retained, however, in some measure, the ferocity of their ancestry';[14] this is enough for us to infer that an implicit parellel is being drawn between the bulls and the Ravenswood family itself. When the bull attacks Ashton, therefore, we cannot but feel that the animal is symbolically expressing the animosity of the ancient estate towards its bourgeois usurper. Edgar's shooting of the bull, moreover, assumes a significance beyond its obvious one (that he abandons his vow of vengeance to save his enemy and his enemy's daughter[15]). By his action Edgar appears to sacrifice the 'natural' enmity that exists between the Ashtons and the Ravenswoods – an enmity which the bull's headlong attack symbolises. This in turn is prophetic of Edgar's later conflicting emotions towards the Ashtons: 'a desire to revenge the death of his father, strangely qualified by admiration of his enemy's daughter'[16] – an inherited, 'natural' hatred for the Ashtons to which his love for Lucy runs counter.

In other ways too, natural events appear to wait upon the actions of the human protagonists in *The Bride*. The gloom of the weather on the day of Edgar's father's funeral suffuses the whole scene, reflecting the state of Edgar's mind in strong contrast to the drunken bravado of his kinsmen during the wake.[17] The preternatural connection between nature and human action in the novel is seen most strongly, however, when a storm hangs over Wolf's Crag during Ashton's visit to the tower. At the moment Edgar kisses Lucy in greeting, a lightning flash illuminates the dark hall and has the effect of freezing the fatal instant into a tableau. The effect of the moment on the castle is equally symbolic: soot 'which had not been disturbed for centuries' flies down the chimney, the castle crumbles further into the ocean as 'several heavy stones were hurled from the mouldering battlements into the roaring sea beneath'; and Scott comments explicitly: 'It might seem as if the ancient founder of the castle were bestriding the thunderstorm, and proclaiming his displeasure at the reconciliation of his descendant with the enemy of his house.'[18] The tentative language here impresses us with Scott's extreme caution in making the supernatural connection too explicit – a tendency which Andrew Hook rightly observes is characteristic of the novel as a whole.[19] This is another great improvement of *The Bride* over *Guy Mannering*: the whole treatment of the supernatural in the later novel is ambiguous and subtly suggestive, rather than overt and manifestly incredible. Sydney Colvin, writing of a memorable discussion with W. E. Gladstone, in which the statesman singled out *The Bride* for its intensity and air of inevitability, concludes with their mutual criticism of Scott for hedging round[20]

> the finely conceived incident of the apparition to the Master beside the Mermaid's well of the spirit of old Alice at the moment of her death with an apology to the rationalist and the sceptic which robs it of half its effect.

On the contrary, it is Scott's provision of an alternative, rational explanation to the romantic incident which seems to strengthen the novel for the modern reader suspicious of Gothic effects. Scott treads a fine line throughout the novel between his contrary modes and the result is, on the whole, brilliantly successful. In many places in the novel realistic details, completely credible in themselves, are subtly invested with symbolic significance. Wolf's Crag, for example, is simultaneously a realistic, poverty-stricken remnant of the Ravenswood estate and also, as Gordon notes, a symbol of the family's social predicament, pushed to the very brink of the country by their (bourgeois) antagonists.[21] Similarly, little Henry Ashton's instinctive fear of Edgar when he meets him is given a rational cause, in that Henry has previously been frightened by the portrait of Malise Ravenswood which Ashton has relegated to the attic, but it also recalls the reader to the circumstances of Malise's revenge on the former usurpers, and suggests a lasting, instinctive enmity through the centuries among the Ravenswoods towards their enemies of which Edgar's physical resemblance to his ancestor is only one sign.[22]

It is a fact of our response to *The Bride of Lammermoor* that these apparently contradictory modes, the 'dark mists' and the 'solid world', mesh in a way that they do not succeed in doing in *Guy Mannering*. A. O. J. Cockshut has attempted to explain why this should be so:[23]

> I suggest the following answer. Scott was not really writing about prophecies and the preternatural at all. Still less was he writing allegory. He was writing with great intelligence and control about the relation between fact and legend. But instead of analysing the difference as most people would do in a like case, he places the fact and the legend side by side at every point in the story. The haunting rhyme [of Thomas the Rhymer] is what the folk consciousness would naturally make up about the later events of the book.

This certainly ties in with Scott's insistence at various points in the novel that he is writing down a tale with its origin in the oral, peasant tradition.[24] In fact this treatment of legend as an element of the traditional folk consciousness has a close parallel in *Guy Mannering*, in the incident where a country girl takes up the words of the traditional ballad about the Bertrams which Brown plays on his flute. I commented on that scene that it was conspicuous partly because of the successful combination of the modes of Romance and historical realism, in that Scott uses Romance 'machinery' there to summon up the lost feudal world. In the same way, Scott's feat of imagination in *The Bride* is in combining with his realistic description of the demise of the feudal order a dramatisation of its destruction as the traditional, feudal consciousness would see it – that is, not as a materialistic struggle, but as an inexplicable, fatal decline. In other words, in *The Bride of Lammermoor*, Scott actually carries out the task he saw Walpole as having set himself in *The Castle of Otranto*:[25]

to draw such a picture of domestic life and manners, during the feudal times, as might actually have existed, and to paint it chequered and agitated by the action of supernatural machinery, such as the superstition of the period received as matter of devout credulity.

This purpose which, as we saw, Scott failed to achieve in *Guy Mannering*, he manages brilliantly in *The Bride*: yet, just as the world of the Ravenswoods is set against the modern, bourgeois world of the Ashtons, so Scott sets his picture of the world in terms of the feudal consciousness alongside his rationalistic and materialistic mode of realism. Possibly Scott learned too from the failure of his ending to *The Heart of Midlothian*: there he dramatised the world from the point of view of his heroine's providential consciousness much as he dramatises the world from the point of view of Edgar's feudal consciousness (and Caleb's and old Alice's) in *The Bride* – the failure of the former novel is that Scott neglects to set Jeanie's world in perspective during the Roseneath scenes. The ambiguity of mode in *The Bride* fulfils this purpose in a highly original manner.

Edgar Ravenswood is, of course, a much more complex character than Jeanie Deans. Hook rightly asserts that the controversy over *The Bride of Lammermoor* centres on the character of the hero – or the anti-hero, as Hook would have him.[26] The poignancy of Edgar's predicament is that he is committed to the old world but feels impelled, in some way, to adjust to the new: ultimately, he is crucified by these opposing tendencies. The earlier part of the novel is concerned with illustrating how Edgar's position, as determined by history, tends uniformly to force him into personal opposition to Ashton. Every incident which occurs gives Edgar a new motive for hating the Lord Keeper: the loss of the estate by legal 'trickery'; the death of his father, and Ashton's attempt to prevent an Episcopalian burial; the constant degradation of his penury in Wolf's Crag; and his class prejudice against Ashton's evident inability to conduct himself like a gentleman. Ashton rapidly comes to represent to Edgar a triumphant and unmerciful personal antagonist, the destroyer of the Ravenswoods and all they stood for. Thus, Edgar's historical position seems bound to doom the desperate young man of the opening chapters to a bitter, hopeless struggle against a foe favoured by the tide of history.

Yet Toryism itself fails to lend Edgar any comfort when the two leading Tories of his acquaintance, the Laird of Bucklaw and the Marquis of A – , make it clear to him what their politics entail. Bucklaw is an example of the degeneracy of the gentry, gambling away his inheritance and squandering the modicum of good sense bred in him in the company of a cynical *poseur* like Craigengelt, the Jacobite agent. For Edgar, the faults which have contributed to the ruin of his class are obvious in the laird – moreover, he comes to see that Bucklaw's Jacobitism, to which he is at first attracted, has no real existence apart from the qualities Craigengelt manifests as he sponges off Bucklaw, offering him a delusion of esteem abroad even as he presses him deeper into desperate straits in Scotland. The marquis, on the other hand, as leader of the Tory faction in the Scottish Privy Council has renounced Jacobitism in favour of an obviously dishonourable compromise with the powers that be in the new Britain. Not only is the marquis implicitly deprived of his traditional aristocratic authority when he lowers himself to the Whig party's level of political intrigue, but his very integrity as a gentleman is compromised in the interests of retaining political power. When Edgar, his kinsman, is grossly insulted by Lady Ashton while a guest of the Lord Keeper's, the marquis has to suppress his natural reaction to leave with Edgar because of political considerations which make an alliance with Ashton desirable.[27] We can never imagine Edgar swallowing his pride in such a way.

Nevertheless, the fact is that Edgar does come to attempt a compromise with the Lord Keeper when he resolves to 'parley with the victors of the day'.[28] The ostensible reason is his growing love for Lucy Ashton, yet this is only one motive among the many Scott gives us for Edgar's action. His sense of degradation – especially as experienced during Bucklaw's visit to Wolf's Crag – depresses him in the absence of any obvious course of action. His defeatist reflections when he sights a hunt from the tower are typical of his state of mind:[29]

The sense that he was excluded by his situation from enjoying the silvan sport, which his rank assigned to him as a special prerogative, and the feeling that new men were now exercising it over the downs which had been jealously reserved by his ancestors for their own amusement, while he, the heir of the domain, was fain to hold himself at a distance from their party, awakened reflections calculated to depress deeply a mind like Ravenswood's.

The use of archaic words here to describe Edgar's thoughts nicely displays the obsolescence of the feudal concepts which possess him. The impression of Edgar the reader has is one of defeatism here: when he discovers that the 'new men' hunting are led by none other than Ashton himself, Edgar's depression is naturally deepened. The feeling that he must be realistic, that he must accept the changes conferred by the passage of time, is a strong impulse, and an apparently sensible one, for him to make a 'compromise.' At the same time, Edgar's love for Lucy seems to represent the possibility of a hopeful future for him in contrast to the doom-laden role bequeathed him by the past. At least at times, their union seems to Edgar to pose an alternative to the obliteration of the old order by the new – a union of the young people who represent the best of both sides of the conflict. In this respect, Edgar's idealism in love is paralleled by his political idealism about the future. He declares to Bucklaw:[30]

> 'I hope to see the day when justice shall be open to Whig and Tory, and when these nicknames shall only be used among coffee-house politicians, as "slut" and "jade" are among apple-women, as cant terms of idle spite and rancour.'

Bucklaw's reply – 'That will not be in our days, Master: the iron has entered too deeply into our sides and our souls' – is only too apposite. The inevitability with which Edgar's fragile, but naïve hopes are torn apart in the rest of *The Bride* is responsible for the pessimism of the novel's total effect.

From the beginning, Edgar's love-affair with Lucy is at odds with, and disrupts, his deeply imbued hatred of Ashton for his ruin of the family. It is because of this weight of historical enmity on Edgar that he comes to feel it dishonourable to come to a reasonable arrangement with Ashton in the manner which he has resolved. During Ashton's visit to Wolf's Crag, Edgar is a victim of his contradictory emotions:[31]

His mortal foe was under his roof, yet his sentiments towards him were neither those of a feudal enemy nor of a true Christian. He felt as if he could neither forgive him in the one character, nor follow forth his vengeance in the other, but that he was making a base and dishonourable composition betwixt his resentment against the father and his affection for his daughter. He cursed himself, as he hurried to and fro in the pale moonlight, and more ruddy gleams of the expiring wood-fire. He threw open and shut the latticed windows with violence, as if alike impatient of the admission and exclusion of air.

Edgar's mental agitation is marvellously transferred here into an 'objective correlative' in his actions: his opposed attraction for peace with the Ashtons and feudal revenge on them are metamorphosised into the contrasting lights (to his conscience) of the 'pale moonlight' and the 'expiring wood-fire'. The contrast between modern, rational thinking and the old heat of revenge could hardly be made more concrete: similarly, Edgar's indecision between admitting and excluding air effectively symbolises his equal dissatisfaction with harbouring his stale malice and disposing of it entirely. This conflict continues in Edgar, however he attempts to conceal it: it is very obviously foremost in his mind during his extraordinary proposal to Lucy, in which he prefaces his offer of marriage with an agonised insistence to her that he is sacrificing the public honour of his family and his own private vengeance for her benefit.[32]

Even the attraction between the two lovers is qualified by the peculiar social and historical context in which it is set. There is little in the lovers' feelings for each other which exemplifies that union of minds which might conquer historical circumstance. The lovers' notions of each other are, indeed, based almost entirely on their fantasy constructions about the other. Lucy's feelings grow from her reading of romances, a pastime which seems to offer her a picture of a world quite different from her immediate environment in the Ashtons' household: 'Her secret delight was in the old legendary tales of ardent devotion and unalterable affection, chequered as they so often are with strange adventures and supernatural horrors.'[33] After he has rescued her from the bull, Lucy dwells in her memory on her short acquaintance with Edgar, romanticising the episode into a tale of knightly rescue. The origins of Edgar's passion for Lucy are more obscure, but throughout the novel he shows a fascination with her appearance, rather than with any deeper character, even to the extent of self-delusion:[34]

> In those features, so simply sweet, he could trace no alliance with the pinched visage of the peak-bearded, black-capped Puritan, or his starched, withered spouse, with the craft expressed in the Lord Keeper's countenance, or the haughtiness which predominated in that of his lady; and, while he gazed on Lucy Ashton, she seemed to be an angel descended on earth, unallied to the coarser mortals among whom she deigned to dwell for a season.

Yet, when, after their secret engagement, Lucy and Edgar come to know each other better, the difference between their backgrounds again asserts its importance. Lucy is frightened by her lover: she finds him 'awesome' as well as loving, and she cannot but be dismayed by the contempt Edgar openly displays for ideas inculcated in her by her family. At the same time, Edgar is dissatisfied with Lucy's passivity, first expressed in her fear of revealing their engagement: 'He felt that his own temper required a partner of a more independent spirit, who could set sail with him on his course of life, resolved as himself to dare indifferently the storm and the favouring breeze.'[35] The lovers find themselves at odds over their differing religious and political beliefs, over their attitude to Lucy's father (whom Edgar continues to despise as a 'porter' during his visit to their house), and over the secrecy of their relationship, which is anathema to Edgar's pride.[36] Gladstone's comparison of the novel with *Romeo and Juliet* is misleading in that it suggests that Edgar and Lucy's love is destroyed only by external conflict.[37] In *The Bride*, historical circumstances affect even the lovers' emotional relationship: D. A. Cameron says that 'love' is an imprecise word to apply to Lucy and Edgar, while Hartveit points out Edgar's difference from Romeo in that he 'never appears as the happy lover'.[38]

Throughout the novel Edgar is wracked by uncertainty about

his relationship with Ashton, and is pained by the consciousness that by allying with the man he would be betraying his own kind. In a notable incident, Edgar joins in the laughter of Sir William and Lucy at Caleb, whose most extravagant lie – the lightning bolt which is supposed to have destroyed a veritable gourmet's dinner – can, indeed, hardly be taken seriously. Yet in laughing at Caleb with the Lord Keeper, Edgar is 'conscious that the jest was at his own expense':[39] that is to say, he joins the Ashtons in mocking both his own penury and the feudal loyalty of his devoted servant. Edgar's doubts only deepen after his attachment to Lucy: even if Edgar tries mentally to pass over his less amenable emotions, Old Alice, the former tenant of the Ravenswood family, shames him with the facts as they will appear to others:[40]

> 'Are you prepared to sit lowest at the board which was once your father's own, unwillingly, as a connexion and ally of his proud successor? Are you ready to live on his bounty; to follow him in the by-paths of intrigue and chicane, which none can better point out to you; to gnaw the bones of his prey when he has devoured the substance? Can you say as Sir William Ashton says, think as he thinks, vote as he votes, and call your father's murderer your worshipful father-in-law and revered patron? Master of Ravenswood, I am the eldest servant of your house, and I would rather see you shrouded and coffined.'

As Hartveit notes, Edgar can only weakly rationalise his position.[41] He attempts to argue with the old woman 'Are you such a wretched Christian as to suppose I would in the present day levy war against the Ashton family, as was the sanguinary custom in elder times?' but Edgar's tone here of attempted detachment and 'civilised' scorn of the feudal ways lacks conviction – the 'modern' consciousness sits badly on him.

Alice's warning, and his treatment by Lady Ashton tend to make him react against the Ashtons into his instinctive conservatism and feudal nostalgia. In neither case, however, can Edgar find peace even in reaction. Immediately after leaving Alice, with every intention of quitting the estate, Edgar is led by events to Lucy at Mermaiden's Well, where the fatal betrothal takes place: during his angry departure from Ravenswood castle in the second instance, he is halted by an apparition of Alice dying. This in turn leads him to his interview with the sexton, a former servant of the Ravenswood family, whose recollections of life in service dispose of any possibility of romanticising the old order. The man gives Edgar a vivid description of how he was pressed into battle against the Covenanters at Bothwell Bridge, little dreaming that he is speaking to his old master's grandson:[42]

> 'There was auld Ravenswood brandishing his Andrew Ferrara at the head, and crying to us to come and buckle to, as if we had been gaun to a fair; there was Caleb Balderstone, that is living yet, flourishing in the rear, and swearing Gog and Magog, he would put steel through the guts of ony man that turned bridle; there was young Allan Ravenswood, that was then Master, wi' a bended pistol in his hand – it was a mercy it gaed na aff! – crying to me, that had scarce as much wind left as serve the necessary purpose of my ain lungs, ''Sound, you poltroon! – sound, you damned cowardly villain, or I will blow your brains out!'' and, to be sure, I blew sic points of war that the scraugh of a clockin-hen was music to them.'

There is absolutely no heroism in this account – the men are pressed into battle in an alien cause – but the sexton's point in telling the tale is to elicit sympathy from the 'modern' listener for his being placed in such an unreasonable situation by feudal servitude. To the sexton, the absolute loyalty demanded of him as a 'vassal' seems in retrospect a gross imposition: his whole grievance is based on the supposition that as he was engaged and paid as a trumpeter, the additional duties imposed on him were excessive and unwarranted. His complaint that the Ravenswoods have ruined him, through Edgar's father 'guiding his gear like a fule' is not lost on the hero: by allowing their servant to be ruined when the family fell, the Ravenswoods have implicitly reneged on their own side of the feudal bond. Edgar can no longer feel that he is entirely the victim of circumstances which were not of his family's making. Hook calls the sexton's speech 'the most brilliantly satirical passage' in the novel:[43] its real brilliance, however, lies in the fact that it is a double satire, both of the sexton's attitude and of Edgar's nostalgic harking-back to the ways of his father. The sexton is a real-life example of the lower orders under the old system whom Edgar imagines to have been 'bound, both by law and gratitude', as he puts it in the fire scene. 'Tory pessimism' may sum up Edgar's attitude in the novel, but scenes like this one effectively place the hero's attitudes in perspective.

The novel's catastrophe, which hinges on Lucy's apparent betrayal of Edgar in her betrothal to Bucklaw, is completely consonant with the movement of the novel up to that point. Lucy's character, as already established, is the least able to withstand the psychological warfare waged on her by Lady Ashton, though she puts up a stubborn struggle. Edgar, on the other hand, embraces defeat when he storms in at the climax of her forced betrothal, the embodiment of injured, aristocratic pride. Gordon finds this final confrontation of the Ashtons a magnificent gesture on Edgar's part: 'He defies them all, overpowering "by the ecstasy of desperation" the "less energetic passions of the others." ' [44] Yet Edgar wrongs Lucy by his mistaken inference. At bay in the camp of his bourgeois enemies, Edgar refuses to humble his aristocratic pride in front of them by insisting that Lucy herself should speak, lest she reject him from her own mouth. Instead, he pronounces himself content with the legal form of her signature on the betrothal document, and retreats in self-righteous disgust. Once again, the Ravenswoods are defeated by a legal contract. [45] It is Edgar's discovery that he has been deceived – or rather that he has deceived himself – after the events of Lucy's bridal night with Bucklaw, which marks the high point of his tragic self-revelation. After this point Edgar seems oblivious to his fate: he accepts the challenges thrown at him by Sholto Ashton and Bucklaw 'with the resignation to Providence that Hamlet showed in going to duel with Laertes', as Frank McCombie says. [46] Even here though, Scott imbues plot details undoubtedly taken from *Hamlet* with social connotations. Just as Lucy's grotesquely stage-managed wedding showed the brittle splendour and pseudo-gentility of the Ashtons, so Sholto's challenge also appears as a hypocritical show of nobility: the duel is no longer a 'gentlemen's affair'. Edgar is not concerned to save himself – choosing the shorter sword of the two he possesses he exclaims to himself, 'Let him have this advantage, as he has every other'.[47] The historical advantage is all with his antagonist. There is a measure of poetic justice in the fact that Kelpie's Flow robs Lucy's brother of his chance to extinguish the house of the Ravenswoods: in the end it is the Ravenswood estate which takes Edgar's life. The symbolic ending, again in fulfilment of an ancient prophecy, reverts to the feudal consciousness of the doom of the old order, while Scott again offers a rational alternative in the reader's knowledge that Edgar is doomed, in any case, in the duel to which he was riding.

Such is the main plot of *The Bride of Lammermoor*. Because of the nature of the historical situation and the social position of the hero chosen by Scott, and because of Scott's determination to carry through the potential of his theme to its bitter conclusion, as he failed to do in *Guy Mannering, The Bride* justly earns the title of tragedy. One of the novel's most interesting links with Jacobean tragedy, however, is not in this main plot at all, but in the almost self-contained, and predominantly comic sub-plot of *The Bride*, concerning Caleb Balderstone and the villagers of Wolf's Hope. Some critics have complained that the portrait of Caleb is overdone,[48] but this is to neglect the way in which Caleb offers a key to the main plot of the novel. Exactly in the manner of Jacobean tragedy, Scott uses Caleb and the comic sub-plot to underline the events of the main action but at the same time to offer another point of view on them.

In Caleb, Scott shows the inevitable degradation of the feudal ideal in the modern age. A picture of absolute fidelity to the Ravenswood family, Caleb's actions are motivated entirely by his desire to uphold the 'honour of the family' and the 'credit of the house'. Yet circumstances are unfavourable to Caleb, and it is an essential irony that Caleb should resort to measures which are completely dishonourable and discreditable in order to maintain a public façade of 'honour' and 'credit.' The substance of the Ravenswoods' ascendancy has gone, but habit has accustomed Caleb to consider a show of power or wealth sufficient to make good this deficiency. At one point he even exclaims that 'in some sort, a gude excuse is better than the things themselves' – a ludicrous justification for his lies of necessity.[49] Edgar, who sees his guests' resentment or, worse, amusement at going without food after Caleb's transparent evasions, cannot share his servant's view of affairs. When a meal of scraps has been presented with great ceremony by Caleb to Edgar and Bucklaw, Scott comments: 'But, alas! how little on such occasions can form, however anxiously and scrupulously observed, supply the lack of substantial fare.'[50] This significant observation is applicable to Edgar's circumstances as a whole: Caleb, pompously covering up for his master's poverty, presents a comic picture which, to the reader, satirises the aristocratic obsession with 'honour'. Caleb forces us to ask ourselves whether Edgar's feudal ideals, equally lacking in material foundations, are not equally suspect. To some extent, Edgar himself seems to feel the implicit indictment of his own situation that Caleb represents: it is another motive provided by his reason, against his instincts, for compromising 'with the victors of the day'.

Caleb's relationship with the villagers of Wolf's Hope serves both to make plain the economic changes which have accompanied, or rather, precipitated the ruin of the Ravenswoods and their class, and also to show the historical process involved from a point of view diametrically opposed to that of the feudal characters. Wolf's Hope, formerly part of the Ravenswoods' domain, is a microcosm of bourgeois Scotland emerging from the shadow of feudalism. Scott painstakingly records the villagers' awakening to the recognition that they have gradually succeeded in freeing themselves legally from their feudal ties, and that only the remains of feudal attitudes among them have allowed Caleb to go on levying dues from them on behalf of his master in Wolf's Crag. Eventually, their grudging submission to these exactions turns to resistance:[51]

> they met with a determined purpose of resisting the exaction, and were only undecided as to the mode of grounding their opposition, when the cooper, a very important person on a fishing-station, and one of the conscript fathers of the village, observed 'That their hens had caickled mony a day for the Lords of Ravenswood, and it was time they suld caickle for those that gave them roosts and barley.' An unanimous grin intimated the assent of the assembly.

It is the cooper's exact ideological expression of the villagers' self-interest in his homely metaphor which elicits the unanimous grin. The cooper's point is that the return on the hens should in future go, not to those who have exercised hereditary rights over them, but to those whose investment is responsible for the birds' production. It is essentially the bourgeois concept of property which appeals to the self-employed fishermen and tradesmen gathered together in Wolf's Hope: the cooper has little sympathy for the poor, propertyless villagers, as we discover when he generously orders, after the marquis's visit, that 'if there is ony thing totally uneatable, let it be gien to the puir folk'.[52] The cooper's suggestion that the villagers employ a lawyer to back their case is also efficacious. Davie Dingwall answers Caleb's veiled (and in fact empty) threats of violence against the offending 'vassals' by warning him:[53]

> 'that new times were not as old times; that they lived on the south of the Forth, and far from the Highlands; that his clients thought they were able to protect themselves; but should they find themselves mistaken, they would apply to the government for the protection of a corporal and four red-coats.'

The lawyer's warning here underlines the fact that the law is supported by the might of the government, and that the government itself (with Ashton as Lord Keeper) is now the guardian of class interests directly opposed to those of the old feudal aristocracy. If Scott's presentation of the Wolf's Hope scenes is not actually sympathetic to the villagers' aspirations, it at least makes them understandable to the reader. Caleb's idealisation of the old days when 'a vassal scarce held a calf or a lamb his ain, till he had first asked if the Lord of Ravenswood was pleased to accept it',[54] and his desperate resort to knavery when all else fails appear at least equally unattractive in contrast.

It is of course true that Caleb is an ambiguous figure: his vices are also his virtues, and Scott's delineation of the feudal mentality in him sometimes evokes pathos rather than laughter.[55] Caleb is a victim of changes he hardly understands. He tells Edgar:[56]

> 'I am a dog, and an auld dog too . . . and I am like to get a

dog's wages; but it does not signification a pinch of
sneeshing, for I am ower auld a dog to learn new tricks, or
to follow a new master.'

Caleb's sardonic characterisation of himself here is sad because
it is so accurate; the absolute loyalty he shows to his master, and
his utter dependence on the house of Ravenswood, seems to
make him, indeed, more dog than man. The final description
Scott gives of Caleb pining and dying within a year of Edgar's
death, 'with a fidelity sometimes displayed by the canine race,
but seldom by human beings', strongly recalls this earlier
passage.[57] It is Scott's wryest comment on the feudal mentality
that Caleb comes to appear to a later age less than a human
being. Even Edgar, riding to his death, is impatient to the point
of cruelty with his old servant. Angered by Caleb's grotesquely
inappropriate plea that 'all will be well' while his master yet
lives, Edgar throws his purse at Caleb – a response which is itself
both inappropriate and unjust. Caleb's loyalty to his master
may be futile and outmoded, but it is completely genuine. The
simple words with which Scott describes Caleb's retrieval of
Edgar's feather from the quicksands: 'The old man took it up,
dried it, and placed it in his bosom',[58] are eloquent of the
depth of Caleb's feelings, as well as their simplicity.

It is dangerous to draw easy conclusions about Scott's views
from *The Bride of Lammermoor*. Gordon's inference from the
novel that the author's principles had themselves undergone a
major upheaval, and that *The Bride* represents a crucial
upsetting of the balance between 'Scott's love of the past and
his acceptance of the present'[59] is only tenable if, like Gordon,
we ignore the elements in the novel which satirise Edgar and
Caleb. On the other hand, Daiches goes too far in the other
direction when he likens Edgar to Sir Arthur Wardour in *The
Antiquary*, on the grounds that 'both retain nothing of value
from the past except an unjustified pride'.[60] Scott's attitude to
the historical changes delineated in *The Bride* is characteristically ambivalent: the interspersing of the main, tragic plot in
which Edgar is protagonist with a comic-satiric sub-plot is the
expression of this ambivalence.

The Bride's excellence as an historical novel owes much to the
previous novels in the Waverley series – indeed, many of Scott's

preoccupations in the earlier novels are apparent in *The Bride*. Gordon's comment that Scott wrote *The Bride* 'from an inner need to confront the fact of historical change with more honesty than he had exhibited in his early novels'[61] is particularly apposite in view of the connections with *Guy Mannering* already noted in terms of protagonists, the supernatural, and the identical historical situation in which the private dramas of both the novels are placed. The defeat of Edgar's idealism in *The Bride*, on the other hand, is reminiscent of the defeat of Morton's idealism in *Old Mortality*: in both cases, the efforts of the hero to compromise are thwarted by an intractable class opposition in his society. The novel's links with *Rob Roy* are less obvious, but the complex ironic attitude Scott adopts towards historical change in *The Bride* is a development of the dualistic contrast between the Scotlands of Rob and of Jarvie in the earlier novel. Finally, Scott is indebted to *The Heart of Midlothian* for the skill with which his hero is presented: the ambiguity of the pardon-scene, in which Scott viewed events through Jeanie Deans's eyes, while at the same time making the limitations of her viewpoint apparent to the reader, closely relates to the ironic treatment of Edgar as both hero and anti-hero in *The Bride*.

If *The Bride* has a claim to individuality among the Waverley Novels, it must be not only because of its unequalled coherence and consistency, but because of the depth of insight with which Scott treats the opposed social classes in the novel. Scott uses the ideologies of the conflicting feudal and bourgeois cultures to define each in its own terms. Thus, for the villagers of Wolf's Hope, historical development is a materialistic affair – for them, the end of the old ways is amply compensated for by their ability to follow the profit motive without interference. For Edgar, a product of the feudal system, and for the other feudal characters, however, the economic causes of their downfall remain obscure: instead, Scott dramatises their decline in the way they themselves experience it, as an inexplicable, fatal, eclipse. For this reason the realistic action of the novel is juxtaposed with supernatural omens, legends and prophecies, all of which offer a superstitious 'explanation' of events. Thus, Scott's ambivalent attitude towards the social transition he treats is reflected not only by his attitude towards the protagonists in the main and sub-plots, but by the conflicting modes of writing. Both 'romance' and 'rationalist' modes are used here to convey the truth of human experience of historical change, as Scott understood it: it is therefore no paradox that Scott's most 'Romantic' novel should also turn out to be his greatest essay in historical realism.

8

Redgauntlet

Five years, and a plethora of lesser novels, separate *Redgauntlet* from *The Bride of Lammermoor*. Scott's decision to return to the field of Scottish history, and to the subject of the Jacobites in particular, seems at first to be at odds with his own admission (in the Introduction to *Ivanhoe*) that the public's interest in Scottish manners had been sated.[1] Certainly contemporary critics of *Redgauntlet* complained of repetition, and did not rate the novel highly.[2] Recent interest in the novel – and its revaluation as a result – has come about because of the idea that, in an essential way, the novel completes the treatment of themes common to all the Scottish novels.[3] The problem with the novel is that Scott's expression of these themes in *Redgauntlet* is not complete: to some extent, the reader has to act as an interpreter of private associations which are only partly dramatised. Robert Gordon has correctly defined the special qualities of *Redgauntlet* as 'arbitrariness, eccentricity, and a strong impression of having been composed to please the author rather than the public or the critics.'[4] The strongly auto-biographical features of the book have been recognised for some while: the characters of the young men, of Saunders Fairford, and of Lilias as 'Green Mantle' are all based on memories which had private significance for Scott.[5] Similarly, Scott's encomium of the 'marriage of reason' in Chapter XVII reads as a personal defence of his own choice of marriage partner against the claims of his earlier, unrequited, romantic attachment. Clearly, however, much of this autobiographical detail is irrelevant to the novel: it concerns Scott in a way that he has not made important to his reader. The private, 'associational' nature of the novel goes even further than this, however: the book is an amalgam of different narrative forms, interpolated tales, and even apparently autonomous characters like Peter Peebles and Nanty Ewart, whose connection with the main plot, and with each other, is far from obvious. Nevertheless, unlike the hackneyed, 'external' plots of *The Antiquary* or *Rob Roy*, the parts of *Redgauntlet* give an impression of being related to the whole in some important way, even if the relationship has to be inferred by the reader to a great extent. In these circumstances, it may be easier to examine the main movement of the novel from those episodes which appear definitely 'relevant', and then finally to discuss more speculatively the part played by other, more impenetrable elements of the novel.

Redgauntlet, set in the late 1760s,[6] is as David Daiches has said 'the story of two worlds':[7] the world of modern Scotland, exemplified by the young men and their way of life in Edinburgh; and the world of the older, feudal Scotland which still exists for the Jacobite characters, and into which Darsie Latimer stumbles during his fateful visit to the Borders. The Fairfords, father and son, manifest the growing confidence of the new middle classes in Scotland – a confidence which is symbolised, as in *The Bride of Lammermoor*, by the characters' positions in the Scottish legal system – Fairford Senior as Writer to the Signet, Alan as a more prestigious Advocate. Scott underlines this implied social significance explicitly later, when he interrupts the narrative to stress the effort required of Alan to assert his equality at the Bar with the sons of the nobility who have previously monopolised the profession.[8] The Fairfords' command of the legal machinery is symbolically important, as the law is the process whereby the new class's economic and political values are legitimised.[9] The portrait of the Fairfords is in many ways a repetition of Scott's portrait of the Osbaldistones in *Rob Roy*, but the characters gain in strength here by being firmly situated in a Lowland Scottish milieu. Saunders Fairford exemplifies the frugal work-ethic of the older, strict Presbyterian type – Alan, despite his occasional rebellions against the severe discipline imposed by his father, is thoroughly imbued himself with middle-class assumptions and values. When Darsie ventures to poke fun at Alan's father's flight from the Highland hordes in 1745, Alan staunchly defends him on grounds of 'common sense': 'I tell you he has courage enough to do what is right and to spurn what is wrong – courage enough to defend a righteous cause with hand and purse.'[10] Certainly Alan intends no bathos here, though the reader's reaction is somewhat different. According to Alan, 'This is civil courage . . .' and at least as admirable as military bravado, while other remarks he makes show his pride in his middle-class background. When later on, for example, the Pretender confuses Alan's family with an aristocratic one of the same name, Alan is at pains to correct the mistake, declaring with no little pride that: 'My father's industry has raised his family from a low and obscure situation'.[11] Given that Alan is so obviously the son of his father, Saunders' worries about his son's stability never strike us as other than unnecessary.

Modern commercial Scotland is also represented by the character of Joshua Geddes, the Quaker. Joshua's pacifism is an extreme manifestation of the tendency towards peace which often characterises the commercial classes in the Waverley Novels: his ethics are totally at odds with the violent code of honour of his own, rapacious, feudal ancestors, though his attempt to repudiate his ancestry by sheer willpower is not always wholly successful. Joshua is nevertheless the unashamed advocate of new ways: Mount Sharon is not only a showpiece of late eighteenth-century picturesque, but also of the newest agricultural innovations with which Joshua fearlessly experiments in spite of the criticism of his traditionalist neighbours.[12] Joshua's tide-nets, which precipitate the attack on the fishing station during which Darsie is abducted, also symbolise the economic changes which are taking place, and on which Joshua has capitalised. The nets ingeniously catch fish more efficiently than the traditional spear-fishers, yet the new process is alienated from the human action of fishing, and is resented by the spear-fishers, whose livelihood it threatens, as unnatural.[13]

Redgauntlet, who first appears as the leader of the spear-fishers, and throughout the novel acts as the spokesman for feudal values, is opposed to Joshua here quite specifically: the point of the tide-nets issue for Scott is that it reveals much deeper, cultural antipathies between the two men.[14]

At the beginning of the novel, however, only Darsie Latimer seems uncomfortable in middle-class Edinburgh, rejecting his legal studies there in favour of apparently aimless roaming, and later similarly renouncing the Puritanical quietude of Mount Sharon. In the epistolary form which opens *Redgauntlet*, Scott succeeds in giving a clear picture of Darsie's character – his restless, flippant, romantic impulses which seem little to suit a career of steady employment. We also infer that the source of Darsie's dissatisfaction is in his alienation from his family origins, a subject on which he constantly harps and which seems effectively to block his acceptance of the Fairford's background as his own. His pride in the one fact of which he is certain – his English nationality – also testifies to his near-obsession with his doubtful identity. Yet in many ways Darsie shares assumptions with his friend Alan without realising. He shares a joke with Alan about the state of the Highlanders twenty years after the Forty-Five:[15]

The Pretender is no more remembered in the Highlands than if the poor gentleman were gathered to his hundred and eight fathers, whose portraits adorn the ancient walls of Holyrood; the broadswords have passed into other hands; the targets are used to cover the butter churns; and the race has sunk, or is fast sinking, from ruffling bullies into tame cheaters.

The light, patronising tone with which Darsie summarises the effects of two decades of subjugation and depopulation of the Highlands bears witness to his absorption of the 'civilised' Edinburgh attitude towards the clans. It is the same attitude of cultural prejudice, half fear and half contempt, which led the British government after 1745 to forbid the wearing of the kilt, the playing of the bagpies, or the carrying of arms (hence Darsie's sarcastic reference to butter churns).[16] The fact that Darsie no longer considers the Highlanders dangerous is a sign of the completeness of their pacification. Similarly, Darsie feels free to affect sympathy for the Pretender's condition, while simultaneously mocking Stuart authority in the form of the fake portraits of legendary kings hanging in the old palace.[17] Darsie may be a romantic youth (*vide* Waverley) but the times are such that even he finds it impossible to take Jacobitism seriously. It is these 'modern' attitudes – implicitly repudiating the feudal past – which ultimately spell doom to Redgauntlet's attempts to involve his nephew in 'the old cause'.

Thus while the novel opens with an exchange of views between Darsie and Alan, which apparently shows them to be very different characters, the reader finds, as the novel proceeds, that the real gulf is not between the two friends, but between both of them as 'modern' consciousnesses and the Jacobite sympathisers and temporisers who constitute the world of 'old' Scotland in *Redgauntlet*. Darsie's bent for romantic adventure may lead him initially into contact with the spectacular spear-fishers and the mysterious inmates of Redgauntlet's household, but his romanticised view of them has nothing to do with the reality of their traditional way of life; once Darsie's illusions have been dispelled, he shows as little sympathy or understanding towards them as Alan does. It is the young men's journey into the world of the past which constitutes the essential action of *Redgauntlet*, but it is also essential for an understanding of the novel to recognise that the young men's perception of the old Scotland is itself limited and prejudiced.

A notable feature of the novel is the number of prevaricating characters whose portraits are skilfully painted, characters torn between their loyalty to the old values and their compromised lives in the new world. If the young men's attitudes come to appear superficial in some ways, we have still to compare them with men whose ideas are sentimental or even hypocritical. Justice Foxley, Provost Crosbie, and Pate-in-Peril are connected characters in that they all represent compromises between the past and the present which are practical but at the same time unattractive. Foxley is a Jacobite J.P. who 'examines' Darsie under the conflicting scrutinies of Redgauntlet and of his own upstart, Whiggish clerk. We immediately recognise the scene as modelled on that of Justice Inglewood and Clerk Jobson in *Rob Roy*, yet it is as though Scott has finally found the right context for a scene which was isolated in the earlier novel. Foxley is ready to confirm Redgauntlet's guardianship of Darsie, after minimal examination, purely out of political favouritism, but the whole scene is disrupted by the entrance of Peter Peebles who makes known Redgauntlet's identity as a wanted man in a way which can hardly be misunderstood.[18] Faced with such a flagrant call to his legal duty, Foxley puts his new position firmly before his old sympathies: once the conspiratorial fiction about 'Mr Herries'' true identity has been exploded, Foxley can no longer turn a blind eye without endangering his new status. The result is an ignominious about-turn with regard to his former ally. Redgauntlet has to resort to brute force merely to keep a supposed sympathiser from betraying him.

Provost Crosbie is a more detailed study of a temporiser, deftly using ambiguous loyalties to further his position. In some ways a typically Whiggish Lowland burgess, Crosbie is suspected of Jacobite opinions because of his connexion by marriage with a Highland family. Maxwell of Summertrees comments to Alan that Crosbie treads the fine line between the party factions in Dumfries so successfully that:[19]

because he is a whilly-wha body, and has a plausible tongue of his own, and is well-connected, and especially because nobody could ever find out whether he is Whig or Tory, this is the third time they have made him provost!

This is no sign of independence or strength of character, however. We soon see that Crosbie's 'plausible tongue' means that he trims his talk to suit his listeners, while at the same time maintaining a bogus reserve of inscrutability to impress his audience. During his dinner with Alan he is torn between expressing his zeal for George III, which he knows will earn his wife's wrath, and his loyalty to Charles Edward, which he rightly expects will cause trouble with the young man. Every utterance he makes is therefore hedged around with qualifications and evasions to a ridiculous extent. For example, while preparing the ground for Alan's introduction to Pate-in-Peril, Crosbie temporarily forgets Alan's background and slips into his Jacobite conspiratorial tone, ending with a wistful lament that the oaths of allegiance to King George, which lawyers take to qualify, 'kept more folk out then than they do now – more's the pity'. Yet when Alan makes clear his disapproval of this apparently open avowal of Jacobitism, Crosbie cleverly changes tack:[20]

'No – no,' answered the provost; 'I am only sorry for folks losing the tenderness of conscience which they used to have. I have a son breeding to the bar, Mr. Fairford; and no doubt, considering my services and sufferings; I might have looked for some bit postie to him; but if the muckle tikes come in – I mean a' these Maxwells, and Johnstones, and great lairds, that the oaths used to keep out lang syne – the bits of messan doggies, like my son, and maybe your father's son, Mr. Alan, will be sair put to the wall.'

In this cunning volte-face, the provost manages to turn his sentimental Jacobitism into a vulgar but shrewd Whig assessment of promotion prospects. It is an argument specifically designed to appeal to Alan, whose professional competition with noblemen's sons has already been noted. Even Crosbie's tone changes here: the distant and respectful 'Mr Fairford' giving way by the end to the ingratiating familiarity of 'Mr Alan'. If this is historical compromise, it leaves an unpleasant taste in the mouth: if Crosbie leaves any decided impression at all, it is that he no longer knows, even privately, where he really stands. Even when his friend's son is threatened with physical danger, Crosbie's less selfish instincts prevail only long enough for him to hint fearfully to Alan that Maxwell's letter of 'introduction' for Redgauntlet should be opened.

Maxwell himself, alias Pate-in-Peril, evokes a different response from the reader, though he too is a man whose former loyalty is continually compromised by the realities of life in the latter half of the eighteenth century. What Maxwell displays most clearly, however, is the folly and unreality of the man who is attached to his former opinions purely by sentimentality. His mind, like his appearance, is studiedly antiquated: at first he asks Alan for news from Edinburgh, but stops him short when he finds that 'the answers all smell of new lords, new lands, and do but spoil my appetite'.[21] Moreover, Maxwell's whole stock of social conversation centres on the story which has given him his nickname – yet this tale, when told, reveals the illogicality of his commitment to the Jacobite cause. The story is entirely one of adventure: the political consequences of the Forty-Five's defeat are irrelevant to it as such. Maxwell's actual motives for involvement in the rebellion are reduced to this one sentence:[22]

I dinna mind very weel what I was doing, swaggering about the country with dirk and pistol at my belt for five or six months, or thereaway; but I had a weary waking out of a wild dream.

The haziness of purpose of the Prince's adherents in 1745, accentuated by the length of time that has passed, makes Maxwell's words here deeply significant. Yet his tale, which has become a bore to his old friends and an irrelevance to new listeners like Alan, is a tribute to the sheer power of memory. Even as he repeats it for the umpteenth time, Maxwell relives the events in his mind, and the pride and excitement of the exploit return afresh to him. The injustice of the executions is felt again, and when Alan refers to them in unsympathetic, coldly legal terms, Maxwell can only drown his unhappiness in his glass. Alan's analysis of Maxwell as 'a discontented man' is more poignantly true than the young man realises.

The effect of these character studies of Jacobitism in Foxley, Crosbie and Maxwell is to prepare the reader for Scott's masterly portrait of Redgauntlet himself, with whom the others both compare and contrast. Simultaneously, Scott prepares Redgauntlet's character through his background, which is slowly revealed. This is partly done through the legendary family history of the Redgauntlets, in a manner reminiscent of *The Bride*. The tale of his ancestor Sir Alberick's murder of his son, for example, reflects on the main narrative in a number of ways. Obviously, the story underlines the traditional fidelity of the Redgauntlets to the Scottish ruling family: a fidelity that is unchanged in Redgauntlet himself, and which underlies the intense pride in Scotland's feudal independence manifest in his moving reprehension of the 'tyrant' Edward I.[23] The story has a second, private relevance, however, in displaying the utter ruthlessness of the Redgauntlets towards filial disobedience. The parallel here between Alberick's attitude to his son and Redgauntlet's relationship with Darsie is explicitly made later, when, crossed by his nephew, Redgauntlet exclaims:[24]

'if Scotland and my father's house cannot stand and flourish together, then perish the very name of Redgauntlet! perish the son of my brother, with every recollection of the glories of my family, of the affections of my youth, rather than my country's cause should be injured in the tithing of a barley-corn! The spirit of Sir Alberick is alive within me at this moment.'

The Alberick story also 'explains' and gives significance to the peculiar link between Darsie, his uncle and the whole Redgauntlet family: the mysterious horseshoe mark visible on their foreheads during moments of anger. The mark is a symbol of Darsie's connection with his family; a connection that cannot be obliterated by the cultural differences that exist between him and his uncle. Thus, significantly, Darsie is halted in the middle of pleading his rights to Justice Foxley as a 'free subject' by his sudden recognition of the familiar mark in Redgauntlet's face. While the mark has a modern, rational explanation in terms of heredity, the legendary explanation offered by the Alberick story embodies the force of feudal traditionalism that bears upon Darsie in the novel.

The other legend which bears directly upon the character of Redgauntlet is Wandering Willie's Tale. The Tale is in many ways the most problematic digression in *Redgauntlet*: some critics have been happy simply to take it as a vivid piece of Scots prose, interpolated into the novel in the eighteenth-century tradition and having reference to nothing outside itself.[25] The introduction of a complete short story – a short story, moreover, which displays Scott's agility in the traditional Scots medium – is certainly formally disruptive. Unlike the tale of Martin Waldeck in *The Antiquary*, however, the Tale on reflection adds depth to the novel in which it is placed. Once again, it provides insight into the family history of the Redgauntlets. Willie's description of old Sir Robert Redgauntlet, hunting down the Covenanters 'with bugle and bloodhound . . . as if they had been sae mony deer' cleverly characterises the family by placing them in the world of *Old Mortality*.[26] This effect is repeated in Steenie's vision of Sir Robert in Hell with other, well-known Cavalier persecutors, including Claverhouse himself: it identifies Herries' fanaticism with the Royalist fanaticism of eighty years before. Steenie's renunciation of his old master also mirrors Darsie's final renunciation of his family's politics, as a number of critics have remarked. Edgar Johnson, for example, sees the Tale as 'a symbolic center of the entire novel, an anticipation of the confrontation and defiance that is ultimately to be demanded . . . of Darsie . . . in resisting the tyrannous claims of a moribund past'.[27] Coleman O. Parsons, in his study of Scott's demonology, comes to the same conclusion.[28] The Tale is also, as Daiches says, 'a critical piece about master-servant relations in old Scotland' and the decay of feudal paternalism[29] and, as Francis Hart says, 'a parable of courage and prudence combined'.[30] The subject of the Tale can be said to be identical to the subject of the novel as a whole: the change in attitudes accompanying the downfall of the feudal order, and the choice between damnation and survival with which social change confronts all men. At the same time, as folk-lore, the Tale reflects these changes as they are viewed and mythologised by the peasantry. For the peasantry, survival is the most important value: the Tale thus celebrates precisely the peasant's native virtues of fortitude and prudence in Steenie's actions. The novel, on the other hand, provides *other* views of the same historical process: Darsie's 'escape' from his hereditary obligations is finally to be weighed against the tragic fate of Redgauntlet himself.

One other related story, apart from these two legends, throws light on the character of Redgauntlet's mind. This is Lilias's account of the events surrounding the coronation of George III, during which Redgauntlet's peculiar hostility to the Hanoverian regime is brilliantly displayed. The mood of the story is important: the Jacobites' discontentment strongly contrasts with the jubilation of the London crowds during the celebration, and Redgauntlet seems to shun the very sight of the people by moving through dark alleys on the way to the palace. This strongly hints at the unpopularity of Jacobite principles in 1760. In the Court itself, Redgauntlet's 'suppressed agitation' bears witness to his near distraction as he points out to Lilias the identity of the men paying homage to George:[31]

> 'See,' he said: 'yonder bends Norfolk, renegade to his Catholic faith; there stoops the Bishop of – , traitor to the Church of England; and – shame of shames! yonder the gigantic form of Errol bows his head before the grandson of his father's murderer!'

Redgauntlet's Shakespearian tone here stresses the dignity of his attitude, but also its obsolescence.[32] His fixity of purpose is fanatical: the years which have passed away since the Forty-Five hardly exist for Redgauntlet at this moment. Yet the most damning proof of the Jacobite conspirators' outdatedness is the mode of their challenge to the Hanoverian regime at the coronation. What they meditate is not assassination, a course of action which, however feasible, is anathema to their feudal notions of honour – Redgauntlet considering Lilias foolish even to suspect him of such a thing. Instead, violence is eschewed in favour of an ultra-traditional challenge to the new monarch: a glove proffered to the king's champion in the chivalric fashion. It is a comment on the unreality of the Jacobite mentality that Redgauntlet and his fellow-conspirators should even imagine that George would hazard his throne over an antiquated ceremony in this way. George does not owe his position to the feudal aristocracy, and so he can hardly be expected to relinquish it in obedience to feudal theory.

Just as Redgauntlet epitomises the old, feudal world of Scotland, so the young men epitomise the new, liberal culture of the middle classes who have displaced the old world. The impact between the opposed cultures is dramatised in the scene of Darsie's ideological argument with his uncle. Angered by his continuing captivity, Darsie is roused to a passionate assertion of his right to independence and freedom:[33]

'Misfortune – early deprivation – has given me the privilege of acting for myself; and constraint shall not deprive me of an Englishman's best privilege.'

Redgauntlet's reply is deeply revealing:

'The true cant of the day,' said Herries, in a tone of scorn. 'The privilege of free action belongs to no mortal: we are tied down by the fetters of duty, our moral path is limited by the regulations of honour, our most indifferent actions are but meshes of the web of destiny by which we are all surrounded.'

'Duty . . . honour . . . destiny:' it is in these terms that Redgauntlet lives. The long, agitated monologue he launches into is the essence of Stuart philosophy at its most doom-laden and medieval, but it also testifies to the depth of feeling attached to this philosophy by the man. Darsie's response, that he hopes he will never be 'obliged to form a decided opinion upon a point [the predestination/free-will issue] so far beyond our comprehension', is in many ways an inadequate reply to Redgauntlet's heartfelt outburst. It is a measure of how little Darsie understands the old way of life that he sees the question only as one of 'subtle metaphysics': it is because of his distance from feudal attitudes that the whole question appears to him academic. This distance is reinforced by the attitude Darsie strikes at the end of his interview, when he reiterates his loyalty to George III as the sentiments in which he has been bred, and which are not open to change. At the same time he dismisses his uncle to himself with the thought that 'He has chosen an antiquated and desperate line of politics'. How little Darsie comprehends Redgauntlet is shown once more in his use of the word 'chosen.' The whole point of Redgauntlet's outburst against free-will is that he feels he has effectively no 'choice'.

Alan Fairford's audience with Charles Edward is yet more illuminating, largely because Scott succeeds in dramatising concretely the issues which remain abstract in Darsie's dialogue with his uncle.[34] Here Scott's treatment is unambiguously comic, even verging on farce. Alan believes to begin with that the 'father' wants to see him to convert him to Catholicism, a purpose of which he is quite unafraid. Just as Darsie's 'open mind' on the question of free-will underlines his distance from Redgauntlet's fatalism, so Alan's declaration that 'in religious matters he had the greatest respect for every modification of Christianity' means in effect that he no longer sees Catholicism as a serious threat because its tenets are irrelevant to his own life and the lives of his peers.[35] The sight of Alan, with his democratic notions, blundering into the Stuart presence, is part of a comedy which mocks Alan's presumption as well as the Chevalier's gravity. Puzzled by the extent to which the supposed priest's tone of authority disarms him, Alan finds himself 'at a loss how to assert the footing of equality on which he felt he ought to stand'. On the other hand, his outspoken pride in his non-aristocratic descent, his chance reference to 'the Pretender', and his protests at Charles's opening Maxwell's letter – despite Charles's dogmatic assertion, 'I have a warrant for what I do' – all this is deeply wounding to the pride of the Stuart monarch. As he warns

Charles that Britain is a free country, and offers to shake his hand, Alan implicitly destroys Charles's pretensions to absolute sovereignty over his subjects.

Alan's bathetic interview prepares the reader for the breakdown of the attempted rebellion at the end of the novel. In a superbly orchestrated build-up to the climax, Scott points the social unreality of the Jacobite enterprise. Alan's search for Darsie slowly reveals the lamentable state of the Jacobites, forced to rely on paid agents like Tom Turnpenny, a disgusting Puritan hypocrite whose motivation is entirely economic, and Nanty Ewart, whose contempt for 'your Jacobitical, old-fashioned Popish riff-raff' is no secret. Nanty's shrewd observations about the Jacobite conspirators' chances undermine our belief in the possibility of their rebellion. Castigating Alan for his supposed adherence to the Jacobite party, Nanty replies to Alan's rebuke on the company he keeps:

'And with whom do you yourself consort, I pray? . . . Why with plotters, that can make no plot to better purpose than their own hanging; and incendiaries, that are snapping the flint upon wet tinder. You'll as soon raise the dead as raise the Highlands; you'll as soon get a grunt from a dead sow as any comfort from Wales and Cheshire. You think, because the pot is boiling, that no scum but yours can come uppermost; I know better, by – . All these rackets and riots that you think are trending your way have no relation at all to your interest; and the best way to make the whole kingdom friends again at once would be the alarm of such an undertaking as these mad old fellows are trying to launch into.'[36]

This is indeed a shrewd observation of the barrenness of any Jacobite hopes based on the troubles in the American colonies and in London over John Wilkes: as Nanty correctly sees, these incidents bear no relation to the social roots of Jacobitism. The irrelevance of Redgauntlet's ideology is further apparent as Nanty goes on mockingly to analyse the motives of the Jacobite 'sympathisers' themselves.

'and he gets encouragement from some because they want a spell of money from him; and from others because they fought for the cause once, and are ashamed to go back; and others because they have nothing to lose; and others because they are discontented fools.'

The end of the novel proves the accuracy of Nanty's sarcastic remarks here. One other remark he makes to Alan also becomes significant later on. He declares 'More shame that government send dragoons out after a few honest fellows that bring the old women of England a drop of brandy, and let these ragamuffins smuggle in as much Papistry and – .'[37] The fact that the government is more interested in suppressing smuggling than in rooting out Catholics and Jacobites is another testimony both to the impotence of Redgauntlet's ideas and to the economic changes (which in turn have ousted feudalism) in the late eighteenth century. The government puts its effort into defending its new source of strength, the commercial economy of England – a strength which smuggling undermines in a way that the Jacobites' half-baked schemes cannot. Nanty's conversation with Alan, apparently a merely 'episodic' incident, in fact prepares the way for the conclusion of the novel.

It is, of course, a central irony of *Redgauntlet* that the rebellion of the last Jacobites is not put down: instead, the internal resolution of the conspirators is shown to be too weak to bring matters to a head. From the moment we see the Jacobites greeting Redgauntlet in Crackenthorp's inn with an 'ominous melancholy', the outcome of their conference is never really in doubt.[38] The conspirators fully deserve Nanty Ewart's satiric description: Sir Richard Glendale is a loyal supporter from the days of the Forty-Five, attending out of a sense of duty; MacKellar, an old laird, declares pathetically that 'they that took my land the last time may take my life this', while Maxwell sardonically comments to himself that 'if Pate were not a fool, he would be Pate-in-Safety'.[39] To these three are added some still more hopeless specimens. Doctor Grumball, the representative of Oxford University, lectures his audience on the rectitude of the University's stand against 'the blasphemous, atheistical, and anarchical tenets of Locke': proof that Oxford is still fighting the intellectual battles of the previous century in splendid isolation.[40] By contrast, the young Lord – has more bravado than sense, challenging Redgauntlet himself to a duel during their fraught conference out of an over-zealous sensitivity in matters of honour. The conspirators are united only by their earnest wish that their meeting should be merely for the purpose of 'consultation': Redgauntlet's sudden announcement of their king's presence tricks them into a commitment for which they have no relish.

The eagerness with which the group grasp at the issue of Charles's mistress as a let-out clause in their contract of support is obvious, but their objection is nonetheless important. The importance lies not in the actual subject of their reservations, however: Charles rebukes Redgauntlet for implying that he values a woman's society more than the aim of reclaiming his kingdom, and even insists that: 'I could part with that person tomorrow without an instant's regret – . . . I have had thoughts of dismissing her from my court, for reasons known to myself.'[41] The real problem lies in the fact that the Jacobites' conditional support undermines the central thesis of Stuart ideology, the doctrine of divine right. When Charles declares that: 'Conditions can have no part betwixt prince and subject', he is expounding the absolutist principle which has consistently dictated his family's position and their fluctuating fortunes over the previous century and a half. Sir Richard Glendale's impassioned plea that his sovereign be 'reasonable' is just not consistent with the Jacobite principles he supposedly admits. As A. O. J. Cockshut puts it, the heated exchanges between Charles and Glendale 'prove to Sir Richard that he was not really a Jacobite at all.'[42] Glendale shows that he is in practice a moderate constitutionalist, a model Hanoverian subject. To this extent, it is not excessive for Charles to criticise Redgauntlet, his only truly loyal follower, for hiding the fact that his supporters 'desired, not a prince to govern them, but one, on the contrary, over whom they were to exercise restraint on all occasions'.[43]

The climactic entrance of General Campbell, which is contradicted immediately by the import of his bathetic message to the conspirators, is one of Scott's most memorable effects. The government's leniency is actually more overwhelmingly crushing, in the circumstances, than any punishment of the rebels could have been; while having the chief of Clan Campbell, traditionally the arch-enemy of the Jacobites, pronounce their complete pardon brilliantly heightens the ironic impact of the scene. According to the general, King George trusts his security, not only to the vast majority who acknowledge his title, but also to the 'prudence' of the few remaining supporters of the Stuart line (a virtue the Jacobites' action at the inn has certainly manifested) and even to the wisdom and compassion of 'his kinsman' Charles himself. George is astute enough to make a 'gentleman's agreement' with the gentlemen here opposed to him. The government's terms, which the bulk of the conspirators hear with ill-disguised relief, are taken by Charles himself to be ironically appropriate: Campbell's affected view of the meeting which has just broken up as a 'cockfight' or 'bearbait' is more accurate than he realises. Redgauntlet too realises the implications of the government's magnanimity at last in his anguished ex-clamation: 'The cause is lost forever!' to which Campbell later adds his choric comment: 'It is now all over, . . . and Jacobite will be henceforward no longer a party name.'[44] The whole scene is Scott's most audacious piece of historical fantasy, yet it succeeds because it is founded securely on the underlying social reality of the period. The British government's attempts to dismantle the social basis of Jacobitism in the Highlands after 1745 were completely successful: in the Lowlands and in England, economic changes had already achieved the same ends. Scott was thus correct to imply that in such circumstances, George III could afford to be lenient. The scene is imaginary, but other, comparable cases of generosity were real. T. C. Smout notes:[45]

> By 1784 it was even considered safe and politic to hand the forfeited estates back on generous terms to the families of their original owners: the Government never had reason to regret this stroke of magnanimity.

This is at least a parallel to the imaginary pardon of the conspirators in *Redgauntlet*.

It is typical of the richness of Scott's mature artistic approach in *Redgauntlet* that the affair of the conspirators is not treated in isolation from the larger social issues surrounding the decline of Jacobitism. The treachery of Cristal Nixon, Redgauntlet's apparently devoted servant, for example, underlines the decay of the ideal of feudal service. Early in the novel, Darsie attempts to bribe Nixon, only to be met with a contemptuous refusal. The man declares: 'And as for me, young gentleman, if you would fill St. Mary's kirk with gold, Cristal Nixon would mind it no more than so many chucky-stones.'[46] His secret attentions to Lilias, however, reveal a streak of ambition which Nixon well knows is unacceptable to his master. His betrayal of the rebellion is a mixture of personal offence at Lilias's rejection of his advances, and a rankling resentment of his subordinate social position:[47]

> 'I have been illpaid for my service among the Red-gauntlets – have scarce got dog's wages, and been treated worse than ever dog was used. I have the old fox and his cubs in the same trap now, Nanty; and we'll see how a certain young lady will look then.'

The dog-metaphor is unchanged from the description of Caleb in *The Bride of Lammermoor*: the fundamental difference here is that Nixon himself feels keenly the degradation of feudal servitude. Nixon's treachery thus deepens our response to the main plot with its theme of 'the end of an era'. Scott's emphasis on Charles Edward's physical change from the dashing young man in *Waverley* to the middle-aged figure in *Redgauntlet*, aged by 'either care, or fatigue, or indulgence', has a similar effect: by this means, Scott symbolically suggests a loss of vigour and hope in the Jacobite movement as a whole.[48]

The abortive rebellion is most immediately set, however, against the activities of the other characters at the inn. Robert Gordon has pointed out that the action here takes on the attributes of farce, even down to Darsie's female impersonation.[49] The sheer irrelevance of the Jacobite plot to the inn's inhabitants succeeds in giving the rebellion a damning insubstantiality. Joe Crackenthorp, the inn-keeper, interrupts Redgauntlet's fraught interview with Charles to protest that his rooms are being taken up with 'prisoners' who don't drink: the everyday business of Crackenthorp's mediocre inn thus, farcically, takes priority over the attempt at high political intrigue. The appearance of Joshua Geddes and Peter Peebles only adds to the confusion: the whole scene is reduced implicitly to the comic level of the inn-romp in *Tom Jones*. Of the 'modern' characters, only Darsie even understands what is

happening, and even he comprehends nothing of the Jacobites'
dilemma or of their emotional conflict when faced with their
king's predicament. At the climax of the scene, when the
conspirators are confounded by Charles's dogmatism, yet
deeply concerned for his safety, Darsie seems a virtual
interloper:[50]

> He [Charles] spoke these words with a determined accent,
> and looked around him on the company, all of whom
> (excepting Darsie, who saw, he thought, a fair period to a
> most perilous enterprise) seemed in deep anxiety and
> confusion.

Darsie's separation from the emotional crisis of the Jacobites
here highlights the essential movement of the novel. He starts
off as a romantic young man, apparently disgusted with the
bourgeois rat-race to gain eminence in the law, and leaves
Edinburgh to search for the clue to his alienation in his
unknown past. When he comes to view the living image of the
past in the form of his uncle, however, he is torn between
incredulity and repulsion. As the novel continues therefore,
Darsie gradually retreats into the very common-sense, rational
values of the culture he has begun by condemning. We have
already seen that his role in the dialogues with Redgauntlet
parallels that of Alan in his interview with Charles; by the close
of the novel, there is little to choose between the two young
men. Darsie's initial romanticism comes to appear merely a
by-product, or reaction, to the way of life in modern
Edinburgh – after 'dropping out' for a short while, Darsie sees
sense and returns. Redgauntlet himself, in a moment of
dispassionate insight, accepts this alignment of his nephew as
inevitable, and even desirable. He makes his family adieus
calmly:[51]

> 'Nephew, come hither. In presence of General Campbell,
> I tell you that, though to breed you up in my own political
> opinions has been for many years my anxious wish, I am
> now glad that it could not be accomplished. You pass
> under the services of the reigning monarch without the
> necessity of changing your allegiance – a change, how-
> ever,' he added, looking around him, 'which sits more

easy on honourable men than I could have anticipated, but some wear the badge of their loyalty on the sleeve, and others in the heart.'

Even if Darsie does not have to alter his personal politics, however, he does repudiate the hereditary politics of his family, and there is a sense in which he is compromised by his final acceptance of the world of the Fairfords. Darsie, like Steenie in Wandering Willie's Tale, repudiates the past in order to survive into the future, but it is an unheroic survival.

Redgauntlet's giant stature, on the other hand, sets him apart from the Jacobite temporisers in the novel: apart even from the honourable but muddled character of Sir Richard Glendale. Redgauntlet's efforts, unceasing and untiring, are admitted by Nanty Ewart: in Nanty's opinion, time would have eclipsed the Jacobite cause long before, were it not for the frenetic activity of this one man. Yet, as his hopes fade, Redgauntlet's desperation is evident: scruples and objections are swept aside in the search for recruits, while he resorts increasingly to a form of terrorism – kidnapping, criminal activity, and personal violence – as a large-scale uprising becomes a hopeless prospect. Redgauntlet's gathering of the Jacobite remnant is itself a huge confidence trick, made possible only by his list of fictitious supporters. It is as a last, desperate measure that Redgauntlet conceals the Pretender's presence from his fellow-conspirators until it is too late for them to withdraw and they have committed themselves by making Charles's appearance the only precondition for action. More astonishingly, Charles reveals that he himself had no personal desire to mount another attempted *coup*: he comes to Britain only out of respect to what he believes is his followers' enthusiasm. This too is the work of Redgauntlet. The whole attempted rebellion is thus eventually revealed to have been the work of one man: Redgauntlet's amazing aim has been nothing less than to conjure up a Jacobite counter-revolution single-handedly, opposing himself to the whole tide of history. When he is overwhelmed at last, we are left at least half-admiring his impossible ambition. The last words of the novel are reserved, not for details of the young men's unsurprising survival, but for the death of the astonishing character of the novel's title. Redgauntlet's zeal seems to outlast even Charles's own pride: the petty squabbles of his monarch's degradation in exile cause his most loyal follower to retire to the cloister, harbouring his regrets to the grave. The inscription on his locket, 'Never to be forgotten', which ultimately denies Redgauntlet Catholic sainthood, is a lasting testimony to the tragic rôle of the man who, faithful to a lost world even in seclusion, refuses either to forgive or forget.

It is not possible to claim that this reading of the novel takes into account all the disparate elements of *Redgauntlet*. More than in any other of his novels, the unity of *Redgauntlet* appears to reside ultimately in Scott's own mental associations, and some of these seem bound to remain obscure. At least two 'peripheral' characters must be allowed at least a speculative significance, however.

Peter Peebles's insistent presence certainly calls for some explanation. Previous critics have detected an ironic parallel between Peter and Redgauntlet: Daiches first noted the similarity of their different obsessions.[52] Devlin and Johnson echo Daiches, pointing out that both Peter and Redgauntlet are fighting for lost causes.[53] Supporting evidence that Scott intended such a parallel can be found in Peter's words on first recognising Redgauntlet:[54]

'I mind ye weel, for ye lodged in my house the great year of forty-five, for a great year it was; the Grand Rebellion broke out, and my cause – the great cause – Peebles against Plainstanes, *et per contra* – was called in the beginning of the winter session, and would have been heard, but that there was a surcease of justice, with your plaids, and your piping, and your nonsense.'

It can hardly be a coincidence that Scott makes 1745 a 'great year' for both men. In this passage he seems to be deliberately questioning the 'greatness' of Redgauntlet's cause by equating it with Peter's.

Peebles has another function, however. He represents the 'unacceptable face of capitalism' in late eighteenth-century Edinburgh society. On his first appearance, Scott informs the reader that Peter's face was 'originally that of a portly, comely burgess' – plainly fixing Peter's status – but it also transpires that the infamous case of Peebles v. Plainstanes is a business case, a monument to the former partners' greed and to their fraudulent commercial practices. It is also revealed later that Peebles was the landlord who evicted Nanty's Mrs Cantrips for her paltry arrears of rent; a cruel action that leads directly to the old lady's death in a workhouse and to Nanty's girlfriend's unhappy career on the streets. In these circumstances, the application of 'justice' to Peter's case (which is implied by Alan's advocacy of his cause) seems wildly inappropriate: the law (and so, by implication, the Fairfords) is shown to be a parasite of the property system. The effect of Peebles is thus to satirise not only Redgauntlet, but also the bourgeois lifestyle of the novel's 'survivors.'

Nanty Ewart's story[55] is more difficult to interpret with any certainty. Daiches's judgment is that Nanty 'comes from the sentimental tradition of the late eighteenth century and has no business in the novel at all'.[56] As a minor character, however, his presence has already been justified in terms of his insight into Jacobitism and the motives of its adherents. The incident of his fight with Redgauntlet at the inn is also indirectly significant in that it exposes the essentially anti-authority stance of the riff-raff who are waiting on the rebellion: their cry 'Down with all warrants!' is the implicit rebuttal of Charles's claim: 'I have a warrant for what I do'.[57] Nanty's interpolated history is a more uncertain addition, however. As a short story it is masterly: Nanty's bitter, cynical tone effectively counterbalances the sentimental story, giving it a depth of emotion new to the tradition. The tale's relevance to the social world of the novel seems to be in Nanty's reaction against the Puritanical discipline of the kirk handed down from the previous century. This discipline was already being undermined by the 1690s when, as T. C. Smout notes, it became possible for richer citizens to avoid the kirk-stool of repentance by paying a fine to the kirk. Nanty bitterly laments:[58]

'A gentleman, in my case, would have settled the matter with the kirk-treasurer for a small sum of money; but the poor stibbler, the penniless dominie, having married his cousin of Kittlebasket, must next have proclaimed her frailty to the whole parish, by mounting the throne of Presbyterian penance, and proving, as Othello says, "his love a whore," in face of the whole congregation.'

To a certain extent, Nanty's rejection of Puritan Edinburgh criticises the city's way of life as Peebles' behaviour does, exposing its essential cruelty and hypocrisy. The artistic problem is that Nanty's history is not sufficiently related to the underlying themes of the novel to make its relevance felt. At best, Nanty testifies independently to the enslaving force of the past: like Redgauntlet, his fate has been sealed long ago by events which he is doomed to remember, but cannot undo.

9

Historical authenticity in the Waverley Novels

Scott's Dedicatory Epistle to *Ivanhoe*

Redgauntlet raises again one of the crucial questions facing readers of the Waverley Novels: what constitutes 'realism' in the historical novel? Robert Gordon puts the problem in a nutshell by asking: 'what are we to make of *Redgauntlet* where a rebellion that never occurred is defeated by an imagined act of royal forgiveness?'[1] In what sense can these totally fictitious events be called 'historical' at all?[2] What grounds are there, if any, for Gordon's subsequent critical judgment that the effect of Scott's inventiveness here is actually 'not escapist but realistic in the profoundest sense?' The defence of Scott's audacity made in the previous chapter rested on certain assertions which require substantiation. Similarly, Scott's defensible fabrications have somehow to be separated from effects which, in other novels, damage the credibility of the whole genre.

These theoretical questions pertain to all historical novels. The problem of authenticity arises from the nature of the historical novel itself, and as the founder of the genre Scott naturally wrestled with its problems. However, with the exception of a short, analytical passage at the beginning of *Waverley*, Scott's approach to the question of historical authenticity in the major Scottish novels seems to have been intuitive rather than conscious. The turning point is *Ivanhoe*, written in 1820 and the result, apparently, of Scott's fear that the public was tiring

173

of 'Scottish manners, Scottish dialect, and Scottish characters'.[3]
Certainly, in breaking with the Scottish milieu in *Ivanhoe*,
Scott's imaginative grasp of his material was for the first time
revealed as insecure, and he may have faced the problems posed
by the novel theoretically in the Dedicatory Epistle because he
felt he had been unable to solve them in practice, in the novel
itself. The result is that the Dedicatory Epistle is only
superficially a defence of *Ivanhoe*: Scott's confident style fails to
conceal his own doubts. In a sense, the Dedicatory Epistle
actually draws attention to the faults in *Ivanhoe*, since the
response to the novel of the public at large was enthusiastic:
Scott admitted that 'it would be ungrateful not to acknowledge
that it met with the same favourable reception as its
predecessors'.[4] The Epistle's lasting interest is in the extent to
which Scott identifies the theoretical problems of the historical
novelist. It is therefore worth considering the points he makes
there in some detail, before suggesting tentative answers of our
own to the questions raised.

Scott opens with two possible criticisms of *Ivanhoe* arising
from the novel's setting in twelfth-century England.[5] He first
puts forward the point of view which holds that the secret of the
previous Waverley Novels' success lay in their Scottish author's
unique national standpoint – his familiarity with the periods
and localities of which he was writing: 'All those minute
circumstances belonging to private life and domestic character,
all that gives verisimilitude to a narrative and individuality to the
persons introduced, is still known and remembered in
Scotland.'[6]

There is obviously some truth in this: the great changes which
had taken place in Scotland in the fairly recent past (even 'Sixty
Years Since') and their accessibility to a Scottish author, are
matters which must have contributed to Scott's success in the
Scottish novels. In the fragmentary 'Ashestiel Autobiography'
in Lockhart's *Life*, Scott had seen the shaping influences on
his life as his enforced childhood sojourn in the Scottish
countryside, where he conversed at length with old Jacobites,
together with the lectures on the history of Scottish law which
he received later from Baron David Hume at Edinburgh
University.[7] Scott certainly also modelled some impressive
incidents of the novels both on his own experience of Scottish

manners (as any reading of Lockhart's *Life* shows) and on the traditional Scottish border ballads and folk stories which he had assiduously collected and committed to his prodigious memory.

Yet this argument from the immediacy of authorial experience is itself insufficient to explain the quality of Scott's achievement. A modern exponent of a similar argument, A. O. J. Cockshut, shows the argument's limitation when he argues that Scott's method could only be truly historical 'when he knew enough and felt enough about the period with which he dealt to recreate the past with imaginative insight. He could only do this for times within about a hundred years of his boyhood.'[8] The problem returns as soon as Cockshut tries to narrow down his general statement (which is obviously true) into a specific critical canon. 'A hundred years' strikes us as an arbitrary length of time: it is beyond either Scott's direct experience or that of anyone with whom he may have spoken as a boy (for even the Forty-Five rebels were old men when Scott knew them, and that event was only forty years in the past.) Cockshut does in fact explain that he has chosen the period of one hundred years because this conveniently allows *Old Mortality* to be included – but this is a circular argument. In fact, *Old Mortality* is an obvious instance of Scott reaching beyond his personal experience, through contemporary accounts which he had read of the period, but still writing with brilliant imaginative realism. Moreover, the simple cut-off date of 1679 does not square with Scott's record of success and failure: of the novels set before this date, at least *A Legend of Montrose* and *The Fair Maid of Perth* attain a fair degree of historical realism, while *The Pirate*, set in the early eighteenth century, nevertheless strikes us as inauthentic. This first argument then which Scott levels against *Ivanhoe*, that of the necessity of direct authorial experience, is at best a broad generalisation. It is not a fine enough instrument with which to analyse Scott's varying achievement in the Waverley Novels as a whole.

The second objection to *Ivanhoe's* setting which Scott raises in the Dedicatory Epistle is based on the suspension of disbelief which is necessary to the reading of any novel. Scott gives the argument a satiric turn, however, by suggesting that, as an historical novelist relying on the art of illusion, the Author of *Waverley* did best to exercise his imagination in areas of the reader's greatest ignorance: 'If you describe to him a set of wild manners, and a state of primitive society, existing in the Highlands of Scotland, he is much disposed to acquiesce in the truth of what is asserted.'[9] Scott's rider is that the English reader will be less tolerant of *Ivanhoe* because of his greater acquaintance with the substance of English history. There is, of course, a relationship between the reader's knowledge of history and his credulity in reading an historical novel, but it is not as simple as Scott here suggests (admittedly tongue-in-cheek). James Hillhouse is certainly right to suggest that Scott's medieval novels have lost credibility in the twentieth century partly because greater public knowledge about the period makes Scott's knights in armour less credible.[10] It could also be argued that the vast industry in 'historical romance' today depends more on historical fantasy than fact. A critic in the *Eclectic Review* seems to have been making this point when he went so far as to conclude that *Ivanhoe* was only 'that mongrel sort of production, an historical novel'[11] because the romantic expectations of the readers for 'a work of pure enchanting fiction' were always at odds with those 'general views of society connected with moral and political considerations . . . [which are] the proper interest of history'.[12]

This line of argument loses its force, however, as soon as it is applied specifically to the greatest of Scott's work. As Scott himself had probably realised as early as 1816, with his apology for the weak plot of *The Antiquary*, his gifts were often best exercised in spite of his audience's expectations. Moreover, *The Antiquary* itself satirises the very view of history based on ignorance which Scott purports to hold in the Dedicatory Epistle: Oldbuck's pleasant day-dreams about the past are continually being broken by the unwelcome intrusion of real, unromantic history, typified by Edie Ochiltree, a real human remnant of the past age. In other words, Scott in the Dedicatory Epistle is wrong about the appeal of the Scottish milieu in his own work: in the great novels, his concern is always to illuminate a past period of society, however dimly the reader may at first view it – never to use the primitive darkness of the past as the setting for a romantic fiction in the Keatsian fashion. Joseph Duncan has argued that even in *Ivanhoe*, where the historical setting is very easily dismissed as cardboard scenery,

Scott's *intention* at least is historical rather than romantic.[13] Scott's historical fiction is a more complex affair than he himself suggests here.

Scott continues the Epistle by advancing some theoretical canons for the historical novelist. Now rejecting the argument that the author must have direct experience of his subject, Scott asserts instead that: 'to those deeply read in antiquity, hints concerning the private life of our ancestors lie scattered through the pages of our various historians. . . .'[14] Yet from this undoubted truth, Scott draws a doubtful conclusion, for he goes on to state that even if he had failed in *Ivanhoe*, he is convinced that 'with more labour in collecting, or more skill in using' the available materials, another novelist would have been successful. Here the imaginative reconstruction of the past in the historical novel is too far reduced to a matter of assiduous research. The reviewer of *Ivanhoe* in the *Eclectic Review* was to draw a crucial distinction between antiquarian effort and imaginative grasp, when he wrote of the author:[15]

> He has probably taken greater pains, if not in writing, yet in order to write the present work, than in the case of any of the preceding tales: accordingly, it contains more information of a certain kind, is in parts more highly wrought, and is richer in antiquarian details, than perhaps any other; *but it has less of verisimilitude. . . .*

The effort of Scott's research in writing *Ivanhoe* notably fails to result in increased historical realism: in fact, the lack of realism is made more rather than less noticeable by the surfeit of bookish detail in the descriptive passages. Where later authors followed Scott's advice about assiduous research, the results are not favourable. Francis Hart actually compares *Ivanhoe* favourably with two such nineteenth-century historical novels, Flaubert's *Salammbô* and Bulwer Lytton's *Last Days of Pompeii*, noting that Flaubert's 'massive particularity of material fact' and Lytton's 'archaeological authenticity' both result in a sterile externality which makes *Ivanhoe* look 'determinedly anti-antiquarian' by comparison.[16] Lukács has similarly observed that the same historical novelists who put their efforts into extreme accuracy of material detail are often those who fail most lamentably to create authentically historical human personalities for their characters.[17]

In fact, Scott partly retracts this implication in the next paragraph of the Epistle, and admits that complete, naturalistic reproduction of the past is impossible. Apart from anything else: 'It is necessary, for exciting interest of any kind, that the subject assumed should be, as it were, translated into the manners, as well as the language of the age we live in.'[18] Here Scott raises perhaps the most important question for the historical novelist, that of the relationship between the past, in which the novel's action takes place, and the present from which the novelist takes his standpoint.[19] Once again, however, Scott's theoretical answer to this question in the Dedicatory Epistle is less than satisfactory. In order to justify his presentation of human beings from the twelfth century in *Ivanhoe*, Scott falls back on the eighteenth-century, neo-classical conception of the uniformity of human nature throughout history:[20]

> Our ancestors were not more distinct from us, surely, than Jews are from Christians; they had 'eyes, hands, organs, dimensions, senses, affections, passions;' were 'fed with the same food, hurt with the same weapons, subject to the same diseases, warmed and cooled by the same winter and summer,' as ourselves.

Despite the elegance of this argument from Shakespeare, Scott's words really do no more than echo Fielding's famous pronouncement in *Joseph Andrews* that his Lawyer 'is not only alive, but hath been so these four thousand years' – an essentially non-historical view of human nature that was also the Augustan orthodoxy.[21] D. D. Devlin, who notes that Scott used the same argument in the first chapter of *Waverley*, also points out Scott's hesitancy about the point, however, and suggests that 'Scott's understanding of history was possible only when he began to qualify . . . the Enlightenment view that human nature was unchangeable.'[22]

We have seen that in *The Antiquary* Scott questions the very possibility of men of the present understanding the past in any way but the superficial, antiquarian manner which Oldbuck and Wardour adopt. Oldbuck's soliloquy, already noted, in which he looks back on his youth in astonishment, asking 'can we be ourselves called the same? or do we not rather look back with a sort of wonder upon our former selves, as beings separate and distinct from what we now are?'[23] implicitly expresses Scott's real dissatisfaction with the neo-classical view of a fixed human nature, for in the same way that Oldbuck looks back 'in cold unfeeling old age' on his 'wayward infancy and impetuous youth', his 'anxious and scheming manhood', so the modern age looks back on past ages.[24] The Scottish Waverley Novels are devoted precisely to the differences between human manners in different ages, to the change in human life which accompanied social change in Scotland.

If Scott's break with the Enlightenment is clear, so too nowadays are the Scottish intellectual origins of that break: Duncan Forbes, Peter Garside and Avrom Fleishman have extensively explored Scott's connection with the 'philosophical' historians of the tradition emanating from Adam Smith, so that the links between the view of history inherent in the Waverley Novels and that of the earlier 'philosophical' school is now well established.[25] The essential qualities of 'philosophical' history, as summed up by Garside, are: a belief in the inevitability of progress (particularly economic progress); an emphasis on the effect of the social environment on 'manners'; and an awareness of the power struggle between men born into different social classes.[26] Leaving the influence on Scott of the 'philosophical' historians in its largest sense aside for the final chapter, we can note here that Scott's rejection of the neo-classical formulation of human nature followed a respectable Scottish intellectual tradition of the late eighteenth century, and that the Dedicatory Epistle is therefore as misleading as Devlin claims.

Of course, modern critics of Scott have not themselves always broken with the Enlightenment view. Hart, for example, only slightly adapts the neo-classical account of human nature to take account of Scott's 'historicity'. According to him, Scott's work[27]

embodies crisis and transformation in timeless personal relationships so that, while dramatised in their own political cultural terms, they are imaginatively grounded in familiar, natural problems of individual human experience.

Yet how far is even this true of the Waverley Novels? We have seen in *The Bride of Lammermoor*, for example, that the relationship between Edgar Ravenswood and Lucy Ashton is conditioned from the very beginning by the lovers' different backgrounds: they are separated by a deep social and cultural gulf which they cannot close by any effort of their individual wills. Because of the uniqueness of the historical situation which permeates their relationship, it seems misleading to call it 'timeless'. Hart also seems to suggest that Scott's method is essentially dual; that he first conceives of the personal relationships and then dramatises them in historical terms, or at least that the two stages in composition are distinct. This underestimates the unity of Scott's approach to history, particularly the extent to which his characters appear the product of their period. Notably, the novels are never successful in one of Hart's terms and unsuccessful in the other: *Ivanhoe*, for example, fails to dramatise the Middle Ages in realistic 'political-cultural terms', but this failure goes hand-in-hand with Scott's failure to invest the novel's protagonists with any convincing personal significance.

Scott's last pronouncement in the Dedicatory Epistle concerns the danger of anachronism in the historical novel. Scott says of the historical novelist:[28]

> However far he may venture in a more full detail of passions and feelings than is to be found in the ancient compositions which he imitates, he must introduce nothing inconsistent with the manners of the age.

It is interesting that Scott notably does not adopt the criterion of strict veracity to fact laid down by some contemporary critics of the novels. The reviewer of *Quentin Durward* in the *New Monthly Magazine*, for example, put forward much stricter precepts:[29]

> The author of an historical novel may omit facts, or add to them inventions which are in keeping with what is known. But he is not at liberty to distort the truth by a transfer of events and personages.

Scott consistently refused to accept such a straitjacket in his fiction. It is certainly arguable that historical realism depends on an imaginative recreation of the period, rather than on a mere extrapolation from historical fact, just as novelistic realism in general differs from documentary. As the critic of the *Eclectic Review* saw it, the historical novelist[30]

> aims to produce the conviction in his readers . . . that the events recorded not merely took place, but took place under such and such minutely defined peculiarities of scene and circumstance.

This aim of producing conviction in the reader will not necessarily be served by reproducing every detail of historical circumstance – indeed, this is unlikely to produce any impression except one of antiquarian pedantry. Scott's own guidelines were that nothing in the historical novel should be inconsistent with the 'manners' of the period portrayed: the 'manners' of the age become, by implication, the most important subject for the historical novelist. It is to a consideration of the importance of 'manners' in the Waverley Novels that we must therefore turn.

'Manners' and historical authenticity

A good starting point from which to approach the problem of historical authenticity, is Scott's concluding point in the Dedicatory Epistle on the permissibility or impermissibility of violating history in the historical novel. There appear to be two types of verisimilitude at which the historical novelist can aim. First, there is factual verisimilitude, a strict veracity to the extent that the historian can ascertain exact facts about the period concerned. This is the canon laid down by the *New Monthly Magazine's* critic. On the other hand, there is a deeper verisimilitude, an imaginative encapsulation of the essence of the period, which Scott's concern with 'manners' epitomises. The two types of verisimilitude are undoubtedly related, but their relationship is, for the historical novelist, an imaginative problem rather than a mechanical or derivative correspondence. Violations of history through anachronism will thus be of two kinds, and both kinds are, in fact, found in the Waverley Novels. Two examples already noted in *Old Mortality* will, however, suffice to show the distinction.

Historical authenticity in the Waverley Novels

In the first type of anachronism, Scott sacrifices strict, factual verisimilitude in the service of a deeper verisimilitude of 'manners'. General Dalzell's presence at the battle of Bothwell Bridge in *Old Mortality*, contrary to historical fact, is this sort of violation. Having read the novel, there is a sense in which the reader feels that even if Dalzell were not present at the scene in reality, he 'should' have been; and this is because, in Scott's hands, Dalzell becomes an open symbol of Royalist authority. Scott's description of Dalzell is, as I have noted in my chapter on that novel, eloquent of precisely those qualities of the Stuart regime in 1679 that Scott is at pains to convey in the novel as a whole. Through Dalzell, Scott shows the character and mentality of the class who held the reins of government under Charles II; and this, the reader feels, is more important than a strict adherence to the actual roll-call on the occasion.[31]

The second kind of violation of history is also represented in *Old Mortality*: the misrepresentation by Scott of the conditions in the Lowlands after the 1688 Revolution, noted in my chapter on the novel. The representation of 'King William's Ill Years' as a time of plenty in which Cuddie and Jenny Headrigg live an idyllic existence is obviously a travesty of factual verisimilitude, although, like Dalzell's transposition to Bothwell Bridge, a travesty which only very few readers would be sufficiently knowledgeable to notice. The essential difference is that the deeper truth to the period at which Scott habitually aims is also undermined by this fabrication. Scott distorts the facts here with the dubious purpose of vindicating the Glorious Revolution as a triumph of moderation, and this, as I have argued in my critique of the novel, is all too obviously an imposition on the reader, an idealist reading of history which is belied by the realistic drama of the novel which precedes it. In this drama, Henry Morton's moderate Presbyterianism in religion, his liberalism in politics, and his general abhorrence of fanaticism are portrayed sympathetically by Scott, but at the same time are shown to be quite incapable of resolving the conflicts of the period. In showing Morton defeated, Scott remained faithful to his representation of the underlying forces in the situation: Morton's failure is less his own than that of the small middle class whose ideology he propounds, and to which his supporters belong. When Scott misrepresents the agri-

182

cultural situation after 1688, he is attempting to persuade the reader that Morton is eventually victorious after all – the far-fetched events of Morton's return from exile have the same aim. Thus, in his enthusiasm for the Revolution, Scott rather crudely contradicts the whole movement of the novel: in particular, he confuses a mainly English event with the action which has previously been confined tightly to Scotland. The violation of history here therefore serves no greater historical verisimilitude; in fact, it only weakens the novel as a whole by undermining the clear, coherent, and illuminating drama of the bulk of the novel.

Of what, then, can this deeper verisimilitude of 'manners' be said to consist? Alexander Welsh comments at one point in his study of Scott: 'The reality celebrated by the Waverley Novels is an abstraction, a projected reality. This reality consists not of things but of relations.'[32] In the preceding chapters I have suggested that the essential relations in the Waverley Novels are relations between classes. It is clear from the work of Forbes and Garside that this is quite consistent with Scott's intellectual context, and the tradition of the 'philosophical' historians. Men like Smith, Ferguson and Millar had already divided the general history of mankind into distinct social stages, progressing from 'savage' and 'rude' through 'feudal' to modern, 'commercial' society; the achievement of the Waverley Novels was brilliantly to map out the human implications of these changes with reference to Scotland's own turbulent history. If Scott's 'manners' therefore are to be understood in the way in which the 'philosophical' historians would have understood the term, the implication of class distinctions and opposed, historical, class organisations of society is already there. The idea of inexorable progress from a more primitive to a more advanced organisation of society, which we have also noted to be a theme of many of the Scottish novels, was also implicit in the Smithian tradition.

Limits to historical authenticity

One advantage of understanding Scott's historical realism in terms of class-relations and historicism is that the problem of a 'time-limit' to Scott's work (in the sense of a limit to the distance Scott was able to penetrate imaginatively into the past) is clarified. The limit is not quantitative (for example, Cockshut's hundred years) but qualitative: Scott's failures occur when he treats historical situations in which the class-relationships familiar to his imagination had not come into being, and to which he could not, therefore, apply himself with any confidence of success.

Broadly speaking, Scott's historical imagination seems to have been limited to the states of society in which the clan (the Scottish patriarchal system), the feudal aristocracy, and the commercial classes held sway, with all the complexities of the interface between these three great social systems in Scottish history. In particular, Scott is at home with the unified Royalist-feudal system which operated in Scotland under the Stuarts from James VI (as recognised by Robertson among the 'philosophical' historians),[33] and with situations in which conflicting classes in Scotland came into contact with each other, as part of the inevitable economic progress of society from its more primitive to its more advanced state. Undoubtedly, this consuming interest of Scott's was based on his own experience both direct and indirect and included not only his wealth of historical knowledge, but also his conversations with old Jacobites as a boy, his understanding of former 'manners' gained from his collection of Border ballads, and his practice in the Scottish law. David Daiches has gone further, relating Scott's interests to his own family's contradictory class position – suggesting that Scott's personal and psychological stance stemmed ultimately from his mixed aristocratic and bourgeois ancestry.[34] All this coalesced imaginatively to inform Scott's portraits of the opposed Scottish classes back to the earliest conflicts between the clans and their historic an- tagonists.

The great problem with *Ivanhoe* is that Scott is dealing with a society to which this intuitive grasp could hardly be applied. It is true, of course, that as Joseph Duncan says, Scott intended to tackle in *Ivanhoe* a serious, historical theme, the relations between Norman and Saxon and their eventual fusion into the English race.[35] Yet Scott's Introduction to the 1830 edition of the novel, while proving Duncan correct, shows that the author conceived of the Norman/Saxon relationship only in the broadest of generalisations:[36]

> It seemed to the Author that the existence of the two races in the same country, the vanquished distinguished by their plain, homely, blunt manners, and the free spirit infused by their ancient institutions and laws; the victors, by the high spirit of military fame, personal adventure, and whatever could distinguish them as the flower of chivalry, might, intermixed with other characters belonging to the same time and country, interest the reader by the contrast . . .

The vague, romantic description of the two races here bodes ill for any historical understanding at a more realistic level. The focus in time in *Ivanhoe* becomes vague, as Scott admitted in the Dedicatory Epistle when he confessed that 'it is extremely probable that I may have confused the manners of two or three centuries'.[37] One reason for the vagueness of *Ivanhoe* is that Scott was unable to visualise the supposed Norman/Saxon conflict in the concrete social terms familiar to him – simply because the later forms of social opposition did not exist between the two races. Lukács's claim in defence of *Ivanhoe*, that the opposition is 'above all one between Saxon serfs and Norman feudal lords' is wide of the mark, as even a cursory reading of the novel will show.[38] Scott was not capable of falsifying the existing evidence to that extent.

The opening chapter of *Ivanhoe* shows the problem with which Scott was faced. After a short introduction, in which he elaborates his thesis of the hostility of the two races after the Conquest, Scott shows us two Saxon serfs, Gurth and Wamba. Scott's instinctive feel for social class leads him to draw special attention to Gurth's status – by describing the engraved ring fastened irremovably around his neck to proclaim his servitude. It turns out that Gurth is the thrall, however, not of a Norman master, but of Cedric, the elderly Saxon protagonist of the novel. Thus it strikes us as somewhat incongruous to hear Gurth and Wamba complaining about the Normans renaming their animals with the names of the dressed meat, because we realise that the actual sheep they are tending are to be slaughtered for their Saxon master's table. The whole 'nationalistic' conflict comes to feel superfluous, particularly later when Gurth and Wamba's social status is forgotten and they become just part of the cast of 'Saxons' like Cedric. The basis of the novel in social realism, in other words, has to be abandoned. It comes as no surprise to find that Scott's whole Norman/Saxon theory was historically wrong-headed. G. M. Young goes as far as to say: 'I am not sure that Scott did not give a lasting distortion to our conception of medieval history, by his fancy that Norman and Saxon persisted as consciously hostile races.' *Ivanhoe* is therefore a good example of Scott losing his grasp on a situation which, socially, he does not understand, and inventing a non-realistic quasi-social struggle in order to give his composition the accustomed animation and interest.

Ivanhoe is not, however, representative of all Scott's work apart from the great novels of the Scottish series which have already been discussed in some depth. There are a large number of novels comprising Scott's 'second rank'; novels that fall between *Ivanhoe* and his greatest work by being partly interesting and convincing, partly trivial and unrealistic. Three examples, *The Pirate, Peveril of the Peak*, and *The Fair Maid of Perth*, may suffice to show some of the ways these lesser novels succeed and fail.

The Pirate (1822) has already been noted as an exception to Cockshut's general proposition that Scott's grasp of events in eighteenth-century Scotland was quite secure. The novel is set in the Shetland Isles – not a part of Scotland Scott knew well, but the problem is not merely geographical. The real trouble is that Scott shows that he does not wholly understand the peculiarities of Shetland society; as Hart says, the manners of the Islanders in the novel were 'as remote and unparticularised for Scott as the manners of twelfth-century England'.[40] This is not to say that Scott does not score some minor triumphs. The satire directed at the inept improver Triptolemus Yellowley and his attempts to 'reform' Shetland agricultural practices is keen enough: Yellowley's ideas, which spring partly from his Lowland upbringing, partly from his personal prejudices, take no account of the relatively primitive social system in the Isles, and the Islanders consistently refuse to be forced into a mainland mould. Similarly, Scott makes the Shetlanders' confused mixture of Norse superstition, Christianity and economic interest (well illustrated in their scruples about saving a drowning man) an interesting subject, and one that does seem to arise genuinely from their historical situation. Yet Scott fails to enter upon even this issue with any real confidence, and his observations on the Islanders' manners remain in the realm of antiquarian curiosity, rather than becoming part of an integrated historical drama. Reading the novel, we continually feel that the plot is merely an excuse for Scott to embark on antiquarian comment: whole descriptive passages seem to be related to the action rather as his Notes to the greater novels usually are – providing incidental, rather than necessary comment. The character of Norna of the Fitful Head only adds to Scott's problems: she is all too fantastic a conception to add anything to the theme of the conflict between superstition and rationalism, as she is doubtless supposed to do. The other characters' attitudes towards her, even Mordaunt's, are less culturally ambiguous than confused, and by the time the cast has followed Norna back to her precipitous Gothic castle, guarded by a dwarf, we feel that we are dealing neither with a realistic character nor a credible situation.[41] With only a limited understanding of the period and setting concerned, Scott instinctively falls back on Gothic horrors, spurious romance, and antiquarian curiosities to sustain the novel for its four hundred pages.

Though also a failure on balance, *Peveril of the Peak*, published in the same year as *The Pirate*, shows touches of the master hand. The opening scenes, which depict a local confrontation between Cavaliers and Puritans at the time of the Restoration, are remarkable for showing Scott's historical imagination working well even in the foreign territory of the English Midlands. The descriptive contrast between the ruined castle of the old Royalist, Sir Geoffrey Peveril, and the newly built hall erected by Major Bridgenorth, a Puritan socially advanced by the period of the Civil War and the Protectorate, is full of symbolic overtones, and serves to introduce the two families who form the centre of the novel. The scene of the 'celebration' of the Restoration at Peveril Castle is vintage Scott: the attempted conciliation inevitably breaks down when the two sides' different feelings about the event, and their differing ideas of 'celebration', come into close contact. The potential of the novel is lost, however, when Scott transfers his young hero. Julian Peveril, first to a sketchily-realised Isle of Man and then to London where he becomes unwittingly and almost unintelligibly involved in the Popish Plot suspicion. Scott's account of the Plot is of a different order from the historical delineation of society in microcosm adopted in the opening chapters: Scott can only show the Plot as a fraudulent, hysterical outburst, with no real social cause.[42] Similarly, because the court circle is portrayed as merely frivolous, the actions of its personages seem trivial and incomprehensible – the Duke of Buckingham even admits that his intrigues are motiveless! By this point the hero's wanderings have also been virtually aimless, and even his eventual marriage to Bridgenorth's daughter seems barren of social relevance by the time we finally reach it.

The Fair Maid of Perth (1828) on the other hand, is a consistently interesting novel. Set in fourteenth-century Scotland, it is perhaps Scott's most audacious attempt to comprehend the medieval past in terms of the class dialectics of the more modern novels. *The Fair Maid* shows the precarious independence attained by the Perth merchants and craftsmen of the day, in opposition both to the power of the predatory Scottish feudal nobility and to the way of life of the clans, who still rule supreme beyond the Highland line.

In many ways *The Fair Maid* is on a level with the best of Scott. The portrait of the Perth burghers is convincing: whether in their hatred of the liberties taken by the aristocracy, epitomised by Ramorny's attempted rape of Catherine Glover; their fear of aristocratic power – subtly conveyed in their choice of a sympathetic nobleman, Sir Patrick Charteris, to act as their spokesman; or in their utter contempt for the Highlanders' uncouth speech and savage manners, in the scenes prior to the Battle of the Inch. The clans themselves are seldom more vividly portrayed by Scott than in this novel: the heartbreak of the old clansman, Torquil, when he comes to believe that his young chief's infatuation with a merchant's daughter has made him a coward; the clan's fanatical loyalty to their chief, notwithstanding, at the staged battle with their rival clan in Perth; but also their inability to see that the battle itself (which they view only as clan feud) is in fact a means chosen by the Scottish King to weaken and subdue the Highlands by encouraging the clans to decimate each other. The attitude of the Perth citizens to the clans is brilliantly characterised by Henry Wynd's last minute participation in the battle in place of a missing clansman – a true historical event which assumes, through Scott's treatment, a social realism and significance. The smith, fighting for his own reasons, is utterly indifferent to the rival clans' quarrel (except inasmuch as his personal rivalry with Conachar for Catherine's affection disposes him against the young chief) and treats the whole affair like an apprentices' brawl. Conachar's suicide in disgrace after abandoning his clan on the field contrasts strongly with the citizens' amused toleration of the same weakness in their own Oliver Prudefute.

All this sets *The Fair Maid* apart as a remarkable novel, comparable to some extent with the best of the Scottish Waverley Novels. The limitation of Scott's technique in the novel is also evident, however. In particular, Scott audaciously 'backdates' the class conflicts with which he is familiar to an extent which, though mainly successful, occasionally fails to convince. For example, he attempts to comprehend the Lollards' religious beliefs (in the person of Father Clement) in terms which more properly apply to later Scottish Protestantism. Simon Glover says of the monk, who is accused of heresy:[43]

> I defy foul fame to show that I ever owned him in any heretical proposition, though I loved to hear him talk of the corruptions of the church, the misgovernment of the nobles, and the wild ignorance of the poor, proving, as it seemed to me, that the sole virtue of our commonweal, its strength and its estimation, lay among the burgher craft of the better class, which I received as comfortable doctrine, and creditable to the town.

This is attractive as an interpretation of how Glover would take Clement's teaching, but more is needed to convince us that it is historically authentic, rather than a bold anachronism. Similarly, Scott's treatment of the king, Robert III, is not convincing because too much emphasis is placed on the king's personal weakness in order to explain his political powerlessness. Here, the explanation seems to lie in Scott's attempt to portray the medieval monarch's situation in the more familiar terms of

Stuart monarchism in the seventeenth century: he is not at home with the different political situation in the Middle Ages, during which the Scottish king was often the pawn of the feudal nobility. Thus, perhaps unconsciously, Scott explains Robert's weakness in personal terms rather than in the broader social context of his reign, with the result that the king's actions seem too idiosyncratic. On the whole, however, apart from these weaknesses (and a certain thinning of realism in the dialogue, where Scott necessarily abandons any attempt to reproduce the medieval Scots dialect), *The Fair Maid of Perth* is a success, though one which marks a limit to the power of Scott's historical imagination.

Characterisation in the Waverley Novels

The link between Scott and the 'philosophical' historians also helps to explain how the riddle of human nature in the historical novel, the contradictory 'likeness and unlikeness' between men and women of different periods, is in practice resolved in the Waverley Novels. The 'likeness' is not the absolute neo-classical uniformity of human nature; it is the relative uniformity of 'manners' in any stage of society, or in other words, of a class outlook throughout history. The clan ethic, for example, motivates characters in the novels who share the same 'patriarchal' social and economic 'state' in spite of their separation by time. The 'unlikeness' is most sharply focused in conflicts between opposed classes, but the wealth and variety of the Waverley Novels also comes about because, as Lukács suggests, Scott shows that the relative power of the classes was constantly undergoing change, and that this change had its effect on the politics, religion, and personal characters even of men sharing the same, basic, class outlook.[44]

Lukács was careful to qualify his view of Scott's characters in terms of historical 'types':[45]

> However, this manner of composition certainly does not mean that Scott's historical figures are not individualised down to their smallest human peculiarities. They are never mere representatives of historical movements, ideas, etc.

F. Jameson, writing in defence of Lukács, says of his theory of 'types':[46]

> Of course this . . . has been mishandled in the vulgar Marxist practice of reducing characters to mere allegories of social forces, of turning 'typical' characters into mere symbols of class, such as the petit bourgeois, the counterrevolutionary, the landed nobleman, the Utopian socialist intellectual, and so forth. Sartre has pointed out that such categories are themselves idealistic, in that they presuppose immutable forms, eternal Platonic ideas, of the various social classes: what they leave out is precisely history itself, and the notion of the unique historical situation.

Scott himself never allows his reader to do this. On the one hand Bailie Nicol Jarvie (for example) shows an indisputable similarity of attitude in many ways with men as distant from him in time as Simon Glover in *The Fair Maid of Perth* and Jonathan Oldbuck in *The Antiquary*: all of them share, for example, a contempt for the aristocracy of the day, and a belief in the superiority of a life gained by individual industry. Yet Scott is aware of the greatly changed complexion of the social situation between the three periods concerned, and this is reflected in the three men's differing personalities. Jarvie's self-confidence, the self-satisfaction of a successful merchant in the booming town of Glasgow, would be totally out of place in the narrow, defensive society of the Perth burghers around 1400. On the other hand, Jarvie's energy and zeal for his own way of life, so evident in his arguments with Rob, could hardly be further from Oldbuck's apathy, a result of his inherited wealth, or from Oldbuck's highly theoretical arguments with Sir Arthur Wardour – arguments which vent themselves in the field of antiquarianism because the lifestyles of the two friends have become otherwise barely distinguishable.

Scott's characterisation is intimately bound up with his historical vision. Tillyard has written:[47]

> I say nothing of Jeanie Deans as a character in fiction and take it for granted that she is a very great character indeed set in a successfully supporting context. It is only because

she is such a character that any political and national significance she can have is more than nominal.

It could equally be argued, however, that Jeanie's greatness as a character is due to the force with which she exemplifies the typical character traits of a Lowland Scots peasant girl of the early eighteenth century. It is to this interaction that Daiches refers when he says of Scott: 'it was his tendency to look at history through character and at character through the history that had worked on it that provided the foundation of his art.'[48]

The failure of characters in the Waverley Novels is often connected with a failure of historical realism in the novel as a whole. Thus, Cockshut has pointed out that although the feudal relationship between Louis XI and Duke Charles in *Quentin Durward* is seriously conceived, what is lacking is the author's grasp of the historical situation in which his protagonists live: 'The deep insight required into the mind of the Duke, and into the nature of the changing society, is lacking'.[49] Similar effects are noticeable in a short story, like the much-praised *The Two Drovers*. The period in which this tale is set is not strongly particularised – the action could take place at any date in the first half of the eighteenth century – and, correspondingly, the principal personages of the story, a Highlander and an Englishman, are not strongly individualised. Scott is concerned only to establish that a cultural gulf separates them in a very general sense. The story has as its point a question of the relativity of justice in different cultures, but Scott does not subsume this question into a larger historical struggle in society at a particular date, as he does in *Waverley*, with the trial of Evan Dhu, or in *Rob Roy*, with the murder of Morris. The result is that, while *The Two Drovers* is a good short story, and makes a simple point well, the massive historical imagination that we find in the great novels is absent.[50]

The speech used by the characters in the Waverley Novels is one highly concrete way of simultaneously individualising a character and identifying him with his social origins. According to Virginia Woolf, Scott[51]

> showed up the languor of the fine gentlemen who bored him by the immense vivacity of the common people whom he loved . . . always the dialogue [of the 'common

people'] is sharpened and pointed by the use of that Scottish dialect which is at once so homely and so pungent . . .

The contrast of racy Scots with the refined language of the upper classes is certainly notable in the Scottish novels, though we may question whether the effect is quite so one-sided. What the contrast does do is reinforce the social distinctions between the characters involved. Waverley's conversation with Jinker (already noted) is a fine example of the contrast between Scots and English being put to good use: the hero's naïve directness of speech is returned by Jinker's canny, dialectal irony. Sometimes, speech seems specifically to reinforce class distinctions: in *Old Mortality* I have noted that Morton's measured tones fail to appeal to the predominantly peasant extremist Covenanters. Scott's achievement in the best of his novels is to make his characters' dialect both comprehensible and apparently authentic. The farther back in time he went the more difficult this obviously became: the mock-medieval 'tushery' of *Ivanhoe* fails because it is studiedly antiquarian, but also, linking back with the main authenticity argument, because Scott had only a hazy idea of how men and women of that age thought. Cockshut has rightly called the language of *Ivanhoe* 'an amalgam of different kinds of unreality'.[52]

I have noted in my chapter on *Waverley* that there is a marked difference of style between the early chapters written in 1805, in which Scott adopts a generalised narrative style, and the more mature work in the novel written in 1814, in which the characters suddenly 'come alive' as dramatic entities.[53] One of the most notable features of the later, inferior Waverley Novels is Scott's tendency again to retreat into unparticularised narrative. A novel like *Quentin Durward*, for example, impresses on the reader its lack of vitality and drama; at points it turns completely into a descriptive general history of the period. The effect is that the hero, Quentin, lacks reality because he never expresses himself: possibly Scott had no idea what he had created Quentin to express. Once again, therefore, we find an integral relationship between characterisation and historical realism: Scott's dramatic style necessarily requires a deep understanding of the period in order that character and incident can become historically significant, rather than aimless or anachronistic.

Such examples seem to underline the fact that character-isation was for Scott the most important expression of his historical imagination. Despite his interest in many of the issues which had concerned the 'philosophical' historians, Scott differs from them fundamentally, in that his approach is the opposite of abstract. The basis of his art is in portraying the concrete circumstances of historical situations as they affected real men and women of the time. Scott would certainly have agreed with Marx's dictum that 'the first premise of all human history is, of course, the existence of living human individuals': Scott's achievement is to have been the first to invest human history with a novelistic authenticity.

10

Scott's outlook on history

Scott's 'historicism'

Georg Lukács's essay on Scott in *The Historical Novel* seems likely to remain the classic revaluation of the Waverley Novels – partly because of the sheer size of the claim Lukács makes for Scott. Lukács's concern is not just to rehabilitate Scott as a nineteenth-century novelist alongside the major figures for whom Leavis was to reserve exclusive praise in *The Great Tradition*. Lukács's criticism aims at nothing less than the construction of an alternative 'Great Tradition' with Scott at its head, seeing in the Waverley Novels the first creative literary expression of the modern, 'historical' consciousness. He is at pains to separate Scott's achievement from the efforts of the writers before him who used history merely as a backcloth for their fiction:[1]

> What is lacking in the so-called historical novel before Sir Walter Scott is precisely the specifically historical, that is, derivation of the individuality of character from the historical peculiarity of their age.

Yet according to Lukács, this inferiority is also noticable in the literary criticism of the eighteenth century, and in the eighteenth-century novel in general:[2]

> even the great realistic social novel of the eighteenth

century, which in its portrayal of contemporary morals and psychology, accomplished a revolutionary breakthrough to reality for world literature is not concerned to show its characters as belonging to any concrete time.

According to Lukács, the society portrayed in novels before *Waverley*, even in 'historical' novels, was 'accepted naïvely as something given': characters in such novels are not depicted as belonging to a particular point in history. Scott's great achievement, then, was to break with this ahistorical eighteenth-century novelistic tradition. Later critics of Scott have been indebted to this basic idea. Karl Kroeber, for example, says of Scott:[3]

> he made it possible to describe any society in its temporal dimensions. Before Scott the novel had been restricted to portraying social organisation as static, as seen only in its contemporary aspect . . . Scott presents society as the product of past experiences and traditions which are in the process of becoming different.

In the forty years which have elapsed since *The Historical Novel* was written, however, Scott's achievement has come to seem a good deal more comprehensible in terms of his era, though no less remarkable. In particular, as has been noted in the previous chapter, Scott's indebtedness to the late eighteenth-century Scottish 'philosophical' historians has come to be properly recognised. According to Duncan Forbes, indeed, Scott in the Waverley Novels 'practised what the Scottish philosophers preached'.[4] Lukács had, in fact, partially anticipated such discoveries, while at the same time warning his reader against any future attempt to explain Scott's achievement in 'idealist' terms, by way of influences:[5]

> [in this way] we should find shrewd hypotheses to show the devious routes by which Hegelian ideas, for example, found their way to Scott; and some forgotten writer would be discovered who contained the common source of Scott's and Hegel's historicism.

Nevertheless, the intellectual links between the Scottish 'philosophical' historians, Scott, and Marx (who, rather than

Hegel, provides the best example of the new 'spirit of historicism') are now pretty well established. Scott's own 'Ashestiel Autobiography' in Lockhart's *Life* tells us that his education at Edinburgh University took place under latter-day adherents to the school of 'philosophical' history such as Dugald Stewart and Baron David Hume, and that the lectures of the second of these on the history of Scottish law made a great impression on him.[6] Scott's interest in the school is also shown when he laments that, on leaving the High School, 'the philosophy of history, a much more important subject [than the 'technicalities of history'] 'was . . . a sealed book at this period of my life.'[7] The influence on Marx of the *economic* writings of Adam Smith (though not, of course, of Smith's unpublished lecture notes on 'philosophical' history, which were unknown to Marx) and of the other Scottish economists has long been well known, on the other hand. When one also considers that Marx was an enthusiastic admirer of Scott (according to his daughter Eleanor[8]), some sort of intellectual influence seems clearly indicated.

Lukác's objection to this kind of scholarship supposedly stems from his 'materialist' perspective: it is, according to him, wrong to separate the rise of the historical novel from changes in society taking place in the late eighteenth century – most notably the French Revolution. Yet the specifics of Lukács's argument here are extremely speculative, verging on the far-fetched: according to his thesis, the revolutionary and Napoleonic wars changed history into a *'mass experience'*, by foisting recruitment (and thus involvement) on the people through conscription.[9] Peter Garside points to just one of the weak links in Lukács's argument when he comments that 'why Scott, an Edinburgh conservative, educated and developing his main interests in the eighteenth century, should be the first receptacle of these ideas' is never really explained.[10]

It is however arguable that the *non-sequiturs* of Lukács's thesis arise not from his 'materialist' premises so much as from his development of them in the argument. In particular, Lukács is side-tracked by his overemphasis on the importance of the French Revolution in the development of the historical novel. He does, for example, come close to admitting the importance of the work of the eighteenth-century Scottish historians in the rise of the new, 'historical' consciousness when he notes that Adam Smith and James Steuart, in their economic writings, posed 'the problem of capitalist economy far more historically' and investigated 'the process by which capital came into being'.[11] Yet, curiously, these names are raised by Lukács only as examples of 'the ideological preparation for the French Revolution': the writers' more extensive effect on the culture of their own country is missed. It is only after 1789 that Lukács sees the main advances towards historicism being made, with Condorcet's conception of 'periods' of history.[12] In fact, similar work had been done earlier in Scotland by the 'philosophical' historians: as Franco Venturi says, 'Ferguson and Millar are of the same world as Filangieri and Condorcet'.[13] The earliest attempt to divide the history of human society into periods or 'stages' was made by Adam Smith in his lectures at Edinburgh during the 1750s and 1760s. It was already Smith's idea, by this time, that both 'manners' and political systems were linked— both being the product of the 'stage' which society had reached at a particular time, and 'suitable' specifically for that period and no other.[14] Adam Ferguson, in *An Essay on the History of Civil Society* (1767) made the school more sophisticated and systematic, though sticking largely to Smith's categories of historical society ('hunting', 'pasturage', 'agricultural' and 'commercial'); while John Millar, in the *Origin of Ranks* (1771) with the emphasis on classes quite evident in his title, took the remaining step of basing these historical 'stages' firmly on the successive forms of social and economic organisation: 'tribalism', 'feudalism' and 'manufacture'.[15] Thus, eighteen years *before* the French Revolution, the move towards historicism in Scotland was well under way.

With the French Revolution 'out of the way', it is tempting to seek a cause for the rise both of 'philosophical' history and of the historical novel in the peculiar circumstances of Scottish society in the eighteenth century. By far the most notable event in a not uneventful century was the Jacobite rebellion in 1745, which affected both Lowland Scotland and England with profound cultural shock only a few years before Smith began his lectures at Edinburgh University. In the Forty-Five, the modern army of 'civilised' Britain was, for a time, routed by the massed forces of the 'primitive' Highland clans. The respectable citizens of Edinburgh had their houses occupied by Highlanders whose 'manners' appeared by contrast utterly savage and uncouth. It is not impossible that it was an awareness of this contrast, forced so irresistibly and unwelcomely on 'civilised' Edinburgh, together with the issue of the rebellion, that stimulated Smith's ideas about the historical process: it is certainly significant that Scott should have chosen the Forty-Five as the natural subject of his first historical novel, *Waverley*. Lukács is surely right in the end to suggest that the rise of the historical novel cannot be explained in 'idealist' terms of intellectual influences unconnected with social change: but it was the social changes in Scotland, culminating in the Forty-Five, that would have vitally affected the Scottish 'philosophical' historians and later Scott himself.

The influence of the tradition of 'philosophical' history on the Scotland of the late eighteenth and early nineteenth centuries is evident, according to Garside, in three main areas: first, in the view of 'social history', the idea that society has historically developed – particularly through distinct 'stages', each of which has had corresponding effects on matters as disparate as men's 'manners' and their political institutions; second, in a feeling for 'determinism', the idea of inexorable progress being made through the often unconscious or 'blind' actions of the people; and third (at least after Ferguson), in a feeling for 'relativism', the attempt to evaluate historical societies without debasing them through hindsight – often in the form of an appreciation of the heroic virtues of earlier societies now lost.[16] It remains to discuss how far Scott's outlook on history conforms to these themes which Scott may have inherited from the 'philosophical' historians.

The idea of 'social history' certainly finds expression in the Waverley Novels. Scott refers unselfconsciously to 'feudal' and 'commercial' societies in numerous prose works, including the famous letter written to Lord Dalkeith in 1806 concerning the depopulation of the Borders, in which Scott speculates on the transition from clan society, based on 'patriarchal right', to the 'feudal' system which was already established in the region outside the Borders, and incidentally notices the gradual change in the 'manners' of the clan chiefs which accompanied the economic change.[17] If, in the Novels themselves, these terms are not found, it can only be because Scott must have considered that a novel was not the place for the jargon of 'philosophical' analysis. Scott often approaches the same ideas imaginatively: for example, I have noted already that in *Rob Roy* Scott explicitly compares the tribalism of the Highland clans with that of the American Indians and the biblical Israelites. In *Rob Roy* too Scott shows explicitly that he considers the clans historically, as a 'stage' in development, when he comments that the clans were 'in a savage, or, to speak more properly, in a rude state'[18] – a distinction which only makes sense as a reference to the 'philosophical' distinction between tribal societies and yet more ancient, 'savage' societies in which even the partriarchal principle had not evolved. In the same way, if the implicit evidence of a connection between 'manners' and the 'stage' of society is not sufficient to convince, there is Catherine Glover's notably 'philosophical' musing in *The Fair Maid of Perth*, noted by Garside, that 'men rarely advance in civilisation or refinement beyond the ideas of their own age' – a reflection that leads her to accept the smith for her husband.[19]

The emphasis on 'determinism' in the Waverley Novels is also obvious. Lukács says of Scott that: 'Historical necessity in his novels is of the most severe implacable kind . . . Yet this necessity is no other-worldly fate divorced from men.'[20] Scott's belief in the irreversibility of change is usually illustrated by the passage in his *History of Scotland* in which he wrote: 'It is seldom that civilisation having once made some progress can be compelled to retrograde'.[21] This is certainly couched in the theoretical terms of the 'philosophical' historians, but for that reason it inadequately represents the 'determinism' of the novels, in which the same idea is found expressed imaginatively, in specific historical situations. A better example is the conversation between Darsie and Lilias in *Redgauntlet*, in which Darsie expresses the impossibility of Redgauntlet's plot succeeding:[22]

'whatever these people may pretend, to evade your uncle's importunities, they cannot, at this time of day, think of subjecting their necks again to the feudal yoke, which was effectually broken by the act of 1748, abolishing vassalage and hereditary jurisdictions.'

'Ay, but that my uncle considers as the act of a usurping government,' said Lilias.

'Like enough *he* may think so,' answered her brother, 'for he is a superior, and loses his authority by the enactment. But the question is, what the vassals will think of it, who have gained their freedom from feudal slavery, and have now enjoyed that freedom for many years?'

Redgauntlet as a whole, of course, records the hopelessness of one such attempt at 'social retrogression' – an attempt to reimpose Stuart absolutism on late eighteenth-century Britain: Scott shows that Redgauntlet is ultimately defeated by the changed social relations of the 'modern' age. While Lukács is right, however, to assert that Scott's determinism is 'no other-worldly fate divorced from men', Scott also suggests, particularly in *The Bride of Lammermoor*, that historical processes may well have appeared to their feudal protagonists as 'fate', just as the changes in the vicinity of Wolf's Crag appear to Edgar and Caleb. We may also see the hand of 'determinism' in the way that characters in the Waverley Novels are themselves moulded by the conditions, culture and ideology in which they have been brought up. In a passage in *Rob Roy* already noted, Rob says of Nicol Jarvie: 'he presses ower hard on the temper and situation of a man like me, considering what I have been – what I have been forced to become – and, above all, that which has forced me to become what I am!'[23]

Also in concert with the Smithian tradition is the strong economic character of Scott's 'determinism'. An early critic of *Rob Roy* pointed out that Scott always portrays the basic economic activities of the people in his novels:[24]

society never stands still and is never lost sight of, that battles may be fought or great men display themselves – the anvil is ringing, as well that the poor traveller's beast may not go unshod as that the soldier may be equipped, who is to fight for a realm.

There is a strong implication in the Waverley Novels that men's ways of livelihood, their economic activities, are in fact a primary influence on their lives, and hence on the outcome of history. In *Waverley*, for example, Scott clearly contrasts the

201

temporary military superiority gained by the Jacobite forces with the long-term economic hegemony of Lowland commerce which continues even at the height of the rebellion's success. Walter Bagehot, who also believed that 'when Sir Walter's own works come to be closely examined, they will be found to contain a good deal of political economy of a certain sort, – and not a very bad sort',[25] gave as an example Scott's description of the Highland clans in *Waverley*. Indeed, by first displaying the clan at the feast to which Edward is invited by MacIvor, Scott emphasises the first reality of the Highlanders' situation: the need for food. The hierarchical social organisation seen at the feast, and the clan's action in general, including their participation in the Rebellion, seem specifically evolved to deal with this problem: hence the real importance (as opposed to the romantic importance with which Edward invests it) of MacIvor's raid on the baron's milch-cows. Nicol Jarvie's arithmetical analysis of the Highlanders' predicament in *Rob Roy* is equally telling: Jarvie hints that George I's decision to withdraw the chiefs' purses at a time when the Highlands can support only half their population will necessarily mean trouble for their neighbours in the Lowlands – the only alternative the clans have is starvation. In *The Bride of Lammermoor* too food is a potent symbol: Wolf Crag's pitiful lack of it steadily undermines any pretensions to status that linger in Edgar's mind. The emptiness of the feudal ideas of 'honour' and 'credit' which mean so much to Caleb is brought home to the reader by Caleb's completely dishonourable and discreditable theft of the cooper's chicken in order to give the Marquis something to eat and so uphold the Ravenswoods' status.

'Relativism' is also a notable component of the Waverley Novels and of Scott's outlook on history. One of the themes of Ferguson's *Essay on the History of Civil Society* was the dubious moral value of 'progress'. Himself a Highlander, Ferguson felt an understandable attachment to the 'superior virtue' of earlier societies, while his criticism of the debilitating effects of 'luxury' in modern life became part of the tradition of 'philosophical' history. In Scott's work, a similar 'relativity' of approach has long been appreciated. In *The Spirit of the Age*, for example, Hazlitt noted that Scott refused to side himself with his opposed protagonists in the novels:[26]

The candour of Sir Walter's historic pen levels our bristling prejudices on this score, and sees fair play between Roundheads and Cavaliers, between Protestant and Papist. He is a writer reconciling all the diversities of human nature to the reader.

Scott has, of course, often been accused of idealising the Middle Ages and feudalism in particular – most famously by Mark Twain, who laid the blame for the Southern mentality in the American Civil War on Scott's novels and their supposed idealisation of chivalry[27] – but modern writers such as Forbes, Garside and James Anderson have provided an ample corrective to this point of view, arguing that Scott's attitude to progress was one of qualified approval.[28] Yet Scott's intellectual acceptance of the necessity of progress did not mean that he did not sympathise with those on the losing side. Men like Rob Roy or Redgauntlet are shown by Scott to be doomed figures, but the judgment that history exercises on them, in terms of social obsolescence, is not for Scott a moral judgment. As Daiches puts it:[29]

> Scott has no historical villains. That is, there are no characters in Scott's novels who are wicked because they belong to a particular side in a historical conflict. People can be trapped by history on one side or the other, and again and again Scott shows with persuasive clarity how people of good will can be manoeuvered into opposite sides.

Unlike the majority of nineteenth-century historians whom Herbert Butterfield criticised in *The Whig Interpretation of History*, Scott does not attempt to subordinate the past to the present, or seek to 'produce a story which is the ratification if not the glorification of the present'.[30] When Scott does try to do this, as in the conclusion to *Old Mortality*, his characteristic historical realism is lost. On the whole, Scott is a model of the historical relativism for which Butterfield argues: it is, for example, fully accepted in the Waverley Novels that 'their generation was as valid as our generation'.[31] Scott's avoidance of Whig simplifications and assumptions explains Lukács's apparently obscure comment that Scott's 'objectivity is further heightened by [his] conservatism'.[32] His human sympathy with the men and women of the past is never crudely undermined by a Whiggish glorification of the historical 'victors'. Edmund Wilson's description of Michelet fits Scott too:[33]

> Michelet is able to put us back at upper stages of the stream of time, so that we grope with the people of the past themselves, share their heroic faiths, are dismayed by their unexpected catastrophes, feel for all our knowledge of after-the-event, that we do *not* know precisely what is coming.

Yet this human sympathy of Scott's with past ages – in a way the focus of his 'relativism' – cannot really be attributed to the influence of the 'philosophical' historians. As Garside points out, the 'philosophical' historians themselves showed 'little overt interest in the imaginative re-creation of past societies, that is, of actual individuals and situations in the types of society described.'[34] Scott's lasting contribution to nineteenth-century historical writing was the lesson that human history was primarily concerned with living human individuals. Even Carlyle, in an essay generally hostile to Scott, was compelled to admit:[35]

> these Historical Novels have taught all men this truth, which looks like a truism, and yet was as good as unknown to writers of history and others, till so taught: that the bygone ages of the world were actually filled by living men, not by protocols, state-papers, controversies and abstractions of men.

Scott's historical novel thus has also to be seen as a continuation of the work of novelists of the eighteenth century like Fielding – and this despite Scott's transformation of Fielding's static conception of 'manners'.

On the one hand, then, Scott feels compelled to affirm the fact of human progress through history; on the other, he is deeply sympathetic to the heroic qualities found in past societies and to people who, through no fault of their own, are bound to be destroyed by the historical process. These contradictory impulses seem to have co-existed in Scott's personality, lending the Waverley Novels a characteristic tension.[36] As a result, Scott in practice rejects Butterfield's notion that history should be considered in a totally detached, relativist, fashion – in other words, that the past and the present are not organically connected. Scott never views the men of the fifteenth century as Butterfield would have them viewed, as 'distant and strange people whose quarrels are as unrelated to ourselves as the factions of Blue and Green in ancient Constantinople'.[37] The conflicts in the Waverley Novels show the 'present' coming into being – at least so far as Scott is able to portray it so doing. The qualifying point about Scott's art, as I have argued, is that he succeeds only as long as he is able to imaginatively relate human conflict to the social and economic forms with which he was acquainted.[38] To the extent that Scott's view of the social classes in history necessarily relates to the historical understanding of his own epoch (including, particularly, the tradition of 'philosophical' history), the past depicted in the Waverley Novels is at least indirectly connected with Scott's own present-day. Just how Scott directly related to his contemporary world is a different problem, and a difficult one (as his biographers have discovered). The question nevertheless bears examining, in conclusion, for the insight it gives into the outlook on history reflected in the Waverley Novels.

The failure to depict contemporary society

It is a very remarkable feature of the Waverley Novels that Scott should portray in them only *past* societies. The ideas of 'historicism' and of 'historical' presentation, particularly the dynamic conception of the conflict between social classes in history, are not themselves tied rigidly to the past. Logically, they are equally relevant to an artistic depiction of contemporary society – yet this is exactly what Scott consistently avoids. Lukács has noted the fact that Scott seldom writes of the present in his novels, and particularly, that he never raises the question of social conflict in contemporary Britain, 'the class struggle between bourgeoisie and proletariat which was then beginning to sharpen'.[39] However, the chapter in *The Historical Novel* does not in the end explain why this should have been the case: Scott's silence on the present in the novels remains a puzzle, particularly as Lukács elsewhere declares that: 'Without a felt relationship to the present, a portrayal of history is impossible'.[40]

Coleridge provides an interesting gloss on this last comment of Lukács's when, in a letter written in 1821, he remarks:[41]

the essential wisdom and happiness of the subject (of the Waverley Novels) consists in this, – that the contest between the loyalists and their opponents can never be *obsolete*, for it is the contest between the two great moving principles of social humanity; religious adherence to the past and the ancient, the desire and the admiration of permanence, on the one hand; and the passion for increase of knowledge, for truth, as the offspring of reason – in short, the mighty instincts of *progression* and *free agency* on the other.

If this is the case, then the critic has to explain why Scott did not write any novel in which these 'great moving principles' were to be seen in action in contemporary society.

The reader turns in vain to the two novels which do, supposedly, depict contemporary society – *The Antiquary* and *St Ronan's Well* – for a view of Scott's own society in dynamic, historical terms. *The Antiquary* (which in any case is set at the close of the eighteenth century) turns out, as we have seen, to be a satirical novel concerned principally with the relation of the past to the 'present'. The satire of the present always takes place with relation to the 'older' values, whether embodied in the persons of Edie Ochiltree and old Elspeth, or in the ritual at the burial of Steenie Mucklebackit, in which Oldbuck takes his place at the head of the funeral party, and the 'old' order is temporarily (if sentimentally) restored. Apart from the single instance of Mucklebackit's grief-stricken outburst against all 'gentles', there is nothing in the novel to suggest that the supremacy of the middle classes to which Oldbuck (and also, in a way, Sir Arthur Wardour) belong is itself subject to historical change. It is the same with *St Ronan's Well*. The fundamental contrast in this novel is between the Auld Town of St Ronan's and the newly-built spa to which the fashionable Edinburgh set are drawn. Meg Dods, the irascible landlady of the Auld Town's only inn, is the repository of 'old' values, in comparison with whom the company of empty-minded ladies, flatterers, fawns and gallants who inhabit the spa carry little moral attraction. In spite of its 'contemporary' setting, however, *St Ronan's Well* really looks backward: the satiric comedy is intended primarily to show how lamentably the products of modern society show up against the remnants of the old, and how peasant virtues are more attractive than bourgeois mores.[42] Notably, Scott depicts the bourgeoisie in the country, on holiday (though admittedly, for some, it is almost a permanent holiday) rather than in their natural environment, the town, where their mode of earning a living, and its consequences for the new, urban working classes employed in industry, would necessarily have been brought to the fore.

Hazlitt commented on Scott: 'He is just half what the human intellect is capable of being: if you take the universe, and divide it into two parts, he knows all that *has been*; all that *is to be* is nothing to him'.[43]

Scott's strong Tory opinions on contemporary political matters were, of course, well known to Hazlitt when he wrote *The Spirit of the Age*, but this did not blind him to Scott's essential limitation. When investigated in greater detail, Scott's political attitudes to his own day do, in fact, themselves appear limited. D. S. Hewitt's study of Scott's attitudes to his own society particularly highlights an unreality in Scott's political opinions that contrasts strongly with the clarity of imagination displayed in the Waverley Novels. A good example is Scott's highly emotive appeal to landlords to protect their tenants against the forces of modern industrialism (as he himself tried to do with his paternalist estate at Abbotsford):[44] an appeal which seems doomed by the very historical processes which Scott himself depicts in his novels. If this attempt to fight the inroads of the new, agrarian capitalism in the Scottish countryside by reviving outdated paternalism seems naïve, Scott's championship of water-powered cottage industry against steam-powered industrialisation and urbanisation seems completely unrealistic.[45]

The correlative to Scott's highly conservative criticism of industrialisation is that, while appalled at the plight of the peasantry during the Highland clearances, he has little or no sympathy for the mass of the urban working class, forced to endure intolerable living and working conditions in the towns and cities, whose ranks were in fact swelled by the flight from the countryside. As late as 1819 and 1820 we find Scott resolutely denying the right of the lower orders to be politically active, arguing only that they should be made to obey their 'natural superiors'.[46] Hewitt also brings out the irony of Scott's reaction to the Luddites, pointing out that, although the machine-breakers actually shared much of Scott's own conservatism and antipathy to change, their expression of these feelings in hopeless violence was sufficient to have Scott calling for heavy retribution against them in alarm at the possibility of a 'Jacquerie'.[47] After this, we are hardly shocked even to find that Scott approved of the Peterloo massacre.[48]

The point is not just that 'the candour of Sir Walter's historic pen' played little part in cooling the outstanding political prejudices of his own time, but also that, in many of his polemical writings, Scott seems confused or sentimental about issues in a way he never is in the best of his novels. While there is obviously something in Francis Jeffrey's remark that it is not easy to judge the real scope of many movements and events until a good while after they have taken place,[49] it is tempting to relate Scott's failure in depicting contemporary society in his novels and in his political understanding of it, to his failure in depicting ancient societies (such as the society of *Ivanhoe*) with any degree of historical realism. It seems that, just as Scott was incapable of exercising his historical imagination on situations prior to the class struggles between the clans, the aristocracy, and the growing Lowland middle classes which he understood so clearly, so also he was incapable of successfully understanding or sympathising with the new protagonists in the struggle just beginning in Scotland between the middle classes and the industrial workforce – a struggle already apparent, for example, in the so-called 'Radical War' which affected Glasgow in 1819–20.[50] The events of the 'Radical War', which included mass meetings, clashes with troops, and the first call to a general strike (on April 1st 1820) are just such as might have been expected to capture the historical imagination of the author of *Old Mortality*, had he been the least sympathetically disposed towards the cause of the working-class participants. In this context, Scott's decision in 1820 to turn towards more ancient history (in *Ivanhoe*) has about it an indubitably 'escapist' air.

We have to conclude that Scott is not quite the 'revolutionary' figure that Lukács makes him out to be (although Lukács does not of course deny Scott's *political* conservatism.) In fact, Scott has a lot in common with the 'Legitimist Romantics' whom Lukács sees as comprising the earlier, reactionary stage in the rise of the spirit of historicism.[51] At least one side of Scott's personality was in harmony with the Legitimists, with their 'falsely idyllic picture' of the Middle Ages, their championship of legitimist monarchs (*vide* Scott's claim to be 'an old Jacobite'), and particularly their affection for the stability of the old feudal order. In the best of Scott's novels, of course, (though not in his political views on contemporary affairs) this tendency of his was kept in check by the other side of his personality – his rationalism which affirmed the necessity of historical change. In his political pronouncements, it often seems as though Scott felt compelled to act the rôle of Redgauntlet in contemporary politics – yet that he had within him a consciousness of the hopelessness of his task. Beyond this contradiction his mind could not progress.

The problem, finally, with Coleridge's talk of 'the two great moving principles of social humanity' displayed in the Waverley Novels is not that it does not throw some light on Scott's genius, but that it is, in the end, too vague to explain Scott's limitations. Coleridge is right to see that the Scottish Waverley Novels embrace, in many forms, the opposition between conservative and liberal philosophies, but he does not see that this is not essentially an 'idealist' conflict, because Scott always shows these philosophies as the ideas of men acting in concrete social situations, and thus associated indivisibly with men's opposed ways of life and social organisation at a particular historical epoch. Correspondingly, Coleridge does not see that Scott could not, in fact, 'carry over' his astonishing historical grasp into his own time because he lacked sympathy with and an understanding of the growing urban working class – a class to whom, indeed, the 'great moving principles' of liberalism and conservatism were to have little to say. We can only say that during Scott's lifetime the stirrings of the new class were too tentative and confused, and Scott's antipathy to them too ingrained, for any such understanding to have become a reality.

Notes

Introduction

1 (J. G. Lockhart), *Peter's Letters to his Kinsfolk*, 'second' edition, Edinburgh, 1819, ii, p. 143.
2 (Thomas Carlyle), '*Memoirs of the Life of Sir Walter Scott, Baronet*' (review), *London and Westminster Review*, Jan. 1838, vi and xxviii, p. 334.
3 Virginia Woolf, *To the Lighthouse*, London, 1927, p. 185.
4 Frank Jordan, 'Scott and Wordsworth; or, Reading Scott Well', *Wordsworth Circle*, 1973, iv, pp. 112–23.
5 Georg Lukács, *The Historical Novel* (1937), (trans. H. and S. Mitchell), London, 1962, p. 35.
6 David Daiches, 'Scott's Achievement as a Novelist' (1951), *Literary Essays*, Edinburgh, 1956, p. 119.
7 Duncan Forbes, 'The Rationalism of Sir Walter Scott', *Cambridge Journal*, Oct. 1953, vii, pp. 20–35.

1 *Waverley*

1 Anon., '*Waverley*: supposed by W. Scott' (review), in *British Critic*, August 1814, New Series ii, p. 205.
2 *Waverley*, II, p. 10.
3 *Ibid*, V, p. 25.
4 *Ibid*., XXII, p. 137.
5 *Ibid*., XL, p. 253.
6 *Ibid*., XL, p. 254.
7 S. S. Gordon, '*Waverley* and the "Unified Design"', in *English Literary History*, 1951, xviii, p. 120.
8 *Waverley*, VIII, p. 42.

9 *Ibid.*, VIII, p. 44.
10 *Ibid.*, XVI, p. 101.
11 Robin Mayhead, *Walter Scott*, Cambridge, 1973, p. 29.
12 *Waverley*, XVI, p. 95.
13 *Ibid.*, XXXVIII, p. 243.
14 *Ibid.*, XXXIX, p. 250-1.
15 *Ibid.*, XXXIX, pp. 246-7.
16 *Ibid.*, LVII, pp. 346-7.
17 *Ibid.*, XX, p. 127.
18 *Ibid.*, LVII, p. 346.
19 *Ibid.*, LIII, pp. 331-2.
20 *Ibid.*, LIII, p. 333.
21 *Ibid.*, XX, p. 124.
22 Mayhead, *op. cit.*, p. 38.
23 *Waverley*, X, pp. 53-4.
24 *Ibid.*, XXVIII, p. 182.
25 *Ibid.*, XLVI, p. 291.
26 *Ibid.*, LII, p. 328.
27 Donald Davie, *The Heyday of Sir Walter Scott*, London, 1961, p. 37.
28 *Waverley*, XXVIII, p. 181.
29 John H. Raleigh, '*Waverley* as History, or 'Tis One Hundred and Fifty-Six Years Since,' in *Novel*, Fall 1970, iv, p. 24.
30 *Waverley*, XI, p. 58.
31 *Ibid.*, LXVI, p. 408.
32 *Ibid.*, LXVII, p. 419.
33 *Ibid.*, LXVIII, p. 422.
34 *Ibid.*, XXII, pp. 136-7.
35 D. D. Devlin, *The Author of Waverley*, London, 1971, p. 64.
36 *Waverley*, XL, p. 254.
37 *Ibid.*, LXXII, p. 448.
38 Maria Edgeworth, letter to 'the author of Waverley', dated 28th November 1814, in *The Life and Letters of Maria Edgeworth* (ed. A. J.C. Hare), London, 1894, p. 226.
39 The uncomfortably assumed attitude of authorial frivolity at the beginning of Chapter XXIV (p. 148) is an example of this.
40 (Francis Jeffrey), 'Waverley, or 'Tis Sixty Years Since' (review), in *Edinburgh Review*, November 1814, xxiv, p. 242.
41 (Walter Scott, with William Erskine and William Gifford), 'Tales of My Landlord' (review), in *Quarterly Review*, January 1817, xvi. p. 469. Scott writes elsewhere in the article, of the 'dramatic shape' of the novels (p. 431).

2 *Guy Mannering*

1 Robert C. Gordon, *Under Which King?*, Edinburgh, 1969, p. 34.
2 Scott, 'Walpole' in *Lives of the Novelists*, vol. II, Paris, 1825, p. 135.

3 Gordon, *op. cit.*, p. 27.
4 Anon., '*Guy Mannering*' (review) in *Augustan Review*, July 1815, i, p. 232.
5 *Guy Mannering*, VIII, p. 50.
6 Duncan Forbes, 'The Rationalism of Sir Walter Scott', *Cambridge Journal*, Oct. 1953, vii, p. 31.
7 A. O. J. Cockshut, *The Achievement of Walter Scott*, London, 1969, p. 35.
8 *Guy Mannering*, VIII, p. 49.
9 Nevertheless, various hints thrown out in the course of the novel fix the date of the main action as the late 1770s: particularly Mrs. Mac-Candlish's reference to 'this weary American war' in Chapter XII (p. 78). The great British advances in India, in which Mannering is supposed to have become famous, took place in the late 1750s, which ties in with this.
10 *Guy Mannering*, II, pp. 6ff.
11 *Ibid.*, II, p. 5.
12 *Ibid.*, XXII, p. 143.
13 *Ibid.*, LVI, p. 415.
14 *Ibid.*, XXXIX, p. 271.
15 *Ibid.*, XXXVI, p. 250.
16 *Ibid.*, VII, p. 43.
17 *Ibid.*, VII, p. 41.
18 Robin Mayhead, *Walter Scott*, Cambridge, 1973, p. 72.
19 Lars Hartveit, *Dream within a Dream: A Thematic Approach to Scott's Vision of Fictional Reality*, Oslo, 1974, makes the point (p. 122) that the smugglers' relationship with the Bertrams too is 'of a semi-feudal nature'. This relationship Godfrey Bertram also destroys.
20 *Guy Mannering*, VI, p. 37.
21 *Ibid.*, XVIII, p. 114.
22 *Ibid.*, XXI, p. 135.
23 *Ibid.*, XXIII, p. 145.
24 *Ibid.*, XXVII, pp. 169–71.
25 *Ibid.*, XLI, p. 289.
26 *Ibid.*, XLI, p. 290.
27 *Ibid.*, XLI, pp. 291–2.
28 *Ibid.*, XLI, p. 293.
29 *Ibid.*, XLI, p. 294.
30 *Ibid.*, XLVII, p. 341.
31 *Ibid.*, XII, p. 83.
32 Gordon, *op. cit.*, p. 34; Mayhead, *op. cit.*, p. 73.
33 Alexander Welsh, *The Hero of the Waverley Novels*, New Haven, 1963, p. 148; Cockshut, *op. cit.*, pp. 31–2.
34 Mayhead, *op. cit.*, p. 79.
35 Gordon, *op. cit.*, p. 35.

3 *The Antiquary*

1 David Daiches, 'Scott's Achievement as a Novelist', *Literary Essays*,

Edinburgh, 1956, p. 105.
2 Introduction to *The Antiquary*, p. v.
3 E. M. Forster's hostile attack on *The Antiquary* in *Aspects of the Novel*,
   London, 1927, pp. 31–8, for example, concentrates entirely on the plot in
   its most external and superficial aspect.
4 (J. W. Croker), '*The Antiquary*' (review), *Quarterly Review* April 1816,
   xv, p. 127.
5 The 'present' of the novel is actually back-dated to the close of the
   eighteenth century. Nevertheless, Scott's Introduction (p.v) makes clear
   that he intended the novel to depict his 'own' age.
6 *The Antiquary*, VI, p. 54.
7 *Ibid.*, XL, pp. 96–7.
8 *Ibid.*, II, pp. 10–11.
9 *Ibid.*, V, p. 40.
10 *Ibid.*, III, p. 21.
11 James Anderson, 'Sir Walter Scott as Historical Novelist,' Part II, in
   Studies in Scottish Literature, October 1966, iv, p. 76; P. D. Garside,
   'Intellectual origins of Scott's view of history in the Waverley Novels',
   unpublished Ph.D. thesis, University of Cambridge, 1970, pp. 93–4.
12 On the Goths see *The Antiquary*, XXX, p. 279 (among other references);
   on Mary: V, 41; VIII, p. 70.
13 Lawrence Poston III, 'The Commercial Motif of the Waverley Novels',
   English Literary History, Spring 1975, xlii, p. 70–1.
14 *The Antiquary*, V, p. 43.
15 Robert C. Gordon, *Under Which King?* Edinburgh, 1969, p. 37.
16 *The Antiquary*, V, 37, XXVI, p. 329.
17 *Ibid.*, VI, p. 52.
18 Karl Marx and Friedrich Engels, *The German Ideology, Part One*, ed.
   C. J. Arthur, London, 1970, p. 49.
19 *The Antiquary*, IV. p. 29.
20 *Ibid.*, III, p. 24.
21 *Ibid.*, IV, p. 31.
22 *Ibid.*, XXIII, p. 218.
23 Joan S. Elbers, 'Isolation and Community in *The Antiquary*', *Nineteenth-
   Century Fiction*, March 1973, xxvii, p. 417.
24 Gordon similarly comments that old Elspeth Mucklebackit 'knows antiquity
   in a way that Oldbuck, scribbling his notes, will never master' (*op. cit.*,
   p. 40).
25 *The Antiquary* XII, p. 105.
26 *Ibid.*, IV, p. 35.
27 *Ibid.*, XII, p. 104–5.
28 *Ibid.*, XXI, p. 202.
29 Daiches, *op. cit.*, p. 107.
30 *The Antiquary*, XXVIII, p. 264.
31 *Ibid.*, XXXI, p. 287.
32 *Ibid.*, XXXI, p. 288.
33 *Ibid.*, XXVI, p. 246.

34 Gordon, *op. cit.*, p. 36.
35 *The Antiquary*, XXXV, p. 320.
36 *Ibid.*, XLI, p. 371.
37 *Ibid.*, XLII, p. 385.
38 *Ibid.*, XXXIV, p. 315.
39 *Ibid.*, XXX, p. 279.
40 *Ibid.*, XXX, p. 282.
41 *Ibid.*, XXXV, p. 318.
42 *Ibid.*, XXXVI, p. 333. It is a further irony that Oldbuck makes his protest not really from any respect for history, but with an eye to the damage the chargers would do to his supply of fodder.
43 *Ibid.*, X, p. 83.
44 *Ibid.*, XVII, p. 151.
45 Elbers, *op. cit.*, pp. 421–2.
46 *The Antiquary*, XLIV, p. 397.
47 Croker, *op. cit.*, p. 125.
48 Thus Oldbuck points out the changes in the law concerning magicians: Douterswivel would no longer be treated in law as an actual witch, but as 'a common cheat and imposter' (XXIII, p. 216).
49 Edgar Johnson *Sir Walter Scott—The Great Unknown*, London, 1970, i, p. 541.
50 *The Antiquary*, VII, p. 63.
51 *Ibid.*, XLV, p. 407.
52 *Ibid.*, XLIV, p. 401.
53 *Ibid.*, XLV, p. 406.
54 Georg Lukács, *The Historical Novel*, trans. H. and S. Mitchell, London, 1962, p. 33.
55 *The Antiquary*, XXXIV, p. 307.
56 W. M. Parker, 'Introduction' to the Everyman edition of *The Antiquary*, London, 1954, p. viii.
57 The question of Scott's view of contemporary society is further examined in the concluding chapter.
58 Lukács, *op. cit.*, p. 33.

4 *Old Mortality*

1 S. S. Prawer, *Karl Marx and World Literature*, Oxford, 1976, p. 396.
2 Karl Marx and Friedrich Engels, 'Manifesto of the Communist Party' (1848), *Selected Works*, London, 1953, i, p. 35.
3 *The Black Dwarf* obtrudes its stunted and obscure presence between these two novels, but it is impossible to claim that this production advanced Scott's art as an historical novelist in any way. The Dwarf's place in history is, as Robert Gordon says, 'quite truthfully nowhere' (*Under Which King?* Edinburgh, 1969, p. 46) but the historical background itself is also trivial. Mareschal's Jacobite 'philosophy', for example, is merely a sketchy backdrop for his characterisation, just as the abortive rebellion is the

backdrop for the story, rather than integral to it. Because none of the characters possess any historical reality (or, in some cases, even plausibility) the result is a Gothic fairy-tale, of drastically limited seriousness.

4 Angus Calder's advice to the reader new to Scott to miss out the first chapter for the time being is typical – but also sensible. See Calder's 'Introduction' to the Penguin edition of *Old Mortality*, London, 1974, p. 9.

5 Hugh Trevor-Roper, 'Sir Walter Scott and History', *The Listener*, August 1971, lxxxvi, p. 228.

6 *Old Mortality*, I, p. 3.

7 *Ibid.*, I, p. 7.

8 Lars Hartveit, *Dream within a Dream: A Thematic Approach to Scott's Vision of Fictional Reality*, Oslo, 1974, p. 159.

9 *Old Mortality*, II, p. 16.

10 *Ibid.*, II, pp. 15–16.

11 *Ibid.*, XV, p. 150–1.

12 Kay V. Mathias, 'A study of Walter Scott's *Old Mortality*', unpublished M.A. thesis, University of Wales, Aberystwyth, 1968, p. 26.

13 *Ibid.*, p. 27.

14 *Old Mortality*, XIX, p. 184.

15 *Ibid.*, XXVI, p. 244.

16 See T. C. Smout, *A History of the Scottish People, 1560–1830*, London, 1969, pp. 64–5.

17 *Old Mortality*, VII, pp. 57ff.

18 *Ibid.*, VII, p. 55.

19 Smout, *op. cit.*, p. 33, notes that in the baron courts 'the lord was naturally happy to act as both plaintiff and judge'.

20 Thomas McCrie, *Vindication of the Covenanters; in a Review of the 'Tales of My Landlord'*, (1817), Edinburgh, 1845; David Craig, *Scottish Literature and the Scottish People, 1680–1830*, London, 1961, p. 147.

21 James Anderson, 'Sir Walter Scott as Historical Novelist', Part III, *Studies in Scottish Literature*, Jan.–April 1967, iv, p. 164. Craig himself seems to admit that the written evidence supports Scott (*op. cit.*, p. 183): his own, surely unverifiable, claim is that the Covenanters did not talk in the style of their extant, written pronouncements.

22 *Old Mortality*, VII, p. 59.

23 Hartveit, *op. cit.*, p. 196.

24 George Goodin, 'Walter Scott and the Tradition of the Political Novel', in *The English Novel in the Nineteenth Century*, ed. Goodin, Urbana, Illinois, 1974, p. 17.

25 Donald A. Cameron, 'Studies in the structure of six major novels of Sir Walter Scott', unpublished Ph.D. thesis, University of London, 1967, p. 368.

26 *Old Mortality*, XXVII, p. 247.

27 David Daiches, 'Scott's Achievement as a Novelist', *Literary Essays*, Edinburgh, 1956, p. 110.

28 Cameron, *op. cit.*, p. 347.

29 See Mathias, *op. cit.*, p. 37.

30 *Old Mortality*, IV, p. 27.
31 *Ibid.*, VIII, p. 70.
32 *Ibid.*, VIII, p. 71.
33 *Ibid.*, X, p. 100.
34 Alexander Welsh, *The Hero of the Waverley Novels*, New Haven, 1963, p. 242.
35 *Old Mortality*, XIII, pp. 126–7.
36 *Ibid.*, XXIV, p. 222.
37 *Ibid.*, XXIX, p. 265.
38 *Ibid.*, XII, p. 112.
39 (Scott, with William Erskine and William Gifford), 'Tales of My Landlord' (review), *Quarterly Review*, January 1817, xvi, p. 472.
40 Mathias, *op. cit.*, p. 96.
41 *Old Mortality*, IX, p. 88.
42 *Ibid.*, II, p. 17.
43 *Ibid.*, XVIII, p. 172.
44 Cameron, *op. cit.*, p. 374.
45 *Old Mortality* XX, p. 192.
46 Karl Marx, 'The Eighteenth Brumaire of Louis Bonaparte', *Selected Works*, London, 1953, i, p. 303.
47 Craig, *op. cit.*, p. 185.
48 See Anderson, *op. cit.*, p. 159, who finds a prototype for Mucklewrath in Meikle John Gibb, 'a lunatic dissenter'.
49 See Mathias, *op. cit.*, p. 77, for the character of the historical Burley.
50 *Ibid.*, p. 29: Mathias sees Scott's intention as 'bringing out the ruthlessness of Burley'.
51 *Old Mortality*, XVIII, p. 173.
52 *Ibid.*, XXI, p. 199.
53 *Ibid.*, VI, pp. 47–8.
54 *Ibid.*, VI, p. 45.
55 *Ibid.*, XIII, p. 124.
56 *Ibid.*, XIV, p. 139.
57 Welsh, *op. cit.*, p. 240.
58 Mathias, *op. cit.*, pp. 38–9.
59 Scott characterises the effects of the 1688 Revolution in just such terms in Chapter XXXVII, p. 331.
60 *Old Mortality*, XXVII, p. 250.
61 *Ibid.*, Note 28, p. 423.
62 Craig, *op. cit.*, p. 183.
63 Hartveit, *op. cit.*, p. 166.
64 Calder, *op, cit.*, p. 563.
65 Mathias, *op. cit.*, pp. 38–9, has drawn attention to Scott's deviation from historical fact here.
66 *Old Mortality*, XXIX, p. 270.
67 *Ibid.*, XXX, p. 281.
68 *Ibid.*, XXX, p. 283.
69 J. L. Adolphus, *Letters to Richard Heber Esq., M. P.*, London, 1822, p. 202.

70 Cameron, *op. cit.*, p. 355.
71 Daiches, *op. cit.*, p. 110.
72 Goodin, *op. cit.*, p. 18.
73 *Old Mortality*, XXXVII, p. 331.
74 Cameron, *op. cit.*, p. 361.
75 Calder, *op. cit.*, p. 579.
76 Scott, Erskine et al., *op. cit.*, p. 479.
77 Mathias, *op. cit.*, p. 169.
78 *Old Mortality*, XXIV, p. 220.
79 Hartveit, *op. cit.*, p. 200.
80 Robert C. Gordon, *Under Which King?* Edinburgh, 1969, p. 63.
81 Calder, *op. cit.*, p. 28.
82 *Ibid.*, p. 28.
83 Smout, *op. cit.*, p. 195.
84 Cameron, *op. cit.*, p. 361.
85 Hartveit, *op. cit.*, p. 182.
86 Daiches, *op. cit.*, p. 110.

5 *Rob Roy*

1 David Daiches, 'Scott's Achievement as a Novelist', *Literary Essays*, Edinburgh, 1956, p. 113.
2 E. M. W. Tillyard, *The Epic Strain in the English Novel*, London, 1958, pp. 100–2.
3 D. A. Cameron, 'Studies in the structure of six major novels of Sir Walter Scott', unpublished Ph.D. thesis, University of London, 1967, pp. 145, 160.
4 *Ibid.*, p. 144.
5 James Anderson, 'Sir Walter Scott as Historical Novelist', Part III, *Studies in Scottish Literature*, Jan.–April 1967, iv, p. 172.
6 Lawrence Poston III, 'The Commercial Motif of the Waverley Novels', *English Literary History*, Spring 1975, xlii, p. 82.
7 Avrom Fleishman, *The English Historical Novel: Walter Scott to Virginia Woolf*, Baltimore, 1971, p. 69.
8 This seems too to be the point of William Cadbury's 'The Two Structures of *Rob Roy*', *Modern Language Quarterly*, 1968, xxix, p. 42–60, though the attempt to see the conflict in *Rob Roy* entirely in terms of literary mode appears excessively formalistic.
9 *Rob Roy*, XXXV, pp. 345–7.
10 *Ibid.*, VI, pp. 49–50. It is almost unnecessary to observe that the simple satire directed at the inhabitants of Osbaldistone Hall completely lacks the sense of profound cultural irony found later in the novel.
11 Scott uses practically the same two characters again in *Redgauntlet*, but in a way more relevant to the main action, as we shall see.
12 Robin Mayhead, *Walter Scott*, Cambridge, 1973, p. 98.
13 *Rob Roy*, XIX, p. 178.

14 *Ibid.*, XXXIV, p. 337; Introduction, p. vii.
15 *Ibid.*, Introduction, p. xxiii; XXIV, p. 337.
16 *Ibid.*, XXXI, p. 299.
17 *Ibid.*, XXII, p. 199.
18 *Ibid.*, XXXIII, p. 322.
19 *Ibid.*, XXX, pp. 284–5.
20 *Ibid.*, XXIX, p. 278.
21 *Ibid.*, XXV, p. 233.
22 *Ibid.*, XXIX, p. 276.
23 *Ibid.*, XXX, pp. 288–9.
24 Anderson, *op. cit.*, p. 169.
25 *Rob Roy*, XXVI, p. 242.
26 Daiches, *op. cit.*, p. 111.
27 *Rob Roy*, XXXV, p. 352.
28 Daiches, *op. cit.*, p. 112.
29 *Rob Roy*, XXVIII, p. 269.
30 *Ibid.*, XXI, p. 192.
31 *Ibid.*, XXII, p. 207.
32 T. C. Smout cites Sabbath observance as one area where economic pressures most often came into conflict with Puritan doctrine: *A History of the Scottish People, 1560–1830*, London, 1969, p. 80.
33 *Rob Roy*, XIX, pp. 177–8.
34 *Ibid.*, XXVI, p. 237.
35 (Daniel Defoe), *A Tour Thro' the Whole Island of Great Britain*, London, 1727 [1726], Volume III, Part II, pp. 89–90.
36 Anderson, *op. cit.*, p. 169.
37 *Rob Roy*, XXVII, p. 255.
38 Edgar Johnson, *Sir Walter Scott – The Great Unknown*, Vol. I, London, 1970, p. 606.
39 Daiches, *op. cit.*, p. 112.
40 A. O. J. Cockshut, *The Achievement of Walter Scott*, London, 1969, p. 161.
41 *Rob Roy*, XIV, p. 134 etc.
42 In the same way, though less successfully, Helen MacGregor comments on Rob's actions: she is the unbending, unforgiving facet of the Highland tradition.
43 *Rob Roy*, XXVIII, p. 264.
44 *Ibid.*, XXVIII, p. 267.
45 *Ibid.*, XXXI, pp. 305–7.
46 *Ibid.*, XXVII, p. 254.
47 *Ibid.*, XXVI, p. 238.
48 *Ibid.*, XXIII, p. 216.
49 *Ibid.*, XXIII, p. 213.
50 *Ibid.*, XXXIV, p. 340.
51 *Ibid.*, XXVI, p. 245.
52 *Ibid.*, XXXIV, p. 332.
53 *Ibid.*, XXXVI, p. 358.

54 *Ibid.*, XIX, p. 178.
55 Georg Lukács, *The Historical Novel*, trans. H. and S. Mitchell, London, 1962, p. 58.
56 See J. E. Medcalf, 'Lukács on Scott', *Notes and Queries*, Nov. 1962, ccvii, New Series ix, p. 402.
57 *Rob Roy*, XXXV, p. 345.
58 Fleishman, *op. cit.*, p. 70.
59 *Rob Roy*, XXXVI, p. 359.

6 *The Heart of Midlothian*

1 Robin Mayhead, *Walter Scott*, Cambridge, 1973, p. 44.
2 F. R. Leavis, *The Great Tradition*, London, 1948, p. 14n.
3 In *Essays in Criticism*, July 1956, vi. pp. 266–77. It is only fair to note that Mayhead's later full-length study of Scott contains a partial recantation: in spite of this, his earlier article retains its interest as a set-piece of 'Cambridge' criticism.
4 *Ibid.*, p. 268.
5 *Ibid.*, p. 277.
6 E. M. W. Tillyard, *The Epic Strain in the English Novel*, London 1958, p.100.
7 See Donald Davie, *The Heyday of Sir Walter Scott*, London, 1961, pp.14–15, for a critique of Scott's narrative style. This is not to say that the description of the Porteous riots is not impressive in its way: T. C. Smout declares that 'there has probably never been so brilliant a piece of historical research so brilliantly disguised as fiction' (*A History of the Scottish People*, London, 1969, p. 498).
8 Lars Hartveit, *Dream within a Dream: A Thematic Approach to Scott's Vision of Fictional Reality*, Oslo, 1974, p. 26.
9 *The Heart of Midlothian*, IV, p. 34.
10 *Ibid.*, III, p. 30.
11 *Ibid.*, XVI, p. 163.
12 Thomas Crawford, *Scott*, Edinburgh, 1965, p. 99.
13 Robert Gordon, *Under Which King?*, Edinburgh, 1969, p. 87.
14 *The Heart of Midlothian*, IV, p. 37.
15 *Ibid.*, IV, p. 40.
16 David Daiches, 'Introduction' (1948) to the Rinehart edition of *The Heart of Midlothian*, New York, 1969, p. vii.
17 *The Heart of Midlothian*, XII, p. 123.
18 *Ibid.*, XV, p. 152.
19 *Ibid.*, XVIII, pp. 200–1.
20 David Craig, '*The Heart of Midlothian*: Its Religious Basis', *Essays in Criticism*, April 1958, viii, p. 220.
21 *The Heart of Midlothian*, X, p. 101.
22 George Bernard Shaw, *The Works of Bernard Shaw*, vol. 19, London, 1930, p. 125.

23 Davie, *op. cit.*, pp. 14–15 nicely points out Mayhead's lack of historical awareness in his attribution of irony to Scott's use of the word 'devoted', when Scott uses it normally in its archaic sense. This is symptomatic of the more general historical naiveté in Mayhead's approach.
24 *The Heart of Midlothian*, IX, p. 80.
25 *Ibid.*, X, p. 95.
26 Alexander Welsh, *The Hero of the Waverley Novels*, New Haven, 1963, p. 129.
27 *The Heart of Midlothian*, XV, p. 159.
28 *Ibid.*, XX, p. 214.
29 Georg Lukács, *The Historical Novel* (trans. H. and S. Mitchell), London 1962, p. 52. Daiches (*op. cit.*, p. xi) also comments that 'The juxtaposition of the unconsciously heroic and the domestic is Scott's way of building up the essential reality of Jeanie's character' – a complementary analysis to Lukács'.
30 W. H. Marshall, 'Point of View and Structure in *The Heart of Midlothian*', *Nineteenth-Century Fiction*, Dec. 1961, xvi, pp. 257–8.
31 See D. Biggins, '*Measure for Measure* and *The Heart of Midlothian*', *Etudes Anglaises*, July – Sept. 1961, xiv, p. 199.
32 W. J. Hyde, 'Jeanie Deans and the Queen: Appearance and Reality', *Nineteenth-Century Fiction*, June 1973, xxviii, p. 87.
33 *The Heart of Midlothian*, XXXVII, pp. 379–80.
34 *Ibid.*, XXXVII, p. 386.
35 *Ibid.*, XXXV, p. 367.
36 A. O. J. Cockshut, *The Achievement of Walter Scott*, London, 1969, p. 186.
37 Marshall, *op. cit.*, p. 261.
38 Cockshut, *op. cit.*, pp. 189–90.
39 *The Heart of Midlothian*, XLVII, p. 477.
40 *Ibid.*, XLIII, p. 439.
41 *Ibid.*, LI, p. 524.
42 T. C. Smout confirms the accuracy of Scott's delineation of the decline of Puritanism in *A History of the Scottish People*, London, 1969, pp. 213–22.
43 Daiches, *op. cit.*, p. x.
44 Hartveit, *op. cit.*, p. 30.
45 Avrom Fleishman, *The English Historical Novel: Walter Scott to Virginia Woolf*, Baltimore, 1971, p. 82.
46 Mayhead, *Walter Scott*, p. 44.

7 *The Bride of Lammermoor*

1 Robert C. Gordon, '*The Bride of Lammermoor* – A Novel of Tory Pessimism', *Nineteenth-Century Fiction*, Sept. 1957, xii, p. 123.
2 See particularly Lars Hartveit, *Scott's 'The Bride of Lammermoor': An Assessment of Attitude*, Bergen, 1962, and Andrew D. Hook, '*The*

Bride of Lammermoor: A Re-examination', *Nineteenth-Century Fiction*, Sept. 1967, xxii, pp. 111–26.

3 The literal source of the novel, a scandal of the Stair family, is not in question (see Scott's Introduction of 1829, pp. ix–xviii): from this story Scott certainly extracted the essential details of a secret betrothal opposed by the girl's parents, and its horrific result. Yet the all important social context of the action in *The Bride* is not suggested in the story – it is purely Scott's addition, and he subtly adapts many details of the original story to highlight the social divisions between his protagonists.

4 Cf. *Guy Mannering*, II, pp. 14–15; *The Bride of Lammermoor*, II, p. 6.

5 *The Bride*, XXVI, p. 245.

6 *Ibid.*, V, pp. 50–2. James Anderson, in 'Sir Walter Scott as Historical Novelist', Part IV, *Studies in Scottish Literature*, July 1967, v, p. 21, notes that Scott's depiction of the Scottish Privy Council after the Act of Union is an anachronism: nevertheless, the political consequences of social change which Scott uses this scene to suggest remained relevant.

7 *Ibid.*, III, p. 29–30.

8 *Ibid.*, III, p. 30.

9 *Ibid.*, II, p. 18.

10 *Ibid.*, XVIII, p. 167.

11 *Ibid.*, V, p. 42.

12 *Ibid.*, XVIII, p. 161.

13 Edgar Johnson, *Sir Walter Scott – The Great Unknown*, London, 1970, i, p. 670.

14 *The Bride*, V, p. 39.

15 Hook (*op. cit.*, p. 125) is surely wrong to suggest that Edgar does not intend to kill Ashton prior to the bull's charge. Edgar has supposedly made a solemn, or even profane vow of vengeance (II, p. 22) and killing Ashton is evidently the 'enterprise' which Bucklaw and Craigengelt are discussing while waiting for him (VI, p. 53). The suddenness with which Edgar fells the bull even suggests he may have had the Keeper in his sights when the bull charged.

16 *The Bride*, VIII, p. 79.

17 *Ibid.*, II, pp 19–20.

18 *Ibid.*, X, p. 106.

19 Hook, *op. cit.*, pp. 113–16.

20 Sir Sydney Colvin, *Memories and Notes of Persons and Places, 1852–1914*, London, 1921, p. 198.

21 Gordon, *op. cit.*, p. 119.

22 *The Bride*, XVIII, p. 160.

23 A. O. J. Cockshut, *The Achievement of Walter Scott*, London, 1969, p. 85.

24 See *The Bride*, II, p. 22 and XXIII, p. 217 especially.

25 Scott, *Lives of the Novelists*, Paris, 1825, ii. p. 135.

26 A. D. Hook, '*The Bride of Lammermoor* again: An Exchange', *Nineteenth-Century Fiction*, March 1969, xxiii, p. 499.

27 *The Bride*, XXIII, p. 216.

28 *Ibid.*, XIV, p. 138.

29 *Ibid.*, IX, p. 93.
30 *Ibid.*, VIII, p. 83.
31 *Ibid.*, XIV, p. 137.
32 *Ibid.*, XX, p. 183.
33 *Ibid.*, III, p. 27.
34 *Ibid.*, XVIII, pp. 170–1.
35 *Ibid.*, XXI, p. 190.
36 *Ibid.*, XXI, pp. 189–90.
37 See Colvin, *op. cit.*, p. 197.
38 Donald A. Cameron, 'Studies in the structure of six major novels of Sir Walter Scott', unpublished Ph.D. thesis, University of London, 1967, p. 465; Hartveit, *op. cit.*, p. 19.
39 *The Bride*, XI, p. 110.
40 *Ibid.*, XIX, pp. 176–7.
41 Hartveit, *op. cit.*, p. 24.
42 *The Bride.*, XXIV, pp. 228–9.
43 Andrew D. Hook, '*The Bride of Lammermoor*: A Re-examination', p. 122.
44 Robert C. Gordon, '*The Bride of Lammermoor* again: An Exchange' *Nineteenth-Century Fiction*, March 1969, xxiii, p. 497.
45 *The Bride*, XXXIII, p. 294.
46 Frank McCombie, 'Scott, *Hamlet*, and *The Bride of Lammermoor*', *Essays in Criticism*, October 1975, xxv, p. 434.
47 *The Bride*, XXXV, p. 311.
48 E.g., Robert C. Gordon, '*The Bride of Lammermoor* – A Novel of Tory Pessimism', p. 117; Johnson, *op. cit.*, p. 670.
49 *The Bride*, XXVI, p. 249.
50 *Ibid.*, IX, p. 93.
51 *Ibid.*, XII, p. 116.
52 *Ibid.*, XXVI, p. 253.
53 *Ibid.*, XII, p. 118.
54 *Ibid.*, XIV, p. 132.
55 Two critics' contradictory responses to the relationship between Caleb and Wolf's Hope may be revealing. To Gordon (*op. cit.*, p. 117) 'Caleb exhibits the virtue of loyalty, and this virtue shines all the more brightly when seen against the dark background of surly self-seeking that makes the village of Wolf's Hope a centre of moral paralysis.' To D. D. Devlin, on the other hand, 'The foolishness of Caleb's concerns is made clearer by the fact that for the people of the neighbourhood, the inhabitants of the village of Wolf's Hope, the changing times have brought nothing but gain' (*The Author of Waverley*, London, 1971, p. 108). This ambiguity arises because Scott succeeds in viewing the conflict between the villagers and the Ravenswoods from both sides.
56 *The Bride*, XXVI, p. 245.
57 *Ibid.*, XXXV, p. 313.
58 *Ibid.*, XXXV, p. 312.

59 Gordon, *op. cit.*, p. 111.
60 David Daiches, 'Scott's Achievement as a Novelist', *Literary Essays*, Edinburgh, 1956, p. 104.
61 Gordon, *op. cit.*, p. 124.

8 *Redgauntlet*

1 Introduction to *Ivonhoe*, pp. ix–x.
2 A summary of contemporary reactions to the novel appears in Robert C. Gordon's *Under Which King?*, Edinburgh, 1969, p. 149.
3 Thus Lukács, arguing that Scott's art is objectively bound up with the historical downfall of feudal society, conceived over several centuries of class struggle, writes: 'The chain of these crises extends from the first great struggles between the rising Scottish middle class and the nobility . . . to the last attempts of the Stuarts to turn back the clock of history, to restore outdated Absolutism in an already far advanced capitalist England [*sic*]' – *The Historical Novel*, trans. H. and S. Mitchell, London, 1962, pp. 56–7. There is another of Lukács's unfortunate slips here: he writes '*Rob Roy* – end of the eighteenth century' to illustrate the latter instance, when he must mean *Redgauntlet*.
4 Gordon, *op. cit.*, p. 149.
5 See for example Edgar Johnson, *Sir Walter Scott – The Great Unknown*, London, 1970, ii, pp. 920–1; David Daiches, *Sir Walter Scott and his World*, London, 1971, p. 111.
6 The date is not specified, as befits the vagueness of the Jacobite conspiracy with which the novel is concerned. Nevertheless, it can be established with some certainty; we are told that Darsie was "not a twelvemonth old" when his father suffered for his part in the Forty-Five (*Redgauntlet*, XVIII, p. 343) while in the opening letter Darsie is twenty-one years old. Nanty Ewart's references to popular unrest (see below) tend to fix the date as 1768.
7 David Daiches, 'Scott's *Redgauntlet*', in *From Jane Austen to Joseph Conrad* (ed. R.C. Rathburn and M. Steinmann Jr.), Minneapolis, 1958, p. 50.
8 *Redgauntlet*, X, p. 237.
9 Possibly Scott was also alluding to the fact that mid-eighteenth-century Scottish lawyers possessed actual, as well as symbolic, political power. According to Anand C. Chitnis, *The Scottish Enlightenment: A Social History*, London, 1976: 'Lawyers were central to the Scottish political process of the time: they managed the electoral machine' (p. 82).
10 *Redgauntlet*, Letter V, p. 40.
11 *Ibid.*, XVI, p. 317.
12 *Ibid.*, Letter VII, p. 72.
13 *Ibid.*, Letter VI, p. 50.
14 See for example, the 'emblematic' contrast between Joshua and Redgauntlet in Letter VI, p. 50.

15 *Ibid.*, Letter III, p. 19.
16 Scott undoubtedly intended his reader to compare Darsie's account with the tragic experiences of the Highlanders themselves in the period which were well-known. T. C. Smout gives an account of the aftermath of the Forty-Five in *A History of the Scottish People, 1569–1830*, London, 1969, pp. 208–9 with which Darsie's speech should be compared.
17 Scott's symbolic use of the Holyrood portraits in *Waverley*, XXXIX, pp. 250–1, has been considered in an earlier chapter.
18 *Redgauntlet*, VII, p. 208.
19 *Ibid.*, XII, p. 266.
20 *Ibid.*, X, p. 243.
21 *Ibid.*, XI, p. 249.
22 *Ibid.*, XI, p. 253.
23 *Ibid.*, XIX, p. 362.
24 *Ibid.*, XIX, p. 367.
25 This is evidently F. R. Leavis's view, as he considers Wandering Willie's Tale 'the only live part of *Redgauntlet*' (*The Great Tradition*, London, 1948, p. 14n).
26 *Redgauntlet*, Letter XI, p. 102.
27 Johnson *op. cit.*, p. 924.
28 'In its warnings, devilish company kept, temptation to dangerous allegiance (diabolical or Jacobite), and escape, the tale reflects, emphasizes, and foreshadows the meaning of the longer narrative' – Coleman O. Parsons, *Witchcraft and Demonology in Scott's Fiction*, Edinburgh, 1964, p. 284.
29 Daiches, *op. cit.*, p. 57.
30 Francis R. Hart, *Scott's Novels: The Plotting of Historic Survival*, Charlottesville, 1966, p. 57.
31 *Redgauntlet*, XVIII, p. 351.
32 Redgauntlet's language here is particularly reminiscent of Richard's denunciation of defectors to 'this traitor, Bolingbroke' in *Richard II*, III, ii. Scott's comparison of Richard to the exiled Jacobite monarch James in *Waverley* has already been noted.
33 *Redgauntlet*, VIII, p. 223.
34 The interview between Alan and Charles is added incidental evidence of Scott's more 'conscious' method in *Redgauntlet*. The ironic nuances of the dialogue are only evident if the reader shares the author's secret that Father Buonaventure is Charles Edward: a second reading is normally necessary.
35 This is yet another angle of Scott's on the growing tolerance of Catholicism in the eighteenth century.
36 *Redgauntlet*, XIV, pp. 297–8.
37 *Ibid.*, XV, p. 305.
38 *Ibid.*, XXII, p. 396.
39 *Ibid.*, XXII, p. 397.
40 *Ibid.*, XXII, p. 399.
41 *Ibid.*, XXII, p. 409.

42 A. O. J. Cockshut, *The Achievement of Walter Scott*, London, 1969, p. 210.
43 *Redgauntlet*, XXIII, p. 414.
44 *Ibid.*, XXIII, p. 427; p. 430.
45 Smout, *op. cit.*, p. 209.
46 *Redgauntlet*, IV, p. 185.
47 *Ibid.*, XXIII, p. 413.
48 *Ibid.*, XVI, p. 315.
49 Gordon *op. cit.*, p. 160.
50 *Redgauntlet*, XXII, p. 409.
51 *Ibid.*, XXIII, p. 430.
52 Daiches, *op. cit.*, p. 55.
53 D. D. Devlin, *The Author of Waverley*, London, 1971, p. 118; Johnson *op. cit.*, pp. 925–6, also sees Peebles as a parody of the Pretender.
54 *Redgauntlet*, VII, p. 208.
55 *Ibid.*, XIV, pp. 290–5.
56 Daiches, *op. cit.*, p. 58.
57 *Redgauntlet*, XXI, p. 390.
58 *Ibid.*, XIV, p. 291.

9 Historical Authenticity in the Waverley Novels

1 Robert C. Gordon, *Under Which King?*, Edinburgh, 1969, p. 165.
2 Donald A. Cameron, in 'Studies in the structure of six major novels of Sir Walter Scott', unpublished Ph.D. thesis, University of London, 1967, makes much the same point by asking, of Scott's tampering with history, 'How can such a form be defended? *Can* it be defended?' (p. 330). Unfortunately Cameron never really answers these questions.
3 Introduction to the 1830 edition of *Ivanhoe*, p. ix.
4 *Ibid.*, p. xii.
5 These are supposedly Dr Dryasdust's objections; Templeton (the author's alias) then answers them.
6 Dedicatory Epistle to *Ivanhoe*, p. xxii.
7 J. G. Lockhart, *Memoirs of the Life of Sir Walter Scott, Bart.*, Edinburgh, 1837–8, i, pp. 23–4.
8 A. O. J. Cockshut, *The Achievement of Walter Scott*, London, 1969, p. 104.
9 Dedicatory Epistle to *Ivanhoe*, p. xxii.
10 James T. Hillhouse, *The Waverley Novels and their Critics*, Minneapolis, 1936, p. 319.
11 Anonymous critic, '*Ivanhoe: A Romance*' (review) in the *Eclectic Review*, June 1820, 2nd Series, xii, p. 531.
12 *Ibid.*, pp. 528–9.
13 Joseph E. Duncan, 'The Anti-Romantic in *Ivanhoe*', *Nineteenth-Century Fiction*, March, 1955, ix, pp. 299–300.
14 Dedicatory Epistle to *Ivanhoe*, p. xxii.

15 Anonymous critic, *Eclectic Review*, *op. cit.*, p. 526 (my emphasis).

16 Francis R. Hart, *Scott's Novels: The Plotting of Historic Survival*, Charlottesville, 1966, pp. 182–4.

17 Georg Lukács, *The Historical Novel*, trans. H. and S. Mitchell, London, 1962, p. 60. Lukács says of the German Romantics: 'They discover the picturesque charm of the Middle Ages and reproduce it with "nazarene" accuracy: everything from medieval Catholicism to antique furniture is reproduced with craftsmanlike precision, which often becomes mere decorative pedantry. The human beings, however, who act in this picturesque world, have the psychology of a tormented Romantic or a freshly converted apologist of the Holy Alliance.'

18 Dedicatory Epistle to *Ivanhoe*, p. xxiii.

19 As Cockshut puts it (*op. cit.*, p. 91): 'The historical novel depends on a synthesis of likeness and unlikeness between the time of writing and the time portrayed.'

20 Dedicatory Epistle to *Ivanhoe*, p. xxv.

21 Henry Fielding, *Joseph Andrews* (1742), Book III, Chapter I; see also, for example, Samuel Johnson, *Rasselas* (1759), Chapter X.

22 D. D. Devlin, *The Author of Waverley*, London, 1971, pp. 39–40.

23 *The Antiquary*, X, p. 83.

24 This passage also has a Shakespearian elegance, of course – referring obliquely to the 'Seven Ages of Man' in *As You Like It*.

25 Duncan Forbes, 'The Rationalism of Sir Walter Scott', *Cambridge Journal*, October 1953, vii, pp. 20–32; Peter D. Garside, 'Intellectual origins of Scott's view of history in the Waverley Novels', unpublished Ph.D. thesis, Cambridge University, 1970, pp. 1–67, 145–197, also see below; Avrom Fleishman, *The English Historical Novel: Walter Scott to Virginia Woolf*, Baltimore, 1971, pp. 39–47.

26 Peter D. Garside, 'Scott and the "Philosophical" Historians', *Journal of the History of Ideas*, July–Sept. 1975, xxxvi, p. 500.

27 Hart, *op. cit.*, pp. 185–6.

28 Dedicatory Epistle to *Ivanhoe*, p. xxvi.

29 Anonymous critic, '*Quentin Durward*' (review) in the *New Monthly Magazine*, July 1823, viii, p. 87.

30 Anonymous critic, *Eclectic Review*, *op. cit.*, p. 528.

31 James Anderson, in 'Sir Walter Scott as Historical Novelist', Part VI, *Studies in Scottish Literature*, Jan. 1968, v, p. 143, makes a similar defence of the scene in *The Bride of Lammermoor* in which the Scottish Privy Council is shown at work, despite the fact that it was in fact abolished in 1708 and the action takes place in 1710. Anderson defends the scene on the grounds that it has 'a psychological appropriateness' given that the source of the novel is largely in the late seventeenth century. In other words, Scott remains true to the 'manners' of the period he describes, the period during which political power passed from the feudal aristocracy epitomised by the Ravenswoods into the hands of the Ashtons and their ilk.

32 Alexander Welsh, *The Hero of the Waverley Novels*, New Haven, 1963, p. 137.

33 See Garside, 'Intellectual origins', *op. cit.*, p. 30.
34 David Daiches, 'Literature and social mobility', in *Aspects of History and Class Consciousness*, ed. I. Mészaros, London, 1971, p. 162.
35 Duncan, *op. cit.*, p. 294.
36 Introduction to the 1830 edition of *Ivanhoe*, p. xi.
37 Dedicatory Epistle to *Ivanhoe*, pp. xxvii.
38 Lukács, *op, cit.*, p. 49.
39 G. M. Young, 'Scott and the Historians', in *Sir Walter Scott Lectures, 1940–1948*, introd. W. L. Renwick, Edinburgh, 1950.
40 Hart, *op. cit.*, p. 290.
41 Forbes, *op. cit.*, p. 31, contrasts Meg Merrilies' effect in *Guy Mannering* with Norna's, concluding that Meg succeeds to the extent that she is portrayed as a study in 'historical ecology' while Norna, lacking that dimension, can only be a Gothic failure.
42 In this, Scott's treatment of the Popish Plot resembles Dickens' treatment of the Gordon Riots in *Barnaby Rudge* (1841), an account of mob hysteria which is itself more hysterical than historical.
43 *The Fair Maid of Perth*, XXV, p. 295.
44 Lukács, *op. cit.*, p. 57.
45 *Ibid.*, p. 47.
46 F. Jameson, *Marxism and Form: twentieth-century dialectical theories of literature*, Princeton, 1971, p. 193.
47 E. M. Tillyard, *The Epic Strain in the English Novel*, London, 1958, p. 112.
48 David Daiches, 'Scott's Achievement as a Novelist', in *Literary Essays*, Edinburgh, 1956, p. 119.
49 Cockshut, *op. cit.*, p. 94.
50 This simplicity, of course, endears *The Two Drovers* to 'thematic' criticism, with its emphasis on universalities: even Leavis singles the story out for praise in *The Great Tradition*, London, 1948, p. 14n.
51 Virginia Woolf, 'Sir Walter Scott', in *The Moment and other essays*, London, 1947, p. 57.
52 Cockshut *op. cit.*, pp. 98–9.
53 Scott himself well understood the 'dramatic' quality of his work: see, for example, his mock-apologetic response to Dick Tinto's assertion that his characters 'patter too much' (*The Bride of Lammermoor*, I, p. 9ff.).

10 Scott's outlook on history

1 Georg Lukács, *The Historical Novel* (1937), trans. H. and S. Mitchell, London, 1962, p. 19.
2 *Ibid.*, p. 19.
3 Karl Kroeber, *Romantic Narrative Art*, Madison, 1960, pp. 180–1.
4 Duncan Forbes, 'The Rationalism of Sir Walter Scott', *Cambridge Journal*, October 1953, vii, p. 23.
5 Lukács, *op. cit.*, p. 30.

6 (J. G. Lockhart), *Memoirs of the Life of Sir Walter Scott, Bart.*, Edinburgh, 1837, i, 43, pp. 57–9. For Scott's links with the better known 'philosophical' historians, William Robertson and Adam Ferguson, see David Daiches, 'Sir Walter Scott and History', *Études Anglaises*, 1971, xxiv, p. 458.

7 Lockhart, *op. cit.*, p. 37.

8 'I should add that Scott was an author to whom Marx again and again returned, whom he admired and knew as well as he did Balzac and Fielding.' Eleanor Marx, quoted in S. S. Prawer, *Karl Marx and World Literature*, Oxford, 1976, p. 386.

9 Lukács, *op. cit.*, p. 23 (author's emphasis).

10 Peter D. Garside, 'Intellectual origins of Scott's view of history in the Waverley Novels', unpublished Ph.D. thesis, University of Cambridge, 1970, p. 2.

11 Lukács, *op. cit.*, p. 21.

12 *Ibid.*, p. 28.

13 Franco Venturi, *Utopia and Reform in the Enlightenment*, Cambridge, 1971, p. 133.

14 See Garside, *op. cit.*, pp. 12–18.

15 *Ibid.*, pp. 36–44.

16 *Ibid.*, pp. 65–6.

17 Letter to Lord Dalkeith, dated 23rd Nov. (1806), in *The Letters of Sir Walter Scott, 1787–1807*, ed. H. J. C. Grierson, London, 1932, pp. 329–334.

18 See *Rob Roy*, XXXV, p. 353.

19 See Peter D. Garside, 'Scott, the Romantic Past and the Nineteenth Century', *Review of English Studies*, 1972, xxiii, p. 156. Incidentally, this passage shows well why Scott usually avoided explicit 'philosophical' references in the novel: in the context of fourteenth-century Perth, it seems anachronistic to place Smithian ideas directly in Catherine's mouth in this way.

20 Lukács, *op. cit.*, p. 58.

21 See Forbes, *op. cit.*, p. 28.

22 *Redgauntlet*, XVIII, p. 354.

23 *Rob Roy*, XXXV, p. 345.

24 (E. T. Channing), *'Rob Roy'* (review), *North American Review*, July 1818, vii, p. 150.

25 Walter Bagehot, *The Collected Works of Walter Bagehot*, ed. N. St John Stevas, London, 1965, i, p. 418.

26 William Hazlitt, *The Spirit of the Age: or Contemporary Portraits*, London, 1825, p. 147.

27 Mark Twain, *Life on the Mississippi*, Boston, 1883, pp. 467–9.

28 See Forbes, *op. cit.*, p. 20ff; Garside, *Review of English Studies*, 147ff, James Anderson, 'Sir Walter Scott as Historical Novelist', Part VI, *Studies in Scottish Literature*, Jan. 1968, v, 147–50.

29 Daiches, *op. cit.*, p. 473.

30 Herbert Butterfield, *The Whig Interpretation of History*, London, 1931, p. v.
31 *Ibid.*, pp. 16–17.
32 Lukács, *op. cit.*, p. 32.
33 Edmund Wilson, *To the Finland Station*, London, 1941, p. 21.
34 Garside, 'Intellectual origins', p. 67.
35 (Thomas Carlyle), '*Memoirs of the Life of Sir Walter Scott, Baronet*', (review), *London and Westminster Review*, Jan. 1838, xxviii, p. 337.
36 In Lukács's words, Scott's art is characterised by 'a dialectical interpenetration of both these sides of Scott's personality' (*op. cit.*, p. 54).
37 Butterfield, *op. cit.*, p. 38.
38 Thus Scott inevitably fails when he does try to depict a society as distant as Constantinople, in his last completed novel, *Count Robert of Paris*.
39 Lukács, *op. cit.*, p. 33.
40 *Ibid.*, p. 53.
41 Samuel Taylor Coleridge, *Letters, Conversations, and Recollections of S. T. Coleridge*, ed. T. Allsop, New York, 1836, p. 41, (author's emphasis).
42 In fact, despite the comedy, *St Ronan's Well* is one of Scott's most pessimistic works – even though his pessimism vents itself poorly through the novel's melodramatic conclusion.
43 Hazlitt, *op. cit.*, p. 131, (author's emphasis).
44 David S. Hewitt, 'Sir Walter Scott and Society', unpublished Ph.D. thesis, Aberdeen University, 1969, p. 151.
45 *Ibid.*, p. 152.
46 *Ibid.*, p. 139.
47 *Ibid.*, p. 176.
48 *Ibid.*, p. 171.
49 (Francis Jeffrey), '*Considérations sur la Révolution Française*' (review), *Edinburgh Review*, September 1818, xxx, p. 279.
50 According to T. C. Smout, in *A History of the Scottish People, 1560–1830*, London, 1969, pp. 418–19, the 'Radical War' showed 'the degree to which the industrial labour force was just starting to recognise a common interest and to respond to a call to act together'.
51 Lukács, *op. cit.*, p. 26.

Bibliography

1 Works by Scott

The Waverley Novels, 25 vols, London, Adam & Charles Black, the 'Dryburgh' edition, 1892–4.
Lives of the Novelists, 2 vols, Paris, 1825.
A History of Scotland, London, 1830–1.
The Letters of Sir Walter Scott, 1787–1807, ed. H. J. C. Grierson, London, 1932.
With William Erskine and William Gifford, anonymously: 'Tales of My Landlord' (review), in *Quarterly Review*, Jan. 1817, xvi, pp. 430–80.

2 Bibliographical works

Anderson, W. E. K., 'Scott' (bibliography), *The English Novel: select bibliographical guides*, Oxford, 1974, pp. 128–44.
Bell, Alan, ed., *Scott Bicentenary Essays*, Edinburgh, 1974.
Corson, J. C., *A Bibliography of Scott: A classified and annotated list of books and articles relating to his life and works 1797–1940*, Edinburgh, 1943.
Devlin, D. D., ed., *Walter Scott (Modern Judgements)*, London, 1968.
Hayden, John O., ed., *Scott: The Critical Heritage*, London, 1970.
Hewitt, David S., 'The Year's Work in Scottish Literary and Linguistic Studies, 1973 – Nineteenth Century', *Scottish Literary Journal*, Supplement no. 1, Summer 1975, pp. 29–36.
Hewitt, David S., 'The Year's Work in Scottish Literary Studies, 1974 – Nineteenth Century', *Scottish Literary Journal*, Supplement no. 2, Autumn 1976, pp. 29–31.
Hewitt, David S. and Campbell, I., 'The Year's Work in Scottish Literary Studies, 1975 – Nineteenth Century', *Scottish Literary Journal*, Supplement no. 4, Autumn 1977, pp. 26–31.

Bibliography

Hillhouse, James T., *The Waverley Novels and their Critics,* Minneapolis, 1936.

Jeffares, A. N., ed., *Scott's Mind and Art*, Edinburgh, 1969.

Renwick, W. L. (introd.), *Sir Walter Scott Lectures 1940–1948*, Edinburgh, 1950.

Williams, Ioan, ed., *Sir Walter Scott on Novelists and Fiction*, London, 1968.

3 Scott criticism (unpublished)

Cameron, Donald Allan, 'Studies in the structure of six major novels of Sir Walter Scott', Ph.D. thesis, University of London, 1967.

Garside, Peter Dignus, 'Intellectual origins of Scott's view of history in the Waverley Novels', Ph.D. thesis, University of Cambridge, 1970.

Hewitt, David S., 'Sir Walter Scott and society', Ph.D. thesis, University of Aberdeen, 1969.

Mathias, Kay V., 'A study of Walter Scott's *Old Mortality*', M.A. thesis, University of Wales, Aberystwyth, 1968.

4 Scott criticism (published)

Adolphus, J. L., *Letters to Richard Heber Esq. M.P.*, London, 1822.

Anderson, James, 'Sir Walter Scott as Historical Novelist' (in six parts), *Studies in Scottish Literature*, 1966–7, iv, pp. 29–41, 63–78, 155–78; 1967–8, v, pp. 14–27, 83–97, 143–66.

(Anonymous), '*Waverley*: supposed by W. Scott' (review) *British Critic,* August, 1814, New Series ii, pp. 189–211.

(Anonymous), '*Guy Mannering*' (review), *Augustan Review*, July 1815, i, pp. 228–33.

(Anonymous), '*Ivanhoe: A Romance*' (review), *Eclectic Review*, June 1820, 2nd series, xii, pp. 526–40.

(Anonymous), '*Quentin Durward*' (review), *New Monthly Magazine*, July 1823, viii, pp. 82–7.

Bagehot, Walter, *The Collected Works of Walter Bagehot*, ed. N. St. John-Stevas, London, 1965, i, p. 418ff.

Biggins, D., '*Measure for Measure* and *The Heart of Midlothian*', *Études Anglaises*, July–Sept. 1961, xiv, pp. 193–205.

Cadbury, William, 'The Two Structures of *Rob Roy*', *Modern Language Quarterly*, 1968, xxix, pp. 42–60.

Calder, Angus, Introduction and Notes to the Penguin edition of *Old Mortality*, London, 1974.

(Carlyle, Thomas), '*Memoirs of the Life of Sir Walter Scott, Baronet*' (review), *London and Westminster Review*, Jan. 1838, vi and xxviii, pp. 293–345.

(Channing, E. T.), '*Rob Roy*' (review), *North American Review*, July 1818, vii, pp. 149–84.

Bibliography

Cockshut, A. O. J., *The Achievement of Walter Scott*, London, 1969.

Coleridge, Samuel Taylor, *Letters, Conversations, and Recollections of S. T. Coleridge*, ed. T. Allsop, New York, 1836, pp. 38–42.

Colvin, Sir Sidney, *Memories and Notes of Persons and Places 1852–1913*, London, 1921, pp. 197–8.

Craig, David, '*The Heart of Midlothian*: Its Religious Basis', *Essays in Criticism*, April 1958, viii, pp. 217–25.

Craig, David, *Scottish Literature and the Scottish People 1680–1830*, London, 1961.

Crawford, Thomas, *Scott*, Edinburgh, 1965.

(Croker, John Wilson), '*The Antiquary*' (review), *Quarterly Review*, April 1816, xv, pp. 125–39.

Daiches, David, 'Introduction' (1948) to the Rinehart edition of *The Heart of Midlothian*, New York, 1969.

Daiches, David 'Scott's Achievement as a Novelist' (1951) in *Literary Essays*, Edinburgh, 1956, pp. 88–121.

Daiches, David, 'Scott's *Redgauntlet*', in *From Jane Austen to Joseph Conrad: Essays collected in Memory of James T. Hillhouse*, ed. R. C. Rathburn and M. Steinmann Jr., Minneapolis, 1958, pp. 46–59.

Daiches, David, 'Literature and social mobility', in *Aspects of History and Class Consciousness*, ed. I. Mészaros, London, 1971, esp. p. 162.

Daiches, David, 'Sir Walter Scott and History', *Études Anglaises*, 1971, xxiv, pp. 458–77.

Daiches, David, *Sir Walter Scott and His World*, London, 1971.

Davie, Donald, *The Heyday of Sir Walter Scott*, London, 1961.

Devlin, D. D., *The Author of Waverley*, London, 1971.

Duncan, Joseph E., 'The Anti-Romantic in *Ivanhoe*', *Nineteenth-Century Fiction*, March 1955, ix, pp. 293–300.

Edgeworth, Maria, letter to 'the author of *Waverley*', dated 28th October 1814, in *The Life and Letters of Maria Edgeworth* (ed. A. J. C. Hare), London, 1894, pp. 226–31.

Elbers, Joan S., 'Isolation and Community in *The Antiquary*', *Nineteenth-Century Fiction*, March 1973, xxvii, pp. 405–23.

Fleishman, Avrom, *The English Historical Novel: Walter Scott to Virginia Woolf*, Baltimore, 1971, pp. 37–101.

Forbes, Duncan, 'The Rationalism of Sir Walter Scott', *Cambridge Journal*, Oct. 1953, vii, pp. 20–35.

Forster, E. M., *Aspects of the Novel*, London, 1927, pp. 46–56.

Garside, P. D., 'Scott, the Romantic Past and the Nineteenth Century', *Review of English Studies*, 1972, xxiii, pp. 147–61.

Garside, P. D., 'Scott and the "Philosophical" Historians', *Journal of the History of Ideas*, 1975, xxxvi, pp. 497–512.

Goodin, George, 'Walter Scott and the Tradition of the Political Novel', in *The English Novel in the Nineteenth Century*, ed. G. Goodin, Urbana (Illinois), 1974, pp. 14–24.

Gordon, Robert C., '*The Bride of Lammermoor* – A Novel of Tory Pessimism', *Nineteenth-Century Fiction*, Sept. 1957, xii, 110–24.

Bibliography

Gordon, Robert C., '*The Bride of Lammermoor* again: An Exchange',
    Nineteenth-Century Fiction, March 1969, xxiii, pp. 493–8.
Gordon, Robert C., *Under Which King?*, Edinburgh, 1969.
Gordon, S. Stewart, '*Waverley* and the "Unified Design"', *English Literary
    History*, 1951, xviii, pp. 107–22.
Hart, Francis R., *Scott's Novels: The Plotting of Historic Survival*,
    Charlottesville (Virginia), 1966.
Hartveit, Lars, *Scott's 'The Bride of Lammermoor': An Assessment of
    Attitude*, Bergen, 1962 [1964].
Hartveit, Lars, *Dream within a Dream: A Thematic Approach to Scott's
    Vision of Fictional Reality*, Oslo, 1974.
Hazlitt, William, *The Spirit of the Age: or Contemporary Portraits*, London,
    1825, pp. 131–56.
Hook, Andrew D., '*The Bride of Lammermoor*: A Re-examination',
    Nineteenth-Century Fiction, Sept. 1967, xxii, pp. 111–26.
Hook, Andrew D., '*The Bride of Lammermoor* again: An Exchange',
    Nineteenth-Century Fiction, March 1969, xxiii, pp. 498–9.
Hyde, William J., 'Jeanie Deans and the Queen: Appearance and Reality',
    Nineteenth-Century Fiction, June 1973, xxviii, pp. 86–92.
(Jeffrey, Francis), '*Waverley or 'Tis Sixty Years Since*' (review), *Edinburgh
    Review*, Nov. 1814, xxiv, pp. 208–43.
Johnson, Edgar, *Sir Walter Scott – The Great Unknown*, 2 vols, London, 1970.
Jordan, Frank, 'Scott and Wordsworth; or, Reading Scott Well', *Wordsworth
    Circle*, 1973, iv, pp. 112–23.
Kroeber, Karl, *Romantic Narrative Art*, Madison (Wisconsin), 1960, pp.
    168–87.
Leavis, F. R., *The Great Tradition*, London, 1948, p. 14n.
(Lockhart, John Gibson), *Peter's Letters to his Kinsfolk*, 'second' edition,
    Edinburgh, 1819.
(Lockhart, John Gibson), *Memoirs of the Life of Sir Walter Scott, Bart.*,
    Edinburgh, 1837–8.
Lukács, Georg, *The Historical Novel* (1937), trans. H. and S. Mitchell,
    London, 1962, pp. 19–63.
McCombie, Frank, 'Scott, *Hamlet*, and *The Bride of Lammermoor*', *Essays
    in Criticism*, Oct. 1975. xxv, pp. 419–36.
McCrie, Thomas, *Vindication of the Covenanters: in a Review of the 'Tales
    of My Landlord'* (1817), Edinburgh, 1845.
Marshall, William H., 'Point of View and Structure in *The Heart of
    Midlothian*', *Nineteenth-Century Fiction*, Dec. 1961, xvi, pp. 257–62.
Mayhead, Robin, '*The Heart of Midlothian*: Scott as Artist', *Essays in
    Criticism*, July 1956, vi, pp. 266–77.
Mayhead, Robin, *Walter Scott*, Cambridge, 1973.
Medcalf, J. E., 'Lukács on Scott', *Notes and Queries*, Nov. 1962, ccvii
    (New Series ix), p. 402.
Parker, W. M., Prefaces to the Everyman editions of the Waverley Novels,
    London, 1954–62.

Bibliography

Parsons, Coleman O., *Witchcraft and Demonology in Scott's Fiction*, Edinburgh, 1964.

Poston III, Lawrence, 'The Commercial Motif of the Waverley Novels', *English Literary History*, Spring 1975, xlii, pp. 62–87.

Prawer, S. S., *Karl Marx and World Literature*, Oxford, 1976, pp. 255n, 386, 396.

Raleigh, John Henry, '*Waverley* as History, or 'Tis One Hundred and Fifty-Six Years Since', *Novel*, Fall 1970, iv, pp. 14–29.

Shaw, George Bernard, 'The Quintessence of Ibsenism' (1891) in *The Works of Bernard Shaw*, London, 1930, xix, p. 125.

Tillyard, E. M. W., *The Epic Strain in the English Novel*, London, 1958, pp. 59–116.

Trevor-Roper, Hugh, 'Sir Walter Scott and History', *The Listener*, Aug. 1971, lxxxvi, pp. 225–32.

Twain, Mark [Clemens, Samuel L.], *Life on the Mississippi*, Boston, 1883, pp. 467–9.

Welsh, Alexander, *The Hero of the Waverley Novels*, New Haven (Connecticut), 1963.

Woolf, Virginia, *To the Lighthouse*, London, 1927, especially pp. 184–5.

Woolf, Virginia, 'Sir Walter Scott', in *The Moment and other essays*, London, 1947, pp. 50–9.

Young, G. M., 'Scott and the Historians' (1946), in *Sir Walter Scott Lectures 1940–1948*, introd. W. L. Renwick, Edinburgh, 1950, pp. 79–107.

5 Other works cited in the text

Butterfield, Herbert, *The Whig Interpretation of History*, London, 1931.

Chitnis, Anand C., *The Scottish Enlightenment: A Social History*, London, 1976.

(Defoe, Daniel), *A Tour Thro' the Whole Island of Great Britain*, London, 1727 [1726].

Fielding, Henry, *Joseph Andrews*, London, 1742.

Ferguson, Adam, *An Essay on the History of Civil Society*, Edinburgh, 1767.

Jameson, F., *Marxism and Form: twentieth-century dialectical theories of literature*, Princeton (New Jersey), 1971.

(Jeffrey, Francis), '*Considérations sur la Révolution Française*' (review), *Edinburgh Review*, Sept. 1818, xxx, pp. 275–317.

Johnson, Samuel, *Rasselas*, London, 1759.

Marx, Karl, and Engels, Friedrich, *The German Ideology: Part One* (1846), ed. C. J. Arthur, London, 1970.

Marx, Karl and Engels, Friedrich, 'Manifesto of the Communist Party' (1848), in *Karl Marx and Frederick Engels: Selected Works*, London, 1953, i. pp. 21–61.

Bibliography

Marx, Karl, 'The Eighteenth Brumaire of Louis Bonaparte' (1852), in
  Karl Marx and Frederick Engels: Selected Works, London, 1953, i,
  pp. 221–311.
Millar, John, *Observations concerning the distinction of Ranks in Society*,
  London, 1771.
Smout, T. C., *A History of the Scottish People, 1560–1830*, London, 1969.
Venturi, Franco, *Utopia and Reform in the Enlightenment*, Cambridge, 1971.
Wilson, Edmund, *To the Finland Station*, London, 1941.

Index

Index

Index